BODY ARTS AND MODERNITY

First published in 2007 by

Sean Kingston Publishing
www.seankingston.co.uk
Wantage

© 2007 Elizabeth Ewart and Michael O'Hanlon

British Library Cataloguing in Publication Data
A catalogue record for this book is available from the British Library.

Printed by Lightning Source

ISBN
978-1-907774-04-1
paperback

Body Arts and Modernity

Edited by Elizabeth Ewart and Michael O'Hanlon

Sean Kingston Publishing

www.seankingston.co.uk

Wantage

Contents

Contributors

Catherine Allerton teaches anthropology at the London School of Economics. Her research interests include kinship, place and children, and she is currently writing a book on the landscape of everyday life in west Flores, Indonesia.

Lissant Bolton is Head of the Oceania Section at the British Museum. She has worked collaboratively with the Vanuatu Cultural Centre since 1989, and is advisor to the Women's Culture Project there. Her research focuses on both indigenous and introduced textiles, and on women's knowledge and practice. From 2005–10 she has a major research project to reconnect Melanesians with collections from that region in the British Museum.

Chloe Colchester received her doctorate at University College London for a study of barkcloth in Fiji. She was a research associate on a collaborative study of the transformation of Pacific textile traditions, and her latest book, *Textiles Today*, is a survey of innovations in the field of textiles.

Beth Conklin is a cultural and medical anthropologist at Vanderbilt University, and specializes in the ethnology of indigenous peoples of lowland South America (Amazonia). Her research focuses on the anthropology of the body, religion and ritual, cannibalism, death and mourning, disease and healing, and indigenous identity politics.

Elizabeth Ewart is university lecturer in social anthropology at the University of Oxford. She has worked with Panará people in Central Brazil since 1996. Her research focuses on concepts of personhood and alterity, material culture, and the spatial organisation of gardens and villages.

James C. Faris (Ph.D., Cambridge) has taught at the Universities of McGill, Khartoum and Connecticut. He is the author of seven books, and many articles on Nuba, Navajo and Newfoundland, and lives in Santa Fe, New Mexico.

Laurence Goldman is adjunct associate professor at the University of Queensland. He works in Papua New Guinea with Huli people and his research focuses on sociolinguistics, dispute settlement, child play, law and social impact analysis.

Peter Gow is chair of social anthropology at the University of St Andrews. He is the author of several books and numerous articles based on his fieldwork in Peruvian Amazonia and in Brazil.

Bruce Knauft is Samuel C. Dobbs Professor of Anthropology and Executive Director of the Institute for Comparative and International Studies (ICIS) at Emory University, Atlanta. His research combines cultural and politico-economic analysis at different scales of ethnographic and comparative analysis.

Michael O'Hanlon is director of the Pitt Rivers Museum at the University of Oxford. He has done long-term, broad-based ethnography in Highland Papua New Guinea, with a particular focus on visual and moral systems, kinship, politics and material culture among the Wahgi people. He has also worked on the ethnography of museums and of collecting.

Plates

1

Body arts and modernity

An introduction

Michael O'Hanlon

In many parts of the indigenous world, the realm of body arts has become an arena variously for innovation, debate, revival and repression under the conditions of modernity. Among some peoples, 'traditions' of body arts which had been suppressed when an indigenous identity was solely a liability have recently been revived: for example in the context of an alliance between local peoples and the global environmental movement (Conklin 1997). Elsewhere, body arts have been the means for creating or renovating identities in response to a developing international tourist market (e.g. Otto and Verloop 1996). Such refurbishing of identities may further entail the modification of the original decorative repertoire, either through the incorporation of fresh elements or through the strategic excision of older ones (Conklin op. cit.). It may also register a shift in the balance of power relationships within a country, as minority groups adopt the decorative styles of more numerous ones (Otto and Verloop op. cit.). Alternatively, where the outward form of decorative body styles is apparently preserved, at least to some degree, performances today may be intended to lampoon what their practitioners now see as their former unregenerate state (Knauft 2002). Again, where an earlier indigenous decorative repertoire has apparently been entirely superseded by industrially manufactured clothing, examination of the latter may reveal it to be less the profound rupture it first appears than one more transformation in a sequence of such transformations (e.g. Gow 2001:309). Everywhere, the relationship with the external environment, whether national or international, has become crucial, mediated through tourism, through photography and through the rapid dissemination of information and images electronically.

This is the topic which this volume seeks to address: the patchily documented intersection where three areas of literature converge but seldom overlap. First, there is the explosion of anthropological interest in 'the body'. However, the topic of body arts tends to arise only tangentially in this literature. Secondly, there is the longstanding Western interest in body ornamentation of the 'Other', recently surveyed thoroughly by Schildkrout (2004). But this literature's coverage of the last twenty years – the period that I suggest is especially characterised by revivals of indigenous body arts, their transformation (whether real or apparent) and accelerated flows of images of them – is still only sketchy. Indeed, the examples Schildkrout cites of such attention to body arts under modernity are sometimes prescient early papers by the contributors to this volume. Finally, there is a substantial cultural and sociological literature on the recent revival of body arts in the limited areas of tattooing, piercing and 'new tribalism'. However, as I suggest later, the focus of this literature has principally been on the West.

What has not been systematically treated is what has happened to body arts among 'classic' anthropological societies as these aesthetic practices have assumed fresh significance in the context of modernity when, as Conklin (this volume) observes, 'visual appearance takes on special significance'. Like the study of fashion itself (see Entwhistle 2000:2), contemporary body arts constitute a 'hybrid subject', as understanding them involves the inter-relationship of otherwise fragmented areas. The case studies in this volume are chosen to reveal different permutations of local incorporation of exogenous elements, of transformation and of inversion, each in tension with encompassing national and global stereotypes of the significance of 'indigenous body art': stereotypes which may in turn both constrain and empower the local tradition. The contributors to the volume also bring to it a set of examples which are representative in regional terms, with case studies from a number of South American societies, from Indonesia and Africa and from Melanesia and Polynesia. This Introduction seeks, first, to place these contemporary case studies in the context of the literature on 'the body' and on 'modernity', as well as in the context of an older literature on body arts. I then turn to the chapters themselves, to suggest a range of concepts which inter-relate the different cases studies, and which are potentially extendable to others.

It is now a commonplace that the topic of 'the body' has become pervasive in anthropology. So much is this the case that the emphasis in recent literature has started to shift from remarking that fact to charting more sensitively what Csordas (1999) terms the body's 'career' in anthropology. The hasty stereotype has it that the topic of the body was largely neglected in anthropology (aside from farsighted precursors such as Mauss, and their latter day successors, such as Mary Douglas) until the present explosion of interest in it. Csordas (1999:172) replaces this with a more nuanced picture in which the body was never absent in anthropology, but always existed as an 'implicit, taken-for-granted background feature of social life'. Then in the

1970s, Csordas argues, 'the body' graduated to become first an ethnographic *topic* in its own right, and second a *problem*, as the body's status as a stable, natural substrate to social life was undermined by work which demonstrated its mutability when considered historically and culturally. Finally, Csordas says, the topic of the body – reconceived as 'embodiment' – has become a standpoint from which to rethink culture and the self more broadly. Other writers have identified similar shifts in the body's role in anthropology, albeit over shorter periods. Reischer and Koo (2004:307), for example, distinguish an older theoretical approach in which the body was dominantly viewed as symbol (a site on which the social situation might be inscribed) from the more recent tendency to treat the body as 'agentic': a recognition that 'bodies inescapably mediate our relationship to the world around us'.

This encompassing role for the body, and for embodiment, has also been evident to some degree in recent explorations of body *arts* (defining these here, as elsewhere, in the broadest terms). There, too, issues of agency and experience have come to the fore. Shilling (1993), for example, sees body modification as part of an intentionally designed 'body project' and bodies as always in the process of 'becoming': as subject to reconstruction on an ongoing basis. Atkinson and Young (2001:118) cite Shilling's work in proposing their own notion of 'flesh journeys', which they define as the 'process of intentionally reconstructing the corporeal in order to symbolically represent and physically chronicle changes in one's identity, relationships, thoughts, or emotions over time'. But as is apparent from both these examples and many others, while an exotic source of many body arts practices may be acknowledged, the emphasis in recent literature has been on their recent upsurge in the West.

Of course, there are good reasons for this focus on the West. If nothing else, the sheer amount of face-painting on children that any visitor to a museum, school or fete is likely to see today leads to the suspicion that – however vigorous a revival of body arts there may be in certain indigenous societies – at least as much of it now goes on in the West. (This casts a fresh light on Kroeber's remark – cited in Turner 1995:146 – that direct alteration of the body surface is one of the few ethnographically distinctive features of 'primitive' society). A variety of underlying reasons has been identified for this upsurge of interest in body arts in the West. Shilling (1993) relates the prominent place the body now has in definitions of self to (on the one hand) the weakening of religious frameworks which located identity as external to the individual, and (on the other hand) to the rise of consumer culture. Moreover, he notes, 'it is the exterior territories, or surfaces, of the body that symbolise the self at a time when unprecedented value is placed on the youthful, trim and sensual body' (1993:2–3). Atkinson and Young (*op. cit.*) distinguished six socio-cultural motives for the piercing, branding, tattooing and scarification practised by 'neo-primitives' in the two Canadian cities they surveyed. Motives ranged from inscribing sub-cultural membership and resistance to collective attempts to overcome the perceived fragmentation entailed in urban life through body marking practices felt to promote personal growth.

What makes it odd that the newer anthropological literature on 'the body' has proceeded in relative isolation from the renewed significance that body arts now have among indigenous societies is the extent to which until relatively recently the topic of 'the body' in anthropology could be *defined* largely in terms of body arts. For example, as late as 1986, Seymour-Smith's solid Dictionary of Anthropology could commence its entry for 'Body, anthropology of the' by noting that 'The anthropology of the human body has been most fully developed in the study of bodily decoration ...' (1986:26). It is clear that what Seymour-Smith had in mind here is a number of focused and widely-cited ethnographic accounts of body arts, published from the 1970s, including Strathern and Strathern (1971), Faris (1972), Seeger (1975), Turner (1980) and Gell (1975). A generation on, it is possible to discern more clearly both the strengths of this earlier literature and what, retrospectively, have proved to be its lacunae which meant that it has featured less prominently in the more recent anthropological literature on the body than might have been expected.

One feature common to this 'first wave' literature was its illustration that societies which might not produce the elaborate sculpture which had tended to define earlier studies of 'primitive art' nevertheless possessed complex aesthetic traditions in the form of body arts. A second common feature was this literature's demonstration that the traditions in question were not merely second order phenomena, wholly reducible to kinship, economy, politics, language etc. For example, the messages conveyed by Hagen body decoration modified or cross-cut those conveyed by other behaviours (Strathern and Strathern 1971:172); Nuba personal decoration could not be reduced to practical functions (Faris 1972:6); and the significance of the Umeda costuming and body arts worn for the great *ida* ritual is not verbally expressible (Gell 1975:209ff). While the traditions of body art so analysed were all shown to be *sui generis*, they were nevertheless also revealed to be richly interwoven with other aspects of political, social, moral and economic life.

There was however a price to pay for this densely textured picture of body arts as possessing a degree of autonomy, yet simultaneously connected to other domains of social life. In seeking sensitively to trace out symbolic meanings, as much of the anthropological literature of the period was attempting to do, there was a tendency to make issues of history and change exogenous rather than integral to the analysis: the same shortcoming for which anthropological functionalism had been criticised a generation before that. This was one of the points levelled against Gell by Brunton (1980a:120–1) in what has become a classic exchange over how to interpret ritual forms and systems more generally in Melanesia and elsewhere (see Juillerat 1980, Brunton 1980(b) and Gell 1980; also Juillerat 1992). It was not that this 'first wave' literature on body arts ignored issues of history and change. As Faris (this volume) notes of his earlier study: 'My own work was never premised on some unchanging traditional system'. However, the fairly universal use of synchronic linguistic models and analogies to interpret body (and other) art forms meant that history and change tended in these 'first-wave' studies to have something of a bolt-on character.

To the extent that this was a failing of the earlier literature, it is one that this volume decisively remedies. History is integral to all of the papers – Allerton's paper, for example, explores the selective adoption of Western cosmetics by the Mangarrai of Flores, while Faris provides a withering survey of the changes to south-east Nuba body art, and more importantly to Nuba life, following his original analysis and the subsequently highly publicised and popularising visits by the photographer Leni Riefenstahl.

A second, and related, shortcoming which this volume similarly attempts to remedy is the tendency of much 'first wave' literature to neglect the topic of indigenous groups' incorporation (or rejection) of manufactured goods worn on the body: most notably of manufactured clothing. For example, Turner (1969, 1980), whose sensitive analysis of Kayapo body adornment made him one of the first modern ethnographers to put body arts at the centre of his analysis, noted only in passing that Kayapo frequently wore Western clothing (Turner 1980:122). While such 'first wave' literature might *record* such innovations as the introduction of Western clothing or other manufactured items, they were often treated as the 'noise' against which the indigenous system of body arts had to be delineated. This overlooked a number of possibilities which subsequent literature, and this volume, explores. The first point, now well recognised, is that exogenous materials when locally adopted are no longer extraneous 'noise' but are incorporated as part of a pre-existing system (which may of course be modified in consequence). To adapt a striking dictum from Nicholas Thomas's work (1991:108): to say that mission dresses (or second-hand clothing or Western cosmetics) were given to indigenes does not tell us what was *received*. Consequently, there is an often-neglected ethnography of imported decorative items. This may relate, for example, to the ownership of such materials, represented in this volume in Gow's passing observation that among the Piro introduced clothing is the 'primary form of the possessed object': never shared, even between siblings and destroyed at death. Alternatively, it may relate to the local modification of introduced fabrics, exemplified here in Bolton's ethnography of how ni-Vanuatu women have indigenised the 'mother hubbard' mission dresses common in much of the Pacific, creating them as a third term between 'tradition' on the one hand and 'modernity' on the other.

If 'first wave' literature did not take full account of history and change, and failed too to appreciate the systemic aspect to the incorporation of new materials, there have also been additional developments, apart from the extent to which 'the body' as a subject has become omnipresent. Of these developments, the most relevant is anthropology's concern in the last fifteen years or so with the topic of 'modernity'.

The ubiquity of the term has hardly been accompanied by any consensus as to what might be meant by it. This is a question that Bruce Knauft, one of the contributors to this volume, has treated at length elsewhere in an edited volume of his own (Knauft 2002b). He distinguishes two broad strands in the way in which the topic has been approached in recent years. Crudely, there is on the one hand the literature that treats modernity as a process that originates in the West and is largely homogeneous, top-down and essentially politico-economic in nature. This is the same whether the essence of modernity is felt to arise from a particular moment in capitalism, to lie in the creation of a fundamental disconnection from a traditional past, or an unlinking of time from space, or to reside in a heightening of individualism. On the other hand, there is the more 'bottom-up' literature which allows greater scope for the way in which global processes are locally internalised. Modernity in this latter literature is conceived as multiple. As Knauft notes, each approach has its own strengths and weaknesses. The latter, 'micro' approach is more sympathetic to anthropological understandings but arguably risks failing to capture major underlying changes which may not be superficially obvious amid a multitude of local differences. The weakness of the 'macro' approach, on the other hand, lies in its neglect of the cultural dimension and in its potential imposing of a Eurocentric master-narrative on the diversity of indigenous experience.

The contributors to this volume (as to Knauft's own) understand 'modernity' in a variety of ways, aside from the loose sense in which some of the papers also undeniably use the term, as denoting that which is generally contemporaneous. Some challenge the utility of the term altogether. Faris, for example, distinguishes between 'hard' modernity (essentially a narrative of social evolution) and a 'soft' version which questions the first. He considers both to be predicated on an unacceptable hierarchical separation between a 'non-local modern (perhaps metropolitan) place or time, and a local, non-modern (perhaps rural) margin'. Gow's view is not dissimilar, at least insofar as 'modernity' is understood as singular and as confronting multiple 'traditions'. This is entirely alien to the Amazonian 'perspectivism' of the Piro, with whom Gow works, and of other Amazonian groups. There is however scope for an understanding of 'modernity' which – in capturing aspects of both the 'top-down' and 'bottom-up' approaches – goes some way towards overcoming these objections. This is the working definition which Knauft himself uses, and will be employed here, in which modernity is conceived as 'a core articulation between regional or global forces of so-called progress and the specifics of local sensibility and response' (cf. also Lipuma 2001:5).

Turning now to the papers themselves, I suggest that essential aspects of them can be mapped and discussed in terms of a number of overlapping dyads or oppositions, and that these may also be useful in describing equivalent situations elsewhere. Linguists have long made careful distinctions between different types of oppositions. Troubetzkoy (1976; discussed in Caws 1988:87–8), for example, distinguishes a whole taxonomy. *Bilateral* oppositions (such as 'male/female') are those that exhaust the basis of comparison (insofar as there are no other sexes in nature) whilst in *multilateral* oppositions (such as 'human/canine') the basis of comparison is potentially shared (in that this opposition can be contrasted with 'human/feline', 'human/ape' etc). Oppositions may also be *isolated* (such as 'husband/wife', which pertains to the field of marriage alone), *privative* (such as 'friend/stranger', where the second term of the opposition can be anything, provided it does not have the character of the first), *graduated* (such as 'friend/acquaintance', where the second term has the same character as the first but to a different degree) or *equipollent* (e.g. 'friend/enemy', where both terms are of equal logical strength). More general utilization of the notion of oppositions went out of fashion with structuralism. However, the notion of oppositions is arguably of particular utility and power when considering a topic such as body arts and costuming, which inherently possess something of an either/or, on/off character. By definition they entail either the addition of something (assuming a decorated state) or the possibility of its removal (returning to an undecorated state), a difference that may locally be elaborated as emerges in a number of the papers.

Visibility/invisibility

The first of the dyads or oppositions, that of visibility/invisibility (an opposition that is 'bilateral' and 'privative' in Troubetzkoy's taxonomy), emerges particularly clearly in different ways in the three Amazonian papers, those by Conklin, Gow and Ewart. Conklin's wide-ranging paper analyses the role played by body arts and costuming in native activism in the contemporary world, in which establishing a local identity has become both more crucial for native peoples (access to resources may turn on it), but also more difficult (in that consumerism makes costumes and artefacts hitherto associated only with particular cultural groups accessible to many). Here, issues of visibility and invisibility emerge with particular sharpness. As Conklin discusses, for many years Amazonian peoples found a degree of safety in cultivated *invisibility*. In broader national society, their dramatic body arts were often regarded as a sign of primitiveness and barbarity; indigenous peoples such as the Wari, with whom Conklin herself worked, responded by abandoning their paint and feathers and adopting jeans and other Western dress, in a strategy of 'dissembling' which also permitted them to retain intact many of their other cultural practices. But as Conklin's paper describes, in the final decades of the 20th century other Amazonian peoples – such as the Kayapo – found it advantageous to reverse this strategy when opposing the Brazilian government's plans to construct dams on tribal territory. The Kayapo greatly heightened their visibility as protestors by selectively re-adopting their body paint and feathered headdresses. This dramatic costume acted as a magnet for media attention and helped the Kayapo construct a potent alliance with the burgeoning international green movement.

Conklin also contrasts the culturally loaded visibility achieved by the Kayapo with that sought by another native activist movement, the Zapatistas in southern Mexico whose flamboyant leader, sub-commandante Marcos, became well known for the trade-mark black ski mask he wore. Cheap, generic and commercially manufactured, the ski mask was explained by Marcos as a means of removing the 'exoticized but anonymous indigenous face from the exploitative, commodifying gaze of more powerful others' (Conklin, this volume). In contrast, what gives the re-adoption of plumes and paints by Kayapo people its appeal in the West is the fact that it plays to our stereotypes of pristinity and cultural uniqueness. However, as Conklin also shows, the Kayapo strategy of heightening their visibility by catering to a Western stereotype is potentially self-constraining. It has required the Kayapo to edit from the traditional decorative repertoire elements such as jaguar teeth whose presence might offend an international green constituency. Again, because the Western stereotype of indigenous body arts is that they are the visible external reflection of real internal cultural differences, Kayapo leaders have found themselves accused of inauthenticity when they are photographed dressed in suits, eating in restaurants, driving vehicles and behaving in other ways which fail to match the stereotype.

Issues of visibility/invisibility also emerge sharply, although in a slightly different sense, in the other two Amazonian papers, those by Ewart and Gow. The context of Ewart's paper is the tragic recent history of the Panará people whose population was reduced by disease to less than one hundred following their first contact with Brazilian national society in the 1970s. This remnant population was then re-located (the trauma made worse by being placed in close proximity to enemy groups) for twenty years, and has only recently been restored to their former territory. Ewart's paper provides an outline of the changes to the decorative repertoire and clothing practices of the Panará. While Panará do still decorate in body paint on occasion, the styles in which they do so are exclusively those of other peoples whom they observed while re-located and which, intriguingly, they declare to be infinitely better than their own. But as Ewart describes, Panará men have also purchased T-shirts, flip flops, football shirts and Panará women have started to make dresses, and it is the selective, tactical and gendered adoption of this exogenous garb that Ewart is particularly concerned to explain.

Gow's rich paper similarly concerns another Amazonian people, the Piro, who have had an equally traumatic relationship with outsiders and who have also for the most part abandoned traditional wear in favour of apparently acculturating shirts, shorts and dresses. Integral to understanding what this transition actually signifies is the Piro's potted version of their history. They see themselves as having originally lived in small, mutually hostile, groups in the forest; then as having been enslaved by rubber barons in the nineteenth century; and finally as having acquired the knowledge and abilities to free themselves and live in the independent villages they now inhabit. Before their adoption of shirts, shorts, dresses etc., Piro wear included body paint and woven cotton robes with striking patterns, and one of Gow's departure points is the fact that the Piro declare that they are afraid of their former garb. This, they say, is because it made them look like jaguars, creatures feared for their carnivorous proclivities, but also for their solitude (the antithesis of Piro sociality) and for their terrible and transfixing beauty. The ceremonies for which Piro traditionally wore fresh body paint and newly decorated cotton robes were exceptionally tense ones, bringing together antagonistic groups: ceremonies in which they appeared to each other in the form of jaguars. Part of the reason why Piro have adopted Western clothing is as a physical manifestation of their transformed relationship with 'Whites' (using this term to encapsulate all non-indigenes). But another part of the explanation lies in the fact that the Piro regard Whites themselves as pathologically violent, asocial beings, whose values are entirely antithetical to their own. In wearing new clothing from Whites for their ceremonies today, the Piro are in fact recapitulating their appearing to each other as of yore, in the guise of hostile jaguars.

How does this relate to the questions of visibility and invisibility which I suggested illuminate Ewart and Gow's papers as they do Conklin's? In both cases, the answer has to do with what Rivière (1994) has referred to as the 'highly transformational world' of Amazonian cosmology, particularly as elucidated in Viveiros de Castro's (1998) contrast between Western multi-culturalism and Amerindian multi-naturalism. Our own intuitive understanding of different peoples' traditions of body paint, costume and dress is that these reflect cultural differences superimposed on the natural bodies which we all have in common. Viveiros de Castro argues that for Amerindians, in contrast, nature is characterised by a unity of spirit, but differentiated by bodies. Donning body paint, a costume or a mask is to activate the powers that go with that body. Viveiros de Castro's analogy here is with a wet suit. Donning a wet suit does not turn its wearer into a fish (as we feel that different traditions of body art reflect the cultural distinctiveness of each): rather, a wet suit allows its wearer to operate in a marine environment. Thus what appears to us to be *highly visible* – the sad homogenisation of unique Amazonian cultures through their assumption of Whites' clothing – is not the case (any more than the Kayapo re-adoption of indigenous costume is an innocent return to pristinity). What is *invisible* to us (other than through Ewart and Gow's respective analyses) is that the selective Panará adoption of manufactured clothing permits them to operate tactically in a white environment; while what appears to be the Piro adoption of manufactured garb is in fact a transformation of indigenous clothing.

Issues of visibility/invisibility manifest themselves equally sharply in Faris's rumbustious, self-acknowledged 'tirade', which is almost as critical of himself as it is of the concept of modernity and of the photography of Leni Riefenstahl whose well-known pictures of the Nuba were taken after Faris himself had worked there. At one level, Faris's chapter is a valuable historical update of his original (1972) account which formed part of what I earlier characterised as 'first wave' studies of body art. Faris's original analysis was linguistically inspired and was intended to demonstrate the pared-down, economical character of the system of south-east Nuba body art: a Nuba artist would not elaborate a design beyond the point at which it became culturally recognisable.

What Faris describes is how this changed, following the arrival among the Nuba first of Riefenstahl herself and subsequently of tourists influenced by the celebratory romanticism of her photographs which Faris regards as successors-in-spirit to her films celebrating Nazi achievements in the 1930s. Riefenstahl introduced to the Nuba new colours, new items of décor, locations she thought more exotic, and artificial light; and she and the tourists who succeeded her wished, in Faris's words, 'to photograph and photograph and photograph the decorating ...'. The effect of this, and of the fact that the Nuba were now paid to be photographed, was to stimulate artists to produce new representational designs and to protract the painting of traditional ones. The older, graphically economical, designs simply did not take long enough to produce now that painting was more or less paid by the hour. But as Faris describes, this aesthetic change shrivelled into insignificance in contrast to the violent political changes which then overtook the Nuba and brought their tradition of body art in that form to an end. The three south-eastern Nuba villages were compulsorily converted into 'peace villages' and used by the severe Sudanese Islamicist government as a buffer in their war against the Sudanese People's Liberation Army, and were consequently subjected to raids by the latter.

While Faris considers that the visibility brought to the Nuba by his own and by Riefenstahl's publications may have been a contributory factor to their being selected as 'peace villages', the villages' proximity to developing oil wells was of greater importance. But the issue of visibility/invisibility emerges in other respects in Faris' chapter, aside from the very obvious fact that the Nuba decorative tradition has now been made invisible through its suppression by the Sudanese government. This lies in the photographic visibility required of the Nuba by Riefenstahl and by the tourists who followed her. As we have seen, the effect of this on the original Nuba graphical system was to inflate it (Faris might say deform it: his vision is bleaker than Conklin's, Gow's and Ewart's, all of whom find some positives or at least continuities in the changes to the body arts of those they document). But more fundamentally, Faris sees in Riefenstahl's, and in much other photography, an intolerable assumption of access to others: an entirely asymmetrical presumed right to render others visible, whether as spectacles or as victims, according to our own codes. As will be seen, both photography and issues of visibility and invisibility are also recurring themes in others of the papers.

Authenticity/irony

The illumination offered by the dyad 'authenticity/irony' arises in part from the significance of 'culture' as a resource for indigenous peoples, which leads to assertions of cultural authenticity, to challenges to its legitimacy and to self-reflexivity in relation to it. This dyad (one that is 'multilateral' and 'equipollent' in Troubetzkoy's typology) emerges particularly strongly in the papers by Knauft, Allerton and Colchester.

Knauft's paper concerns the Gebusi, a lowland people inhabiting a remote part of Papua New Guinea who had had very limited contact with outsiders before Knauft first worked with them at the start of the 1980s. Knauft's early work documented the rich array of spirit séances, sorcery accusations, ritual homosexuality and initiation then practised by the Gebusi (fieldwork that was lavishly 'authentic', in another sense of the word). The Gebusi also possessed elaborate traditions of body decoration and costuming worn on such occasions. But when he returned to the area in the later 1990s, Knauft found Gebusi life startlingly changed. Much of what he had earlier observed had been swept away, replaced by new residential patterns, a preoccupation with Christian sin and with sport, and with what elsewhere Knauft (2002a) has termed the Gebusi's 'recessive agency': their patient and passive waiting for enlightenment and development to come from external authority figures. Though the Gebusi now dressed for most of the time in imported Western garb, elaborate body arts were still in evidence. However, they were now deployed in contexts which radically altered their significance. Rather than accompanying the most profound moments of cultural life, body arts now appeared in skits which lampooned and ironised much that had been central and sacred to their culture.

Knauft's account of this transition from authenticity to irony leads him to suggest a valuable typology of orientalisms (which he defines for this purpose as 'the construction and projection of stigmatized Otherness through the cultural assertion of "progress" versus "backwardness" in body decoration and sartorial style'). Most orientalism, he notes, is 'projective': it entails attributing backwardness to others, whether beyond the nation-state or within it. (Orientalism deployed within a state Knauft dubs 'internal orientalism'; the Sudanese state's view of Nuba body arts as backward and requiring prohibition is another instance of 'internal orientalism'). Those subject to orientalist discourse can, however, subvert it by assertively reclaiming the disparaged sartorial styles, a process Knauft dubs 'counter-orientalism' (Conklin's description of the selective re-appropriation by Kayapo of aspects their traditional costume is one example of counter-orientalism). The Gebusi's lampooning of their own traditions thus becomes an example of '*auto*-orientalism'.

Similar issues of authenticity and irony emerge equally clearly in Allerton's paper which focuses on the Manggarai, rural inhabitants from the far west of the Indonesian island of Flores. The Manggarai situation, however, is the reverse of that of the Gebusi, in that the Manggarai are, at one level, in the process of adopting body art rather than abandoning it. Aside from filing and blackening their teeth, and from the elaborate sarongs they wore (which are more in the nature of a second skin rather than an embellishment of the first one), the Manggarai had little in the way of 'body art', in the sense of the paint, decoration and plumes as traditionally worn by classic body arts peoples such as the Gebusi. In recent years, however, Manggarai have been making increasing use of Western cosmetics: rouging their cheeks, powdering their faces, using scented soaps and lipstick. This applies in particular to young children and to brides: both of whom, for the Manggarai, are the epitome of the undamaged body, unmarked by the labour which scars – even invisibly – the bodies of all those caught up in the round of agricultural labour and reproduction.

The Manggarai preference for paleness in their use of cosmetics relates to Dutch colonialism and to the perceived power of Europeans and may be linked, too, to an indigenous category of spirits. But it also has to do with how the Manggarai experience modernity. This resides in the contrast between their own rural existence and what Allerton refers to as the 'heady perfume' of town life of Indonesian officials and salaried workers, with their different styles of dress, dancing and food, and ideal body image of smooth, pale faces with straight black hair and neat clothes. Manggarai brides today favour Catholic weddings in 'town' style, for which they wear white wedding dresses, veils, stockings and lacy gloves and pancaked face make-up (such white weddings are also followed later by weddings in customary style). However, Manggarai adoption of cosmetics and Western-style weddings is taking place against a background of official Indonesian approval of local dress which is 'authentic' in the sense that it is customary. But Allerton also detects in the Manggarai adoption of town fashions a measure of quiet, conscious irony of which town visitors to the village may be unaware.

Irony is again in play in Colchester's paper where the focus is shifted to the 'town' end of the urban/rural dichotomy which Allerton's paper explored. Colchester's fieldwork site is Otara market in a distant industrial suburb of South Auckland, now the world's largest Polynesian city. At this Saturday market, Whites mingle with second- and third-generation descendants of immigrants from Western Samoa, Niue, the Cooks and other Polynesian islands. The original immigrants (who came to New Zealand during the boom years of the 1950s and 1960s) remained oriented to their different islands of origin and held together in their respective communities by church, by marriages and funerals and by the despatch of remittances home. However, more recent years have seen a decline both in the diasporic community's economic fortunes and in the strength of their affiliation to church. Bonds to islands of origin have also weakened, and there has been a rise in intercommunity tension accompanied by a sharp awareness on the part of the islanders of their immigrant status in bi-cultural New Zealand.

In the busy multicultural market which comprises her field site, Colchester's analysis focuses on clothing which, she suggests, brings 'contentious issues of adaptation and change to the surface where they matter, that is directly in the scenes of social encounter, and in the midst of a new kind of gift exchange'. On sale in the market is cheap foreign clothing retailed by members of the white and Asian communities, 'island prints' sold from Fiji–Indian run stalls, and handmade textiles and Tongan-style barkcloth produced by older Polynesian women. But Colchester's particular concentration is on the graphic humour of T-shirt designs produced by New Zealand-born Pacific islanders, especially by Samoans. These designs draw their force from identity politics, reworking and subverting commercial logos to address the relationship of islanders to each other, to mainstream culture and the latter's stereotypes of islanders. Many are also rich in self-deprecating irony, bearing legends such as 'Overstayer', 'Coconut' and 'Freshy' (for 'fresh off the boat') which appropriate stereotypes of islanders as provincial, irresponsible and violent (a further instance of Knauft's 'counter-orientalism').

Real/ideal

As earlier suggested, body arts have an inherent 'toggle switch' dimension to them. The state of being in ordinary dress, undecorated, necessarily raises by implication the potential of the adorned state and vice versa, and the switch between the two states may be culturally highly elaborated. The decorated state is also generally more highly valued, possessing an idealised and other-worldly or 'fictional' character. Aspects of this dyad (which is again 'multilateral' and 'equipollent' in Troubetzskoy's terms) have emerged, of course, in earlier papers. There is an element of this in the way that Manggarai villagers, described by Allerton, dress young children and brides, suggesting as it does to them that momentarily they are urban sophisticates. In an entirely different sense, the same dyad emerges in Riefenstahl's photography, as scathingly related by Faris. With its 'long lens, corny posing, artificial lighting, [and] flat flash', Riefenstahl's photographs conscript the real Nuba to play the roles of idealised noble savages in what Faris terms her 'pastoral racist' vision.

However, it is in Goldman's remarkable paper that we see the most extensive local cultural elaboration of the real/ideal dyad. Goldman's focus is on the Huli people of the New Guinea Highlands, a region which is as great a *locus classicus* for analyses of 'exotic' body arts as is Amazonia. But what also marks Huli out among New Guinea Highlanders is their quite exceptional elaboration of verbal forms, something which Goldman's earlier work analysed in depth (e.g. Goldman 1983). In his paper in this volume, Goldman begins by looking at the relationship between Huli verbal and decorative genres. The Huli have an extensive repertoire of myths, folk tales and sayings which feature decorated beings. These verbal genres not only define the decorated state as an absolute contrast with the undecorated state, but they also tend to represent it as having a potency which mortals cannot achieve with their own decoration. In a striking metaphor that reminds us of the transfixing beauty that jaguars are felt to possess by Piro people (Gow's paper), one Huli verbal form describes a mythical being as moving so fast that the colours in her decoration merge, 'like snakes when they extend their necks causing the skin colours to blur', the sight being powerful enough to knock a small boy unconscious. Goldman's analysis of Huli discourse about decoration reveals it to have a strong 'as if' component to it. It creates, he says, 'a fictional [or ideal] space into which audiences are invited by means of implicit solicitations – "let's say x is the case...let's pretend...let's treat as if.."'.

Recent years have however seen major changes to the Southern Highlands Province, where the Huli live, and the final part of Goldman's paper relates these to changes in decorative practice. There have been considerable oil, gas and gold finds in the area and these have spurred the Huli, and a number of their less numerous neighbours, to lobby the national government to be constituted as a separate province. Provisionally named Hela Province, the new entity would aim to control these mineral resources (the name 'Hela' draws on an origin story that has been refreshed to incorporate all the groups in whose territories mineral resources lie). Meanwhile, converging changes have also taken place in the realm of decoration. Images of Huli, especially of Huli men wearing their famous crescent-shaped headdresses, have become *the* idealised and exotic face of Papua New Guinea in promotional literate for tourist and other purposes. At the same time, Huli decorative practices have been radically simplified. A host of former dances and decorative styles have been abandoned but Mali, the one that has been retained, is significant. Traditionally, an anticipatory dance performed in connection with warfare, Mali is now done at political rallies, festival openings, and large inter-clan and inter-tribal compensation exchanges. Mali is also less complex than other dances, easier to learn and, significantly, permits the inclusion of an undetermined number of participants, echoing the elasticity of the anticipated Hela Province. As Goldman observes: 'the decorated remain imbued with narrative authenticity as storied beings, but invested with the political potency of Hela.'

Interiority/exteriority

The final dyad which I suggest helps illuminate the papers is that of interiority/exteriority. At its crudest, adorning the body entails by definition the overlaying of an existing surface with something else. To that extent body arts are inherently likely to provoke a dialectic between interiority and exteriority. Equally obviously – as analyses of body arts from the 'first wave' literature onwards have demonstrated – the implications or content of 'interiority' and 'exteriority' may vary culturally. They may stand for a disjunction between the hidden and the revealed, the natural and the social, the private and the public etc.: or, indeed, for the absence of any such disjunction. In this volume, for example, an instance of 'interiority' would be the preservation of indigenous culture by the Wari, where 'exteriority' is constituted by the dissembling cover of manufactured clothing visible on the outside, as described by Conklin. Or, in the case of the Manggarai described by Allerton, the face make-up now worn by brides and by children encapsulates the fleeting potential for their living heady town lives, as against the invisible accumulation of internal physical damage which their lives of rural labour engenders. And 'polarities', as it were, can always switch. Elsewhere, Lipuma (1999:201ff) describes such an instance in relation to the pearl shells worn by the Maring people of Highland New Guinea. Obtained from outside Maring society, pearlshells traditionally symbolised the multiple links with the external world. However, from the middle of the twentieth century pearlshells were steadily displaced as a valuable by state money. But the shells did not disappear. Rather, they became confined to the ceremonial arena, and their valency switched. State money now took on the role of representing links to the outside, and came to stand for modernity, for exteriority, for business, and for the emergence of a national identity. Pearlshells, which had hitherto had this role, now came to represent tradition, interiority and local identity.

In this volume, the paper in which the dialectic of interiority and exteriority is manifested most clearly is, similarly, Melanesian in regional terms: that by Bolton. Her paper also illustrates the potential for further mediating terms. Bolton's focus is on the 'island dresses' made from imported fabric by women in Vanuatu, especially in central Vanuatu. Dressmaking skills were taught to Vanuatu women by the wives of Presbyterian missionaries in the nineteenth century. These dresses are exactly the kind of thing neglected by an earlier anthropology for their 'inauthenticity'. Bolton's paper – part of the wider re-appreciation of the indigenous significance which imported clothing may come to possess (see also Hansen 2004, Colchester 2003, Küchler and Were 2005) – shows that for all their external origins and manufacture from imported fabrics 'island dresses' have become very local artefacts. Thus women in peri-urban parts of Vanuatu exchange new dresses for pandanus textiles with women living further from town (the pattern of exchange is restricted: dresses exchanged only against pandanus fabric, shirts exchanged against the beverage kava); shadowy analogies are made between dress styles and flying foxes; women in parts of Vanuatu where red and yellow were colours that had to be earned in the local system of grade-taking tried to wear those colours on their dresses; and the paths along which new dress styles travelled are remembered, in the same way that the paths of particular ritual practices are recalled.

However, as Bolton shows, 'island dresses' have not become exclusively local artefacts, for they prove to occupy an unacknowledged mediatory position in ni-Vanuatan efforts at self-definition. Here Bolton outlines attempts by ni-Vanuatu intellectuals to distinguish not only indigenous practices (*kastom*) from practices that are purely exogenous but also to identify those imported practices that have been localised and come to stand for Vanuatu. At Independence in the 1970s, 'island dresses' were identified as 'national' and this, she suggests, comprises 'an interesting third to the binary opposition between inside and outside, between *kastom* and *fasin blong ol waetman* ... "National" is something distinctively of Vanuatu, but which may have been adopted in, rather than being autochthonous'.

This Introduction began by arguing that what has been neglected in all the recent anthropological attention given to 'the body' more generally, and to the efflorescence of tattooing, piercing and the new tribalism in the West, has been systematic attention to the revival and transformation of 'body arts' in the classic anthropological societies where those arts were originally described. This, I suggested, was odd, given the extent to which attention to 'the body' in anthropology was for much of the 1960s and 1970s substantially represented by detailed accounts of masking, head-dress construction, face and body painting, and dancing in exotic Africa, Melanesia and Amazonia. In discussing the papers in this volume – designed as they are to describe and analyse the different ways in which body arts have more recently emerged as a focus for innovation, debate, revival and repression in such societies in the context of modernity – I have found useful a number of overlapping dyads or oppositions: between visibility/invisibility, authenticity/irony, real/ideal and interiority/exteriority: body art itself having an intrinsically 'switchable' character.

Time will tell whether or not these oppositions are found productive in mapping and organising similar data elsewhere. Before turning to the papers themselves, however, one final, more general point might be made. This exercise has been in part an updating one: an account of what has happened under the conditions of modernity to a particular cultural area – bodily based arts – among a number of the 'traditional' societies whose study anthropologists formerly made their speciality. But just as some of the ideas originally developed in relation to the 'new tribalism' (such as the concept of 'flesh journey') are potentially applicable to the kinds of societies anthropologists originally studied, so the data presented in the papers in this volume has the capacity to enrich the study of body arts everywhere, including in the West. To suggest that this might be so is not to rehearse the old argument about traditional societies being in some sense foundational. Rather, it is to point out that comparative information in observed practice is not often readily available from longitudinal perspectives from other kinds of societies. In this sense, classic ethnographic accounts and the reappraisals represented by the papers in this volume can throw into relief more general issues of change in body arts.

Bibliography

Atkinson, M. and Young, K. (2001) 'Flesh journeys: neo primitives and the contemporary rediscovery of radical body modification', *Deviant Behaviour* 22: 117–46.

Brunton, R. (1980a) 'Misconstrued order in Melanesian religions', *Man* (n.s.) 15(1): 112–28.

—— (1980b). Correspondence: 'Order or disorder in Melanesian religions', *Man* (n.s.) 15: 734–5.

Caws, P. (1988) *Structuralism: the art of the intelligible*, Atlantic Highlands, New Jersey: Humanities Press International.

Conklin, B. (1997) 'Body paint, feathers and vcrs: aesthetics and authenticity in Amazonian activism', *American Ethnologist* 24(4): 711–37.

Colchester, C. (ed.) (2003) *Clothing the Pacific*. Oxford and New York: Berg.

Csordas, Thomas, J. (1999) 'The body's career in anthropology' in H. Moore (ed.) *Anthropological Theory Today*. Cambridge: Polity Press.

Entwhistle, J. (2000) *The Fashioned Body: fashion, dress and modern social theory*. Cambridge: Polity Press.

Faris, J. (1972) *Nuba personal art*, London: Duckworth.

Gell, A. (1975) *Metamorphosis of the Cassowaries*, London: Athlone Press.

—— (1980) Correspondence: 'Order or disorder in Melanesian religions' *Man* (n.s.), 15: 735–7.

Goldman, L. (1983) *Talk Never Dies: the language of Huli disputes*, London: Tavistock Publications.

Gow, P. (2001) *An Amazonian Myth and its History*. Oxford: Oxford University Press.

Hansen, K. T. (2004) 'The world in dress: anthropological perspectives on clothing, fashion and culture', *Annual Review of Anthropology*, 33: 369–92.

Juillerat, B. (1980) Correspondence: 'Order or disorder in Melanesian religions', *Man* (n.s.) 15: 732–4.

—— (ed.) (1992) *Shooting the Sun: ritual and meaning in West Sepik*, Washington: Smithsonian Institution Press.

Knauft, B. (2002a) *Exchanging the Past: a rainforest world of before and after*, Chicago: University of Chicago Press.

—— (ed.) (2002b) *Critically Modern: alternatives, alterities, anthropologies*, Bloomington: Indiana University Press.

Küchler, S. and G. Were (2005) *The Art of Clothing: a Pacific experience,* London: UCL Press.

LiPuma, E. (1999) 'The meaning of money in the age of modernity' in Akin, D. and J. Robbins (eds) *Money and Modernity: local and state currencies in Melanesia*, Pittsburgh: University of Pennsylvania Press.

—— (2001) *Encompassing Others: the magic of modernity in Melanesia*, Ann Arbor: University of Michigan Press.

Otto, T. and Verloop, R.J. (1996) 'The Asaro Mudmen: local property, public culture?', *Contemporary Pacific* 8(2): 349–86.

Reischer, E. and Koo, K.S. (2004) 'The body beautiful: symbolism and agency in the social world', *Annual Review of Anthropology* 33: 297–317.

Rivière, P. (1994) 'WYSINWYG in Amazonia', *Journal of the Anthropological Society of Oxford* XXV(3): 255–62.

Schildkrout, E, (2004) 'Inscribing the body', Annual Review of Anthropology, 33: 319–44.

Seeger, A. (1975) 'The meaning of body ornaments: a Suya example', *Ethnology* 14: 211–24.

Shilling, C. (1993) *The body and social theory*, London: Sage.

Seymour-Smith, C. (1986) *Macmillan Dictionary of Anthropology*, London: Macmillan Press.

Strathern, A.J. and Strathern, M. (1971) *Self-decoration in Mount Hagen*, London: Duckworth.

Thomas, N. (1991) *Entangled Objects: exchange, material culture and colonialism in the Pacific*, Cambridge, Mass: Harvard University Press.

Turner, T. (1969) 'Tchikrin, a central Brazilian tribe and its language of bodily adornment', *Natural History* 78: 50–9.

—— (1980) 'The social skin' in J. Cherfas and R. Lewin (eds) *Not Work Alone: a cross-cultural* view *of activities superfluous to survival*, London: Temple Smith.

—— (1995) 'Social body and embodied subject: bodiliness, subjectivity and sociality among the Kayapo', *Cultural Anthropology* 10(2): 143–70.

Viveiros de Castro, E. (1998) 'Cosmological deixis and Amerindian perspectivism', *Journal of the Royal Anthropological Institute* 4(3): 467–88.

2

Ski masks, veils, nose-rings and feathers

Identity on the frontlines of modernity

Beth A. Conklin

'Modernity' is often equated with cultural homogenisation, the erosion of distinctive local identities and trends toward increasing sameness. Body decoration is widely seen as one of the most potent markers of difference and distinctiveness, and the abandonment of distinctive local body decorations in favour of Western clothing is a widespread concomitant of modernisation and globalisation. T-shirts, jeans and business suits are the uniforms of cosmopolitan global citizenship.

Indigenous people have many reasons to abandon traditional styles of dress or undress. In the Brazilian Amazon where I work, most Indians must deal regularly with outsiders who see nudity as a sign of sub-humanity, barbarism, poverty and inferiority, and see body painting as bizarre and uncouth. Virtually every native group in sustained contact with outsiders has adopted T-shirts, shorts, skirts, jeans and other Western styles of dress to some extent.

Yet alongside the spread of jeans and T-shirts, the past two decades have seen a resurgence and efflorescence of indigenous body arts. Native peoples who once took pains to hide external signs of indigenous identity behind mass-produced Western clothing now proclaim their distinctiveness with headdresses, body paint, beads and feathers. This is taking place not just (or even primarily) in 'traditional' communities, but on what might be called the frontlines of modernity. In the public arenas of national and transnational political activism, native peoples are negotiating new relations to the nation-state and struggling to forge new identities that assert their citizenship in modern society. Distinctive costumes and body adornment express a new self-consciousness and pride in being indigenous, and offer a site for asserting shared identities and solidarity. And in an era dominated by visual media, dramatic body arts are one of the most effective political tools to claim public attention for indigenous causes.

The political potency of body images is evident in two of the most successful indigenous movements of the past fifteen years: native activism in Brazil and the Zapatista movement in Mexico. In both cases, indigenous people are fighting against invisibility, struggling to make native people and their problems visible to the outside world. In both cases they have used dramatic, attention-getting costume as a focal strategy, but the costumes themselves could scarcely be more different. Brazilian activism capitalises on the display of (often semi-nude) indigenous bodies adorned with exotic feathers, beads and handmade decorations. In Mexico, Zapatistas cover their faces with black ski masks or red bandanas. Though the images differ radically, both visual strategies have developed partially in reference to Western stereotypes of primitivism, exoticism and the supposed opposition between tradition and modernity. Both movements use dress and body imagery to claim space in the media-driven public arena and convey messages to challenge, critique, expand and redefine popular understandings of what it means to be indigenous.

Visual appearances as sites of identity and critique

The emphasis on distinctive costuming for native activists is part of a larger global phenomenon in which visual appearance takes on special significance in the social conditions of modernity. The accelerated flow of information, images, technologies and people across social and geographic boundaries is a defining feature of the processes we call modernity or post-modernity. With the spread of mass media, especially the visual media of television, film and video, individuals have access to multiple perspectives, ideas and symbolic vocabularies for imagining ways of living different from their own. Arjun Appadurai (1996:7) and others have noted the 'growing evidence that the consumption of mass media throughout the world often provokes resistance, irony, selectivity and, in general, *agency*.' Much of that exercise of agency focuses on (re-)defining identities and group boundaries.

In a world of rapid transportation, migration, diaspora and movement, encounters with strangers and others different from oneself become more frequent, as does the need to quickly locate oneself in relation to others. Local identities are complicated and sometimes thrown into question, while commodification and consumerism make cultural artefacts formerly associated with specific groups available to anyone with money to buy them. Yet at the same time, other globalising forces – especially the expansion of literacy, communications, human rights discourses, legal mechanisms for disempowered peoples to claim rights and changes in the internal dynamics of nation-states – create political and economic incentives to assert claims based on distinctive group histories and cultural features, even though in reality many group boundaries are increasingly blurred. In the face of these contradictions, marking identity and affiliation on the body is one of the most convenient and effective ways to claim and communicate identity.

The body, dress and adornment have always been prime sites for marking an individual's relation to a group and a group's differences or similarities to other groups (El Guindi 1999:59). These aspects of identity, affiliation and boundary-marking are precisely the issues increasingly thrown into relief, destabilised and unmoored from certainty in the contemporary world. Modernity is partly about the proliferation of possibilities and materials (both tangible and symbolic) for individuals to construct a variety of identities. Capitalism and consumerism promote consumption and concern with appearances and encourage individual choice focused on fashion –changing body images in response to commercial and cultural trends – and style, cultivating an individual image.

At the same time that identity comes to be experienced subjectively either as more of a choice or as one among multiple pragmatic or imagined alternatives, movements affirming cultural identities consciously in the making are proliferating around the globe. The ethnic separatist movements of Eastern Europe, Quebec and elsewhere come immediately to mind, as do the campaigns for rights and recognition being mounted by minorities and marginalised peoples in many countries. Some of this falls under the rubrics of multiculturalism and identity politics, which aim to mobilise group identity to claim rights and resources in nation-states that distribute entitlements on the basis of classifications and policies regarding group identity (Appadurai 1996:15). But identity politics is just one facet of a larger trend in which groups of many sorts are newly self-conscious about their identity, culture and heritage, and are mobilising cultural elements in deliberate, strategic ways. James Clifford (2000:8) notes that 'in contrast to the nation-state building projects of the '50s and '60s, which involved reducing or eliminating retrograde "tribalisms"...Today, newly configured projects of the indigenous, the local and the different pull against such [orthodox] modernizing attitudes.'

For transnational migrants who desire to maintain a distinctive identity and affirm ties to homeland, dress offers a framework for expressing identity. Commenting on the use of Palestinian apparel at Arab–American events in Los Angeles, Fadwa El Guindi (1999:58) observes that 'dress survives destabilized geography and borders to communicate messages about identity and to serve as an embodiment of a group's memory.'

For people trying to forge new ways to be 'alternatively modern' (Knauft 2002:26), body image can be a site for creativity and contestation. Non-western or non-mainstream dress, adornment and body modifications are prime sites to stake claims to distinctive identities, cultural projects and political positions opposed to the dominant trends of global capitalism and cultural homogenisation. The use of dress to express cultural resistance often focuses especially on women, who in many societies are seen as repositories of cultural tradition, responsible for maintaining family heritage and honour at the same time that they must enter the labour force in new ways (Appadurai 1996:45) that threaten male control over women in the family. Women sometimes negotiate these tensions by adopting dress that conveys their adherence to family tradition and separation from men in public.

The resurgence of veiling among Islamic women, especially in urban contexts, is a paradigmatic example. The return to veils, head coverings and modest Islamic dress began in Egypt in the early 1970s not in 'traditional' or rural communities, but among university students in urban centres such as Cairo, Alexandria and Assiut. At the time, veils had virtually disappeared in Egyptian cities and nearly all women wore Western dress (Ahmed 1992:216, 220). Young, highly educated female students led the revival of veiling as an expression of piety and assertion of pride in a separate, assertively Islamic and nationalist identity–an identity that they explicitly contrasted with the commercialism and sexual exploitation of Western fashions (Ahmed 1992:194). This was not a return to tradition but an invention of 'styles of dress that are essentially quite new, neither the traditional dress of Egypt nor the dress of any other part of the Arab world, or the West, though they often combine features of all three' (Ahmed 1992:220).

Traditional dress is associated with the lower classes, whereas the new style of modest 'Islamic dress' conveys modernity and mobility.

Urban Egyptian women who wear Islamic dress typically are

> educationally and professionally upwardly mobile...and are
> confronting bewildering, anonymous, cosmopolitan city life for the
> first time, a city life in which vivid inequalities, consumerism and
> materialism, [and] foreign mores...are glaringly apparent. The women
> are generally the first generation of women in their family to emerge
> socially into a sexually integrated world–where men and women are
> intermingled on the university campuses, in the crowded transport
> system, and in the professions. (Ahmed 1992:222–3)

Similarly, in Singapore, 'Veiling in the new and conservative sense is mostly centered among highly educated women who are career-oriented and articulate about their religious world view and lifestyle' (Stimpfl 2000:176).

These are women on the frontlines of modernity. Modest Islamic dress, including the veil, is a pragmatic coping strategy; it allows women to move through the male-dominated worlds of education, commerce and the professions in a manner consistent with social mores. In adopting Islamic dress...women are in effect 'carving out legitimate public space for themselves'...and public space is by this means being redefined to accommodate women. The adoption of the dress does not declare women's place to be in the home but, on the contrary, legitimizes their presence outside it' (Ahmed 1992:224).

The resurgence of veiling spread among Islamic women in many countries. In a movement that has been one of the most visible expressions of emergent Islamic consciousness. 'Hijab [covering the head and body] became the object and the symbol for the new consciousness and a new activism' (El Guindi 1999:143). The resurgence of modest dress mutated into many different local forms with distinct local gender politics. In some contexts (as in Iran and Taliban-ruled Afghanistan), veiling became much more coercive and restrictive than the voluntary movement that originated in Egyptian universities (Ahmed 1992:232). Everywhere, however, 'encoded in the dress style is a new public appearance and demeanor that reaffirms an Islamic identity and morality and rejects Western materialism, consumerism, commercialism, and values' (El Guindi 1999:145).

The question of how the body is covered and adorned has become a key and contested political symbol both within the Islamic world and in non-Muslims' attitudes toward Islam. Aiwa Ong (1995:187) sees debate over veiling in Malaysia as part of 'nationwide struggles over a crisis of cultural identity, development, class formation and the changing kinds of imagined communities.' In the United States, the news media post-September 11th seemed to have a near-obsession with the issue of veiling, which many Americans identify as a prime symbol of oppression, backwardness and the supposed chasm of cultural differences between 'us' and 'them'.

Exoticism as an index of authenticity

A very different context in which we see contemporary groups using body adornment to mark identities opposed to mainstream norms is in the various alternative subcultures that take 'tribal' cultures and trappings of the 'primitive' as symbols and inspiration (Torgovnick 1992). Urban subcultures such as punks, skinheads, Goths and others use permanent marks of tattooing, piercing and scarification to set themselves apart from the mainstream. 'Modern Primitives' see their experience of undergoing painful and permanent body modifications such as piercing and tattooing as a kind of rite of passage and an act of self-redefinition (Torgovnick 1992). The term 'primitive' has been appropriated to signify something that is original, authentic and definitive, as opposed to derivative (Rowanchilde 1993), and body modifications are seen as an index of the depth of an individual's authentic commitment to an alternative mode of being.

These subcultural uses of 'tribal' body images point to the strength and salience of cultural codes that identify the primitive and the indigenous with visual difference and exoticism. In a study of reader responses to *National Geographic* magazine, Catherine Lutz and Jane Collins found that readers perceived clothing to be the single most important marker of cultural identity: 'Exotic dress alone often stands for an entire alien life-style, locale, or mind-set... Local costume suggests something about the social stability and timelessness of the people depicted' (1993:92). The loss of traditional costume is seen as an index for the loss of cultural traditions: 'Clothing identified as Western seemed often...to be a sign of cultural degradation, while non-Western clothing was taken as a sign of authenticity' (Lutz and Collins 1993:247).

Throughout the Americas, public attitudes toward native people are permeated by two opposing stereotypes: the 'good' Indian: a pure, noble savage living close to nature; and the 'bad' Indian: primitive and backward, or degraded by the ills of civilization (Berkhofer 1978:27–8; Ramos 1998:62). Dominant racial discourses posit a binary logic in which the primitive and the modern are opposed and incompatible. Jonathan Warren describes attitudes in north-east Brazil:

To be an authentic Indian, one must live like a primitive in a traditional manner. One must embody the antiself of civilization, which in Brazil means living in a hut in the middle of the forest, naked, and with no contemporary technological conveniences... Indians are imagined as 'primitive/traditional' in the sense of being outside of and in binary opposition to 'civilization/modernity.'...If Indians participate in professions, use technology, wear clothes, and inhabit urban geographies (which denote modernity), then they are not considered Indian,

regardless of their bloodlines or physical features.

Thus imagined as antithetical to the modern, Indians become locked in time as static beings of a distant, lost past...The more someone deviates from this image of the past, the less Indian that individual is deemed to be. Change and adaptation are conceived of as racial contamination by non-Indians. (Warren 2001:173, 172, 176).

In North America, similar sensibilities locate authentic indigeneity in opposition to change and modern consumer goods, with costume treated as a prime index of authenticity. Lucy Lippard (1992:26–7) observes:

Even today, when Zunis wear rubber boots or sneakers at Shalako [ceremonies], or when an Apache puberty ritual includes a six-pack of soda among the offerings, tourists and purists tend to be offended. Such 'anachronisms' destroy the time-honored distance between Them and Us, the illusion that They live in different times than We do.

Not all mixing of the 'primitive' and the 'modern' offends Western sensibilities, however. Primitive/modern juxtapositions have been a long-running theme in *National Geographic* magazine photography (Lutz and Collins 1993:110–12) and are increasingly prominent in advertising and fashion. For example, the photograph selected as the all-time favourite from *National Geographic* shows a naked Olmec boy having his body painted in a jaguar design applied with a Coke bottle. Rather than marking the 'natives' as active participants in the modern world system, such images tend to portray them as passive, childlike (and often confused or amazed) receptors of Western artefacts and the gaze of Western viewers (Conklin 1997:715). Appreciation for juxtaposition runs in only one direction: exotic, 'primitive' indigenous body plus 'modern' Western technology or hyper-commercial artefact. An indigenous man in a business suit holding a bow and arrow mixes the primitive and the modern as surely as when he appears in body paint and feathers working at a computer. Yet the two images carry very different messages and visual appeal. How does this uni-directional coding for authenticity affect indigenous individuals as they navigate the social and political spaces of the dominant society?

Risks of visibility and invisibility

In Brazil, the centrality of exotic body image in defining authentic indigenous identity is deeply entrenched. 'Real' Indians should 'look Indian', which means going naked or wearing feathers, beads and paint. Most native people, however, have good reasons not to 'dress Indian' much of the time. In face-to-face dealings at the local level in Amazonia, negative stereotypes are rife; to many non-Indians, nudity connotes barbarism, poverty and distance from civilization, and body paint and piercings are bizarre and uncouth.

I work with the Wari', a population of over 2,000 people who live in the rainforest of Rondônia in western Brazil. When Wari' entered sustained contact with Brazilian national society in the late 1950s and 1960s, they were inundated with unwanted attention because of their nudity: it became fashionable for army officers and their wives to take Sunday excursions upriver to stare at the naked savages. Wari' quickly understood the value of wearing clothes to manage their interactions with outsiders; they now wear Western clothing at all times. Many other aspects of their lives also changed after the contact, but Wari' maintain a high degree of social and cultural integrity. The native language is the only language spoken in most Wari' households and there is little out-migration or marriage with outsiders; everyone continues to make a living mostly by traditional subsistence activities of farming, hunting, fishing and foraging. Visitors to Wari' villages are frequently disappointed because 'they don't look like real Indians', but Wari' themselves suffer little confusion about their own ethnicity (Conklin 1997:716).

Like Wari', most native people find that it helps to dress like non-Indians in order to function in mainstream society. In Brazil, looking exotic attracts unwanted attention and makes one a target for discrimination and paternalism. Indians who need to sell their products in town, deal with government agencies, get jobs, or attend public schools usually find that they have a better chance of being taken seriously if they look 'normal' and dress like whites most of the time.

Western clothing carries many complex and varied meanings for native peoples. One role of clothing is as a tool to gain greater respect and equality in dealing with outsiders. Jeffrey Ehrenreich (n.d.) notes that among the Awá of eastern Ecuador, Western dress is part of a broader strategy of dissembling – of trying to appear as 'normal' as possible in the eyes of outsiders, to avoid hostility and interference. Under a visual veneer of sameness, the Awá are able to preserve important traditions, including their language and shamanic practices. '[T]he cultivation of an appearance which mirrors that of outsiders, serves to promote the cultural survival of the group at large', Ehrenreich (n.d.:11) writes. '...The use of [Western] costume to disguise ethnicity in fact protects it.' In addition to its strategic value, clothing and bodily practices are key elements with which groups like the Huaorani of eastern Ecuador construct identities as civilized and modern (Rival 2002:165).

In shaping their body images to downplay exoticism and suppress visual markers of their distinct ethnic identity, however, Indians run another risk, of being perceived by outsiders as degraded and inauthentic, not real Indians. Native individuals who live in Brazilian cities constantly confront questions about their identity, authenticity and bodily appearance. '(W)e spend most of our lives trying to reaffirm that we are Indians', says Eliane Potiguara (1992:46), an urban native activist, 'and then we encounter statements like, "But you wear jeans, a watch, sneakers and speak Portuguese!"...Society either understands Indians all made-up and naked inside the forest or consigns them to the border of big cities.'

For native Brazilians themselves, the emphasis that outsiders place on nudity and visual exoticism as an index of authenticity often has little to do with their own sense of self-identity. Few Indians see modernisation and change as incompatible with being indigenous; they tend to see the loss of traditions and pressures to wear Western clothing as signs of racism and repression rather than indicators of inauthenticity (Warren 2001:189). In the highly charged racial politics of Brazilian society, however, to dress in Western clothing is to run the risk of being seen as not *really* Indian, or not the right *kind* of Indian. Brazilian Indians who do not 'look Indian' are not respected for trying to pass as whites, but are seen as corrupt and degraded, losers in both societies (Ramos 1998:77).

Social classifications have serious consequences. In the late 1970s, Brazilian officials proposed criteria to determine whether someone qualified as Indian, with the intent to terminate special legal status for acculturated individuals. This was a kind of true–false test for Indianness composed of a motley set of several dozen criteria, among which physical appearance and dress were treated as prime indexes (Ramos 1998:249–50). A barrage of criticism from anthropologists scuttled the rating system, but the fact remains that most Brazilians still see bodily appearance as a central criterion for defining authentic Indianness. Native individuals who are not recognised as Indians tend to be categorised with the generic poor on the lowest rungs of the social ladder.

Looking or not looking indigenous can be a matter of life and death. An appalling event in 1997 highlighted the links between visibility, vulnerability and violence. In Brazil's national capital, an Indian man was burned alive as he lay sleeping at a bus stop at 5 a.m. Galdinho Jesus dos Santos was a member of a Pataxó delegation who had come to see officials about land rights issues. Returning from a meeting late at night, he got lost in the unfamiliar city. By the time he arrived at the pension where he was staying, the doors were locked and he lay down to sleep on a bus stop bench. Five teenage boys cruising the streets saw him, went to a gas station and purchased two litres of fuel, doused the sleeping man from foot to head and set him afire. Galdinho died soon after, with burns covering 95% of his body (Pinheiro and Camarotti 1997).

Public outcry was intense. Media commentaries and letters to the editor focused first on lamenting what the incident revealed about class relations and a crisis of values among alienated adolescents. The case was especially riveting because the murderers were not shantytown gang members but privileged sons of upper-middle class families; ironically, one was the stepson of a judge who in 1989 had issued an important judicial ruling in favour of Yanomami Indian rights. That the boys could view a sleeping man as an object for lethal sport seemed to many Brazilians to encapsulate the brutality of a deeply divided class system. This perception intensified when a judge dismissed the murder charges, saying there was insufficient evidence that the boys intended to kill and that they had no way to know the man was Indian (Hollanda and Andrade 1997; Pinheiro and Camarotti 1997).

Galdinho's murder pointed to the complex relations between ethnicity and class, between being Indian and being poor, and the role of bodily appearance in marking and separating these categories. One boy said that they burned the man because they thought he was a beggar; if they had known he was Indian, they wouldn't have done it. From the way Galdinho looked – dressed not in paint and feathers but in T-shirt, slacks and flip-flop sandals – they assumed he was just another bum. Attacking street people turns out to be a not-uncommon form of entertainment for some urban adolescents.

Galdinho's death pointed to the liability of not looking 'Indian' enough. Ironically, this is an issue that Pataxó have confronted many times. The Pataxó are a highly acculturated, detribalised people who lost their territory to Brazilian settlers many years ago. Since the 1970s, they have been at the centre of a bitter, often violent conflict over land rights. Their opponents have repeatedly questioned the Pataxó claim to be Indians. In 1984, a Congressman named Mario Juruna – himself a Xavante Indian – led a Congressional delegation to visit the Pataxó while they were under siege in a life-and-death standoff, surrounded by 3,000 armed settlers determined to evict them. Afterward, Juruna enraged indigenous rights advocates when he told reporters that the Pataxó were not real Indians. 'Indians don't have beards, or mustaches, or body hair', Juruna asserted (CEDI 1984:293). Subsequently, Pataxó activists recognised the salience of visual appearance in signifying authenticity and began to appear in public wearing feathered headdresses and grass skirts (see photographs in CEDI 1984:292 and 1991:513, 525; Pinheiro and Camarotti 1997; DFAIT 2003). This renewed use of native dress has served two roles: it has helped Pataxó attract media attention for their cause, and it has become a focal element in the revitalisation and reconstitution of their own sense of identity and solidarity.

Cultural pride and political empowerment

In many native Brazilian societies, the body is considered intimately connected to personhood, identity and social status. Adorning the body with paints, dyes and ornaments is not just a matter of aesthetics, but a fundamental part of the socialising processes through which persons are made (cf. Conklin and Morgan 1996; Conklin 2001; Seeger, da Matta and Viveiros de Castro 1979). Body decorations identify the individual with the group, its ancestors and sources of empowerment. Among the Xavante, for example, the act of applying body paint and putting on feathered ornaments connects the wearer with other Xavante and with mythic traditions that celebrate the triumphs of heroic individuals. Dressing in native garb, Xavante mark themselves as distinct from outsiders and self-confident in their identity (Laura Graham, personal communication).

This native Brazilian cultural emphasis on the body and body arts converges in interesting ways with the visual emphasis of media-oriented identity politics that capitalize on the attraction of tribal imagery. For Xavante, who pioneered media-savvy political theatre in which dozens of boldly painted warriors confronted government officials, the success of their visual tactics reinforces confidence in the continuing relevance and efficacy of their traditions (Conklin and Graham 1995:699).

Many native activists find colourful body arts to be an asset in their struggle to attain visibility and support. Visual images can communicate certain things more directly and immediately than verbal language ever can, and attractive body images open possibilities for empathy and humanistic identification across distances of space, language and cultural difference. The political power of visual imagery is intensified by the fact that Indians' alliances with international supporters are channelled primarily through non-governmental organizations that rely heavily on voluntary contributions from sympathetic donors. Pictures with 'good visuals' are important tools in public relations and fund-raising and media coverage tends to gravitate to the most strikingly costumed individuals (Conklin 1997:722).

Some native individuals who formerly tried to blend in using Western dress have returned to using colourful body arts. The Kayapo of central Brazil are a prime example. Like the Wari', for several decades Kayapo leaders tried to blend in in their dealings with outsiders, dressing in Brazilian-style outfits, with long pants, long-sleeved shirts and Brazilian-style haircuts.

> Today, however, the same chiefs and other men are again wearing
> their hair long...[and] when chiefs go to a Brazilian city, they make
> a point of wearing shorts (or sometimes long pants) and shoes, but
> no shirt or jacket. Their faces, arms, and upper bodies are painted,
> and they wear traditional shell necklaces and bead earrings. The
> whole ensemble is often topped off with a feather headdress. (Turner
> 1991:299)

This revival of pride in ostentatious displays of their distinctive body images reflects a shift in the balance of power between Kayapo and their Brazilian neighbours. Since the late 1980s, Kayapo activists have been spectacularly effective at mobilising mass protests and media events and forging alliances with influential outsiders like the rock singer Sting. The strategic value of exotic appearance was exemplified in 1989, when Kayapo activists organised a huge protest in the town of Altamira in opposition to a proposed dam that would have flooded their land. Thousands of non-Indians staged their own demonstrations, but the media – especially international reporting – focused almost entirely on the 700 Indians with their dramatic headdresses, body paint, lip plugs and war clubs (Fisher 1994:222). Indians from other tribes who came to Altamira in solidarity found themselves being urged by the Kayapo to take off their Western clothing and put on native decorations. As other native activists have seen the success of such tactics, some have felt empowered to experiment with more indigenous body arts in their own dealings with outsiders.

This politicised revival of indigenous body arts is not just a return to tradition, for it favours only certain body images. The activist dress code favours semi-nudity (for men), colourful feathered and beaded ornaments, and temporary body paints. Traditional aesthetic elements such as permanent dyes, radical haircuts, strong-smelling body oils and necklaces made of monkey and jaguar teeth are generally left at home (Conklin 1997:723). Lip disks, which signify the ability to speak well (Seeger 1981:85), have been abandoned by most Kayapo, Suya and Panará. Elizabeth Ewart (personal communication) observes that in dealing with government officials and other outsiders today, speaking is not the main source of native leaders' power, since language barriers and the need for interpreters make elders' speech less powerful. Instead, the key to success is media visibility; hence the concern with careful management of visual images. Lip disks no longer make sense, while headdresses do, since they satisfy public expectations.

There is a gendered dimension to the body images that have become fashionable and proved effective in native Brazilian activism. Men and women have different options for self-presentation, for men can bare and display parts of their bodies that women cannot. In addition, the consumption of commercial goods and imperative to maintain tradition may be coded differently for men and women in native communities (cf. Wardlow 2002:152), further complicating the meanings of body images.

Body images as targets for criticism

One troubling dimension of the reification of certain body images is that it devalues the choices of indigenous people who do not conform to those styles. Particular constructions of indigenous identity privilege those who correspond best to the idealised image (Thomas 1994:189). In Brazil, Kayapo-style headdresses have become the standard for activist apparel, but not all Indians have such headdresses. Wari', for example, use feathers as head ornaments in just two ways: they stick bits of down onto oiled hair, or they insert a single scarlet macaw feather at the back of the head – a look that anyone raised on cartoon images of Plains Indians will find hard to take seriously. Neither traditional style translates well to media politics. Yet when indigenous people search for effective public images, they are accused of being charlatans.

Hostility and ambivalence toward native activists often are expressed through discourses about native dress. Diane Nelson (1994) described the proliferation of jokes in Guatemala about Rigoberta Menchu, the Mayan leader who won the 1993 Nobel Peace Prize. Rigoberta wears her community's distinctive *traje*, and jokes told by Ladinos (non-Indian Guatemalans) typically revolve around puns about her dress – implying, for example, that she is 'hiding' something beneath her skirts – in other words, that she is not who she presents herself to be.

For Amazonian activists whose native costumes include dramatic headdresses and semi-nudity, another liability is that they must deploy body ornaments and dress selectively in different contexts. All of us do this every day, of course. Dressing for an awards ceremony, a U.S. President puts on a tuxedo and a Kayapo leader puts on a headdress. The next morning, both may appear in T-shirt and jeans. We think nothing of the President's strategic use of costume, but the public tends to have different expectations for Indians. Contextual usage of indigenous body arts contradicts stereotypes of 'authentic' Indians as 'natural' people whose use of body ornaments expresses deep spirituality and cultural roots (Conklin 1997:725). In Brazil, enemies of indigenous rights have repeatedly seized upon this supposed contradiction to claim that Indian activists are frauds, 'staging' their Indianness for a gullible foreign public (Gomes and Silber 1992; see McCallum 1995). A series of vicious journalistic 'exposés' have used photographic layouts in which pictures of exotically costumed Kayapo activists were juxtaposed against pictures of the same individuals 'off-stage', dressed in Western clothes and engaged in 'civilised', modern activities – driving a car, eating at a fancy restaurant, using high-tech equipment (Conklin 1997:725–6).

Bizarrely, Brazil's largest news magazine's coverage of the horrific burning of Galdinho used the same technique to question Pataxó legitimacy by calling attention to the constructedness of activists' public images. Although nothing in the article about the burning referred to debates over Pataxó legitimacy, a sidebar titled 'Life Imitates Art' presented three images: a passage describing sixteenth century Portuguese encounters with naked Indians, a nineteenth century painting of Indians in grass skirts, and a 1997 photo of Pataxó in grass skirts and headdresses. The caption concluded, 'In 1997, centuries after abandoning the nudity of their ancestors, the Pataxo of today adopted grass skirts...to cover their lower parts and *pretend to be Indians*' (Pinheiro and Camarotti 1997; emphasis added). Exotic native bodies appear again and again at the centre of public discourses about Indians good and bad, authentic and inauthentic.

Expanding public notions of indigeneity

Thus far, I have emphasized how outsiders' racist and romantic stereotypes force indigenous people to manage their appearances to work around those stereotypes, deploying the visual code of primitivism, exoticism and authenticity to make themselves visible. This is not the whole story, however. In a multitude of ways, native activists are trying to challenge, critique and expand public concepts of what it means to be indigenous. One technique is to foreground images that combine symbols of tradition and modernity.

Native Brazilian activists tend to mark their autonomy, agency and modernity by presenting themselves not as 'pure' primitives but as people familiar with multiple cultural systems. They mark their cosmopolitan competence and complexity on their bodies with wristwatches or business suits combined with indigenous ornaments or body paint, and they make a point of displaying their familiarity with complex technology. The Kayapo, for example, have trained a number of video cameramen and film editors, pioneering the use of video technology to make their own records of community rituals and political events and exert some control over how their culture is represented to the outside world. Turner emphasizes that not only do Kayapo want to film their own videos, they also want their cameramen to be photographed in the act of filming (Turner 1992:7). Their visual display of technological competency aims to subvert limiting stereotypes that equate being indigenous with being anti-modern.

Zapatista masks: subverting the dominating gaze

Like Amazonian activists, the Zapatista movement in southern Mexico has used dramatic costuming and symbolic juxtapositions to subvert limiting stereotypes, gain visibility and stake claims to indigenous modernity and political participation. But instead of playing up primitivist exoticism, Zapatistas remove indigenous faces from outsiders' gaze by covering them with black ski masks or red bandanas. Generic, cheap and commercially manufactured, ski masks and bandanas are the antithesis of Amazonian feather headdresses.

The masked face has become the identifying symbol of the Zapatista movement in the eyes of the world. Zapatista spokespersons use the metaphor of the masked face brilliantly in a host of ways to articulate their critique of racism and oppression (cf. Ponce de Leon 2001, Ruggiero and Sahukla 1996). References to faces and masks pervade the speeches and writings of the mestizo (non-Indian) leader who goes by the name of sub-comandante Marcos. A former university lecturer who clearly has read his Foucault and Gramsci, Marcos explains the mask as a way to remove the exoticised but anonymous indigenous face from the exploitative, commodifying gaze of more powerful others. At the same time, the mask calls attention to indigenous people's position – faceless, invisible to society, ignored until they put on a threatening symbol of criminality that negates the stereotype of Indian passivity. The mask asserts agency and the demand to be taken seriously.

Another metaphorical valence of the mask is the idea that it negates individual identity to affirm a collective, broadly humanistic solidarity. The mask negates prior personal differences, say Zapatistas, especially gender distinctions between male and female. Hiding individual identity, the mask also is said to prevent the kind of cult of personality that turned individual Kayapo activists like Payakan into media stars.

Like Amazonian activists, Zapatista leaders are trying to expand public notions of what it means to be indigenous and relocate indigenous people from the periphery to the centre, asserting their full participation as citizens in national and global society. They express this claim in their bodily self-presentation: like the befeathered Kayapo cameramen who want to be filmed in the act of filming, indigenous Zapatista leaders combine traditional clothing with defiantly 'non-indigenous' elements. The elderly Tzotzil woman leader who goes by the name of Ramona, for example, always appears in public wearing an embroidered blouse and flowered skirt along with her ski mask. The face masks, weapons, cell phones, laptops and other technologies that Zapatistas display communicate complexity, agency and modernity. The novelty and media appeal of Zapatista images derive partly from such juxtapositions of the indigenous and the commercial, the handmade and the high-tech.

The non-indigenous leader subcommandante Marcos has constructed his famous self-image out of other juxtaposed elements. Jose de la Colina (2002:365) describes his symbolic *assemblage*:

> ...the cartridge belts worn in an X 'like that of Emiliano Zapata,' the lit pipe as a distinctive amulet of an intellectual, a handkerchief tied about his neck perhaps in coquettish remembrance of Pol Pot, the barrel of a shotgun at his shoulder, signalling that this thing is seriously happening, and some auxiliary new age technology attached to his belt, signalling that this is an era of an intercommunicated planet.

The Zapatistas' extensive use of the Internet and the theoretical sophistication and poetic nuances of their rhetoric – not just in Marcos's speeches, but in the native leadership's communiqués as well – are other ways of putting the world on notice that indigenous people are active participants in modernity.

Carlos Monsivais, a prominent Mexican writer and one of Marcos's intellectual mentors, sees Zapatista supporters' bodily self-presentation as tangible evidence of how the movement's success has altered indigenous consciousness. In February 2001, 15,000 to 20,000 mostly indigenous people gathered in the plaza of San Cristóbal, Chiapas, at the send-off rally for the March for Indigenous Dignity, a.k.a. the ZapaTour, in which Zapatista leaders and thousands of supporters marched from Chiapas to Mexico's national capital. Observing the crowd, Monsivais (2002:124) saw in their dress an index of changing relations to modernity, capitalism and the national society. 'Nearly all of them are quite young, they've given up traditional clothing,' he wrote.

> ...Their bandanas and ski masks show they are members of the EZLN's [Zapatistas'] community base of support, and their secondhand clothing indicates a nearly furtive entrance into modernity, into the Eden of late consumption, where museum-piece sweaters, jackets, and Levis, so very out of fashion, find resurrection.

Monsivais (2002:124) continued:

> These Zapatistas, most of them men, have changed... in the seven years since they let their springs of aggressiveness fly like panthers set free. Their body language has changed...and most unexpected is their gaze. These young people look and accept being looked at. They convey a sense of newness: no longer do they consider themselves perennially excluded from the vision of others. They know they are perceived, and the end of their invisibility makes them happy and reinforces their adherence to the EZLN.

Indigenous rights struggles are a fight against invisibility, against being ignored by the larger society. In the media-oriented politics of the late twentieth century, the very different strategies represented by Zapatista masks and Amazonian headdresses have helped native activists claim public attention and forge new paths to political participation.

Solidarity behind the mask

Zapatistas do not speak just for indigenous causes; they assert a broad critique and moral rejection of neoliberalism with which many non-Indian supporters identify. Masks offer a tangible symbol to affirm that solidarity. Anyone can don a mask: Zapatistas say the mask invites other oppressed and dissatisfied people to feel part of the struggle. 'Behind our masks is the face of all excluded women', proclaims a 1996 EZLN declaration,

> of all the forgotten native people, of all the persecuted homosexuals, of all the despised youth, of all the beaten migrants, of all those imprisoned for their words and thoughts, of all the humiliated workers, of all those dead from neglect, of all the simple and ordinary men and women who don't count, who aren't seen, who are nameless, who have no tomorrow. (Ruggiero and Sahukla 1996:24–5)

In Mexico, the idea of a masked figure protecting the interests of the poor resonates with the populist politics of a cadre of masked super-heroes (e.g., Super-Barrio, Super Eco, El Chupacabras Crusader) who have become popular figures on the streets of Mexico City since the late 1980s, showing up at demonstrations and media events to confront government officials and exploitative business interests (Taylor 1997). After the Zapatista uprising, black ski masks became symbols of dissent for a wide spectrum of the Mexican populace. Ski masks have repeatedly sold out in shops all over the country.

At the international level, the Zapatista uprising has been the most prominent new leftist movement of the past decade, and black ski masks have become key symbols of dissent and anti-capitalist critique. Some commentators have suggested that one reason for their popularity is that the Zapatistas appeared at a historical moment when there was a symbolic void on the left, after the Soviet Union's disintegration had toppled older socialist icons. 'That may be why the ski masks worked so well', one observer of the ZapaTour commented to Monsivais. 'After the fall of the Berlin Wall, a new stage-set was needed, one without the Caudillo's beard or Papa Joe Stalin's whiskers' (Monsivais 2002:128).

Black ski masks have been ubiquitous at recent anti-WTO protests, to the point that during the Summit of the Americas in Quebec City in 2001, officials in one suburb tried to ban possession of ski masks, scarves and other face coverings (ISR 2001). In addition to their symbolic resonances with the anti-capitalist, outsider positions of both Zapatistas and urban criminals, face coverings help protestors avoid being identified in police photographic surveillance and offer some protection against tear gas.

Distinctive costume makes a convenient target for hostility and cynicism. As with Guatemalans' jokes about Rigoberta Menchu's skirts and Brazilian journalists' use of photographic juxtapositions to challenge Pataxó and Kayapo legitimacy, Mexicans' scepticism about the Zapatistas has been articulated in questions about the mask. Why does Marcos wear a mask, what is he hiding? ask his critics. Che Guevara never wore a mask; even Emilio Zapata showed his face (Feder 2001).

Zapatistas turn such questions around. 'Why so much scandal about the ski-masks?' Marcos asks. 'Isn't Mexican political culture a "culture of hidden faces"?'

> ...I am willing to take off my mask if Mexican society takes off the foreign mask that it anxiously put on years ago...it has been sold an image of itself that is fake, and the reality is more terrifying than people supposed. If we show each other our faces...civil society will have to wake up from the long and lazy dream that 'modernity' imposes on everything and everybody. 'Sup-Marcos' is ready to take off his ski-mask; is Mexican civil society ready to take off its mask? (Ruggiero and Sahukla 1996:88)

Zapatistas repeatedly affirm their hope to arrive at the day when, with Mexican society having recognised the rights of indigenous and other oppressed peoples, they will be able to remove their threatening masks and live as ordinary people with full citizenship in a modernity reshaped and redefined by their movement.

At the beginning of this chapter, I suggested that the social conditions of modernity itself–the intensified mixings of people, ideas and images, and the influence of global communications, especially visual media – make definitions of identities and boundaries a matter of concern, and make the body arts prime channels to construct and communicate group identities and boundaries and expand the possibilities for identification and solidarity across those boundaries. As people move in and out of interactional spaces configured around varying identities and cultural codes, dress serves as one of the most convenient and immediate modes of self-representation. Visual appearances communicate across social and linguistic divides, and attention-getting images that claim public and media attention help circumvent power relations that otherwise suppress the voices of marginalised groups. Capitalizing on the fascination of dramatic bodily appearances, indigenous causes may gain social visibility and a visual vocabulary to communicate and redefine what it means to be indigenous in the twenty-first century.

Groups as different as Islamic women, urban punks, Amazonian activists and Zapatista insurgents have used distinctive styles of dress and body ornamentation to express their critiques of dominant social patterns and construct positions in opposition to the mainstream. Whether it's done with a ski mask, a veil, a nose-ring, or feathers, distinctive body arts are powerful ways to assert identity on the frontlines of modernity.

Bibliography

Ahmed, L. (1992) *Women and Gender in Islam*, New Haven, CT: Yale University Press.
Appadurai, A. (1996) *Modernity at Large*, Minneapolis, MN: University of Minnesota Press.
Berkhofer, R. F., Jr. (1978) *The White Man's Indian*, New York: Vintage Books.
CEDI (1984) *Povos Indígenas no Brasil/1984*. Aconteçeu Especial 15 (São Paulo).
—— (1991) *Povos Indígenas no Brasil: 1987, 1988, 1989, 1990*. Aconteçeu Especial 18 (São Paulo).
Clifford, J. (2000) Taking identity politics seriously: "The contradictory, stony ground...", in P. Gilroy, L. Grossberg and A. McRobbie (eds) *Without Guarantees: Essays in Honour of Stuart Hall*, London: Verso.
Colina, J. de la (2002) As time goes by: Marcos, or the mask is the message, in T. Hayden (ed.) *The Zapatista Reader*, New York: Nation Books.
Conklin, B. A. (1997) 'Body paint, feathers and vcrs: Aesthetics and authenticity in Amazonian activism', *American Ethnologist* 24(4):711–37.
—— (2001) *Consuming Grief: Compassionate Cannibalism in an Amazonian Society*, Austin: University of Texas Press.
Conklin, B. A. and L. R. Graham (1995) 'The shifting middle ground: Brazilian Indians and eco-politics', *American Anthropologist* 97(4):695–710.
Conklin, B. A. and L. M. Morgan (1996) 'Babies, bodies, and the production of personhood in North America and a native Amazonian society', *Ethos* 24(4):657–94.
DFAIT [Department of Foreign Affairs and International Trade, Canada] (2003) Pataxo. Aboriginal Planet. http://www.dfait-maeci. gc.ca/aborginalplanet/750/archives/june2003/art7_main-en.asp
Ehrenreich, J. (n.d.) The Awá body transformed: Identity, dissembling, and resistance among an indigenous people of the "true" rainforest. Ms.
El Guindi, F. (1999) *Veil: Modesty, Privacy, and Resistance*, New York: Berg.
Feder, D. (2001) The Zapatista movement completed a historic caravan across the Mexican south in Mexico City. The Student Underground (Boston University) 32 (April 6):1–4. (www.thestudentunderground.org.article. phpe?Issue=32$Article ID=5)
Fisher, W. (1994) 'Megadevelopment, environmentalism, and resistance', *Human Organization* 53:220–32.
Gomes, L. and P. Silber (1992) 'A explosão do instinto selvagem', *Veja* (São Paulo) 25(24):68–84.
Hollanda, E. and P. Andrade (1997) 'Dignidade incendiada', *Istoé* 1439 [30 April]:20–3.
ISR (2001) 'Stop the FTAA', *International Socialist Review* 17, April–May. www.isreview. org/issues/17/stoptheftaa.html [accessed 14 November 2003].
Lutz, C. and J. Collins (1993) *Reading National Geographic*, Chicago: University of Chicago Press.
Knauft, B. (ed.) (2002) *Critically Modern: Alternatives, Alterities, Anthropologies*, Bloomington: Indiana University Press.
Lippard, L. (ed.) (1992) *Partial Recall*, New York: New Press.
McCallum, C. (1995) 'The Veja Payakan', *CVA Newsletter* 2/94:2–8.
Monsivais, C. (2002) From the subsoil to the mask that reveals the invisible Indian, in T. Hayden (ed.) *The Zapatista Reader*, New York: Nation Books.
Nelson, D. (1994) 'Rigoberta Menchu jokes', *Anthropology Today* 10(6):3–6.

Ong, A. (1995) State versus Islam: Malay families, women's bodies and the body
    politic in Malaysia, in A. Ong and M.G. Peletz (eds) *Bewitching Women, Pious
    Men*, Berkeley: University of California Press.
Pinheiro, D. and G. Camarotti (1997) 'Planalto selvagem', *Veja* 1493 [30 April]:24–8.
Ponce de Leon, J. (ed.) (2001) *Our Word is Our Weapon : Selected Writings /
    Subcommandante Marcos*, New York: Seven Stories Press.
Potiguara, E. (1992) 'Harvesting what we plant', *Cultural Survival Quarterly* 16:46–8.
Ramos, A. R. (1998) *Indigenism: Ethnic Politics in Brazil*, Madison, WI: University of
    Wisconsin Press.
Rival, L. (2002) *Trekking Through History: The Huaorani of Amazonian Ecuador*, New
    York: Columbia University Press.
Rowanchilde, R. (1993) Cross cultural body modification: A literature review, www.
    bmezine.com/ritual/970101/cc001.html (accessed 2 June 2002).
Ruggiero, G. and S. Sahukla, (eds) (1996) *Zapatista Encuentro: Documents from the
    1996 Encounter for Humanity and Against Neoliberalism*, New York: Seven
    Stories Press.
Seeger, A. (1981) *Nature and Society in Central Brazil*, Cambridge, MA: Harvard
    University Press.
Seeger, A., R. da Matta, and E. B. Viveiros de Castro (1979) 'A construção da pessoa
    nas sociedades indígenas brasileiras', *Boletim do Museu Nacional* (Rio de
    Janeiro), Antropologia, n.s. 32:2–19.
Stimpfl, J. (2000) Veiling and unveiling: Reconstructing Malay female identity
    in Singapore, in L. B. Arthur (ed.) *Undressing Religion: Commitment and
    Conversion from a Cross-Cultural Perspective*, New York: Berg.
Taylor, L. (1997) 'Update: Better than Batman', *New Internationalist Magazine* 296.
    www.newint.org.issue296/update.htm, accessed 29 October 2003.
Thomas, N. (1994) *Colonialism's Culture: Anthropology, Travel and Government*,
    Cambridge, UK: Polity Press
Torgovnick, M. (1992) 'Skin and bolts', *Artforum International* (December):64–5.
Turner, T. S. (1991) 'The social dynamics of video media in an indigenous society',
    Visual Anthropology Review 7(2):70.
—— (1992) 'Defiant images: The Kayapo appropriation of video', *Anthropology
    Today* 8(6):5–16.
Wardlow, H. (2002) 'Hands-up'-ing buses and harvesting cheese-pops: Gendered
    mediation of modern disjuncture in Melanesia, in B. M. Knauft (ed.)
    Critically Modern, Bloomington: Indiana University Press.
Warren, J. W. (2001) *Racial Revolutions: Antiracism and Indian Resurgence in Brazil*,
    Durham, NC: Duke University Press.

3

Black paint, red paint and a wristwatch

The aesthetics of modernity among the Panará in Central Brazil

Elizabeth Ewart

This chapter focuses on the use of clothing among Panará people, an indigenous group living in Central Brazil. This region and the peoples classified as speakers of Gê-languages have been the focus of a number of anthropological studies on indigenous body art. Among others, Gê-speakers include Panará as well as Kayapo, Suya and Timbira people (Grupioni and Lopes da Silva 1995). In particular, the various Kayapo groups have become rather well known for their elaborate body painting while the Suya have also been discussed in terms of the meaning attributed to body ornamentation.[1]

One of the seminal studies in this context remains Terence Turner's paper 'The Social Skin' (1980) in which he discusses body adornment as a means of socialising the essentially natural body. He describes the use of the colours red and black for painting particular parts of the body. Black he suggests is symbolic of the natural, unsocialised interior of the body while the red peripheral parts such as hands, feet and eyes are at the interface with the social. In the same vein he suggests that the use of penis sheaths, lip disks by men and ear ornaments by both men and women can be seen as modifying an essentially natural or pre-social body and thus rendering it ever more social (Turner 1980, 1995).

Again among the Kayapo, this time among a sub-group known as the Xikrin, body painting has been studied in detail by Lux Vidal. She makes the important point that the aesthetic and moral values of bodily presentation are inextricably linked to one another. In this sense, to be 'beautiful' carries with it profound social and moral connotations. She also points out that the act of painting is itself an act of intimate social exchange between the painter and the painted while the hand of the painter stained black is a constant visual sign of her role as skilled painter (Vidal 1992b).

Similarly, Seeger, discussing the meaning of Suya body ornaments shows how the practice of ear piercing and the use of large lip disks by men emphasise the faculties of hearing and speech, which are considered markers of mature adult status. Both men and women wear ear ornaments and Seeger suggests that the act of piercing the ears inscribes on the body the importance – in physical, social as well as moral terms – of good hearing (Seeger 1975). Therefore, a key point made by Seeger is that bodily adornments are not randomly applied but rather, the body parts given attention in this way when taken as a system of interrelated phenomena can tell us interesting things about the moral and aesthetic values of the society in question.

Seeger's argument applies to 'traditional' Suya body ornamentation such as lip disks and ear plugs but here I want to suggest that just as there is a logic behind why Suya men pierce their lips while women do not; why ears are elaborated with large plugs by both sexes whereas nobody pays attention to the ornamentation of eyes, so there is also an element of continuity in why indigenous people, here the Panará, choose certain items of Western clothing over others. Why men wear underwear when women don't, why women sew their own dresses in a certain style while men's clothes, shorts and T-shirts are never home-made. Thus whereas forms of body decoration easily associated with indigenous 'traditional' practices have been extensively studied, this is not true of what might be called more 'innovatory' forms of bodily adornment. This chapter intends to focus on these latter types of body art.

From the literature mentioned above the consensus seems to emerge that the use of body decoration among Gê-societies may be seen as a form of imposing a 'social skin' to follow Turner (1980), on an essentially natural body. In other words, body ornaments[2] are necessary to transform an essentially natural, asocial body into a fully social human being capable of fully social interaction with other human beings and possessing all the moral values associated with such human beings. In this vein one might say that body painting and ornamentation can be read as necessary to enabling a raw, non-social body to become a fully social, real human person.

Clearly, in trying to understand the role and significance of body ornamentation we are faced by the underlying issue of the nature and status of the body in Amerindian thought. Thus Vilaça (2005) has argued that for Amazonian peoples, bodies, are not necessarily best understood as a natural substrate for the cultural elaborations provided by paint, feathers and piercings. Instead of forming an undifferentiated base, she argues that Lowland Amerindian bodies are 'chronically unstable' and liable to transformation. Arguably the propensity for transformation and corporeal fabrication are two sides of a single phenomenon.

Although fabrication has been the issue in many of the analyses of indigenous body adornment mentioned above, the implicit assumption has been that while body painting and lip and ear piercing can be discussed in terms of a socialisation process, as part of the process that makes an as yet undefined body into a real human person, more recent additions to the repertoire of bodily adornment, such as dresses and shorts, flip-flops and

T-shirts, watches and baseball hats cannot. If body paint and feathers are understood as part of and as emerging from within the cultural logic of a given indigenous group, wristwatches, jeans and dresses are not. I suggest this assumption is implicit since the ethnographies of Central Brazilian indigenous peoples are noticeably quiet on the subject of non-indigenous trade goods including clothing.

When Western trade goods are mentioned they are discussed in terms of the dependency generated by the arrival of items such as firearms or fish hooks (e.g. (Fisher 2000; Turner 1992a). While initial assumptions regarding dependency on trade goods may well have been that this dependency would lead to the gradual decline and disappearance of indigenous groups, Turner argues that this has not occurred because indigenous people, in his case the Kayapo, have appropriated the very architecture of dependency and made it their own. So rather than depending on state handouts and the goodwill of NGOs, the Kayapo appropriated a goldmine, receiving royalties from the gold found as well as signing a number of timber concessions with logging companies. With the proceeds which flow both through a community account and individual leaders' accounts, they have managed to largely satisfy their consumer needs as regards non-indigenous trade goods (Turner 1993).

However, what we do not find in Turner's analysis is an account from an indigenous point of view which would answer such questions as: why are the Kayapo interested in particular kinds of consumer goods? What happens to these items within the Kayapo economy? What is the nature of their dependency?

Nevertheless, while non-indigenous trade goods do feature in Turner's analysis this is not very common in the ethnographic accounts of Amazonian societies, as Hugh-Jones suggests. Having noted the strength and persistence of indigenous demands for trade goods from anthropologists in the field, he then points out:

> Yet when it comes to the main text of the standard monograph, the
> presence and impact of foreign goods are often strangely absent.
> As if to bring the image of a 'traditional' society into sharper focus,
> the ethnographer has tidied away these intrusive objects, like the
> television cameramen who hide the tin cans from view and plead
> with Indians to remove their clothes to better present the viewer with
> untarnished images of the good life. (Hugh-Jones 1992:43)

In this article I therefore propose to think seriously about the nature of Panará people's interest in the types of bodily adornment that they most commonly wear today, such as dresses and football shorts.

This is not to say that Panará people are no longer interested in body painting, feathers and beadwork. In fact it is precisely in their interest in these aspects of bodily modification that we can see the continuity between 'pre-contact' forms of bodily modification and those of today. The Panará do paint themselves and make body ornaments from beads and feathers and other materials but during my fieldwork from 1996–8 and again in 2003, they were singularly uninterested in discussing them beyond saying that what they were doing was not actually Panará style painting, *panará yon hokjy*, and that the ornaments were upper Xingú or Kayapo ornaments.[3] On some few occasions they did paint Panará style but again the conversations I managed to have about it appeared to me at the time to be singularly unsatisfying and more often than not the conversation would quickly turn to something more interesting such as what made white people's children[4] so fat or why I had not brought back more beads and flip-flops from my most recent trip to the city.

Fairly quickly it became rather obvious to me that Panará people were more interested in acquiring cloth, shorts, T-shirts and flip-flops than they were talking about indigenous body decoration. How then are we to engage with this interest given that in the late twentieth and early twenty-first century acculturation is no longer really a concept that anthropologists in general have found useful, even if the flip-side of this has sometimes been to simply dodge the issue by ignoring the Western paraphernalia strewn about indigenous villages (Hugh-Jones 1992)?

With regard to the Pacific, Nicholas Thomas provides useful hints when he argues that we cannot assume that the meaning of an item discarded by one society will remain unchanged when the same item is adopted by another: 'objects are not what they were made to be but what they have become' (Thomas 1991:4).

Apart from this point regarding the transformation in meaning that occurs when objects move through time and space and across societies, a further persuasive reason to approach this matter through an anthropological lens is Panará people's own enduring and intense interest in non-Panará objects. During fieldwork this was most apparent in their unceasing interest in discussing how to acquire Western goods, how these are made, why white people know how to make all these things and in general how beautiful other people's – not just white people's but also other indigenous peoples' – things are.

> Puooh, why do white people know everything? Nothing was left for
> Indians. Look at a bicycle, so many small pieces. How do you make
> the transparent parts of glass? The thing I most wonder about is
> fishing line. How do you make it? If you make it in a factory, do you
> earn money? [P., approximately eighteen-year-old man]

Now it seems to me that among a people where great attention is paid to what goes on on the surface of the body and where surface modifications of the body play a significant role in the beautification of persons and the generation of moral well-being, one might gainfully take contemporary bodily modifications such as the wearing of shorts and dresses, the interest in football strips or the use of new hairstyles more seriously as topics for anthropological analysis. Equally it may well be necessary to re-examine the distinction between indigenous and non-indigenous bodily modifications, given that as Conklin has pointed out, there may be strong political motivations involved when indigenous groups adopt the featherwork of those indigenous groups that have been successful in attracting media attention and securing important rights for themselves (Conklin 1997). The question that poses itself is whether from the point of view of indigenous people, this adoption of feather headdresses or styles of painting from other indigenous groups is considered to be of a different nature or adopted for different reasons than for example the acquisition of white people's clothes, such as jeans and T-shirts. Furthermore, given the close relationship between social, moral and aesthetic values, how useful is it to separate out for example the political dimension of bodily adornment as distinct from its moral or aesthetic role? I return to some of these questions below, but first it will be useful to address the ethnography on which this discussion is based.

The Panará

The Panará entered into sustained and largely peaceful relations with Brazilian national society in 1973 when a Brazilian government Indian agency (FUNAI) contact expedition first presented the Panará with white people's presents face to face.[5] At this time, government policy in those cases where there was perceived to be an interest in establishing peaceful relations with a particular indigenous group, pursued a policy of swamping indigenous people with presents, first hanging them up in the forest for the Indians to collect and then distributing goods in the villages. These processes have been well documented in Adrian Cowell's documentary film as well as his book (Cowell 1995 [1973]) *The Tribe that Hides From Man*. They are also described in Cowell's more recent film, *The Last of the Hiding Tribes* (Channel 4 1999) which is about what happened to many of these formerly 'isolated Indians' in the years after their respective 'first contacts'.

The Panará contact in 1973, precipitated by Brazilian government plans to build the Cuiabá-Santarem highway through Panará territory, brought with it a demographic disaster of sheer unimaginable proportion. Estimated at being a population of between 300 and 400 in the late 1960s, the Panará had shrunk to seventy-nine survivors by 1975, decimated mainly by diseases, failing or even absent medical support and the fact that in this period no women gave birth. At this point the decision was taken by the Brazilian authorities to remove the Panará from the territory they had been living in and through which the Cuiabá–Santarem highway was being built. As a result, in 1975, seventy-nine Panará survivors were flown to the Xingú Indigenous People's Park, some 300 kilometres to the south-east. Here the Panará, formerly accustomed to living pretty much alone, at most fighting with, stealing from or simply avoiding other groups, found themselves living in close contact with fifteen different indigenous groups, some of whom had been their former enemies, with whom they shared a long history of mutual raiding.

The importance of visual appearance in determining the nature as well as social and moral status of what is perceived, is underlined by a Panará account of how they came to move to the Xingú in the mid-1970s. At the time of the move, two Panará elders were taken to the Xingú for an advance reconnaissance trip. They came back to the other Panará in the Peixoto saying that they had seen people (*panará*) in the Xingú, people who cut their hair above their eyes and painted with red face paint. In the words of an older Panará woman:

> Krekon said: 'let's go and get white people's things.' He came back (from the Xingú) and said: 'they have red face paint, they cut their hair above their eyes. There are panará (i.e. people) over there a long way away.'
>
> ...
>
> They were not panará, they had long hair, they were Kayapo, they cut fringes over their eyes and were Suya. Krekon and Hatuja were called liars.

Analysing the nature of bodily coverings in Trio mythology, Peter Rivière has famously pointed out that 'what you see is not necessarily what you get' and appearances can be deceptive (Rivière 1994). As he suggests it is the outcome of an encounter which determines what lies behind the outer appearance. Arguably this is precisely what the Panará experienced when they contemplated and then moved to the Xingú Park. In making the decision to move to their new environment the Panará were influenced by the appearance of the people some of them had met there previously. These encounters suggested to them that they were meeting real human beings like themselves, but it was their social practices and the kinds of relationships they were able to establish with these people that later revealed them to be fundamentally different.

In the context of the various groups occupying the Xingú Indigenous Peoples' Park, the Panará found that people that looked rather like them were in fact quite different. More or less simultaneously, they also started creating a new category of otherness encapsulating these same yet different people. In so far as Panará people, according to their own accounts had previously divided the animate world into *panará* and *hipe* they now started to insert an intermediate category, namely that of 'Ugly Things' (*sotangka*) which refers to other indigenous people and which they translate into Portuguese as *indios* (Indians). In certain contexts, this category may include Panará people, while in others they use it to refer to non-Panará indigenous people. The category of 'ugly things' is often also subdivided along the commonly used ethnonyms of the various indigenous groups. In the words of one Panará man: 'before, we called them all *hipe*.[6] It is only today that we know that they are Kayapo, Kajabi, Suya and Juruna.'

The Panará were moved to the Xingú Indigenous Peoples' Park in 1975 but it was to be another several years before they began their slow but impressive road to recovery in every sense – physical, psychological (after a number of suicides appear to have occurred), social (when they started building their own village and gardens) and cultural (as they began resuming gardening practices and performing ceremonies). However, from Panará people's own point of view, they were not yet living well, not yet feeling the sociable energetic strength that characterises Panará life when life is good. It was only in 1997 when they completed a lengthy move back to a part of their old territory in which they had been living pre-contact that they started to say that now, they were once again feeling good.[7]

In the current context the significance of recent Panará history, since the early 1970s, is that in the multi-ethnic Xingú Indigenous People's Park, the possibilities of seeing different painting styles and different ways of modifying the body increased significantly and this resulted in some striking changes in the visual appearance of Panará people. We shall return to this point below.

The things of others

As it happens and – most likely not coincidentally – the FUNAI strategies for contacting and pacifying indigenous people corresponded rather neatly to indigenous expectations of what 'others' have to offer. The policy of flooding villages on the verge of being contacted, and just after contact had been established, with trade goods fed in rather well to a wider concern among many (or even most) Amazonian groups with the material but also non-material culture of others. For instance, among the Kayapo as well as among the Panará, warfare is considered to be one of the prime means of gaining access to other people's valued goods such as headdresses, feather ornaments and baskets for carrying garden produce. Hence the Suya, as Anthony Seeger shows in an article of his (Seeger 1993), were deeply interested in Karl von den Steinen's expedition camped across the river from their village and used the opportunity of having these strangers around to steal whatever they could from them. The Kayapo captured women from other groups not least to learn new songs and dances from them. Nowadays the appearance of others can be captured in new ways, by means of video footage and photographs. Thus after viewing a video film showing other indigenous people including the Wayapí who live north of the Amazon River, Panará women copied Wayapí facial designs in the following days. On another occasion, young men came back from indigenous teacher training courses where they had met men from other groups and immediately set to fashioning Ikpeng earrings for themselves and getting their wives and sisters to paint them with imitation facial tattoos. Interestingly enough they never wished to actually have the permanent tattoos done but they did want to imitate the visual design in the form of facial painting. Thus here the visual appearance of the design on the skin was the issue and not the act of tattooing itself and hence the more permanent inscription of design under the skin.

In the same way as visual designs are acquired from other groups, nowadays the existence of tape recorders in the villages means that different indigenous groups' music can be acquired and listened to and ultimately also imitated. The same can also be said of non-indigenous music and the majority of 'Panará' dances and festivals I witnessed were in fact ceremonies learned from other people, be they Suya rituals, evenings spent dancing to *forró*, music from north-eastern Brazil, or the performance of Kayapo ceremonies. Equally, the Panará, especially younger men, expressed a very keen interest in some tapes of Hindi film music I happened to have with me in the early months of my fieldwork. I suspect that their interest may have been sparked by my description of this music as being *musica da India*, which they may have interpreted as music by female Indians, as opposed to music from the sub-continent. Certainly, there was more enthusiasm for my Bollywood hits then there was for Johann Sebastian Bach's Suites which some people described as *triste* (sad).

A Panará wardrobe

While music and dance are but one dimension of Panará people's interest in other people's things I want to now turn to take a closer look at the use of clothing among the Panará. As indicated in the introductory paragraphs to this chapter, what I want to focus on is the way in which non-indigenous body decoration such as shorts, T-shirts, sneakers, dresses, shirts and leather boots are used. How useful is it to see these more recent types of bodily coverings as symptoms of a modernity that is transforming or perhaps even eroding 'tradition'?

Panará people use a number of different items of clothing on a more or less daily basis. Men wear underpants, shorts, T-shirts, flip-flops or boots for working in the forest or gardens. They also wear football kit for the frequent games of football that punctuate village life. Women wear only dresses and flip-flops. The dresses are hand-made[8] from thin cotton or synthetic materials and all of them essentially follow one of two styles (described later in this chapter).

At the one level Panará people's approach to the use of clothing is highly utilitarian or pragmatic in the sense that when women swathe themselves in loads of clothing when assisting youths who are hornet-bashing, a ritual performed by young men during which they plunge their fists into a hornet's nest, the women avoid getting stung quite as much. Similarly, women like to wrap their babies in towels or make tiny dresses for them, because that way they won't get bitten by quite so many sandflies and mosquitoes out in the garden or forest.

In the village, young children looking after babies and young mothers sometimes entertain themselves by dressing up the babies in shop-bought clothing such as tiny trainers, little T-shirts and trousers. Similarly babies are often hung about with necklaces and bracelets which are soon discarded or removed again. When women are engaged in painting sessions prior to a festival, they also frequently paint bits of design onto their young babies and it is common to see infants with just fragments of design on them, either because the babies refused to lie still or because the mothers had to go off and do other things, such as paint themselves.

With relation to indigenous style body painting it has been suggested that the modification and embellishment of the body renders a basically asocial, 'neutral' or undetermined body, into a properly human body. So by painting and adorning the body Panará people acquire and manifest the moral, aesthetic and social values of real humans. Now what happens when they clothe their bodies in Western-style clothing? Here I argue that we cannot fully understand the interest in and use of clothes among the Panará if we think of them strictly in terms of coverings to hide the body nor strictly as mere signs of social change.

I suggest that just like the designs on the body which make an indeterminate body into a fully human body, endowing the person with the capabilities and attributes of being fully human (i.e. *panará*), so clothing is also a means of acquiring certain attributes that allow you to operate in the social world of those who produce and wear these clothes, namely white people (*hipe*).

In the following I want to try and show how this is so: to start with, I would want to emphasise that the use of clothing among the Panará does not seem to be in any way linked to an idea of 'turning into white people' and therefore it is in no way linked to a notion of changing self-identity or loss of indigenous culture. What goes on, I suggest, is more complex, more interesting and has much more to do with Panará notions of who real people, i.e. *panará*, are and how to relate as 'real people' to white people.

Firstly, there is clearly a political dimension to the ways in which people present themselves as well as the ways in which their bodily presentation is viewed and received and it seems to me to be useful to briefly discuss some work which has been done on the use of clothing as a way of affirming or creating an ethnic identity within the wider field of indigenous politics and hence claims to be recognised as legitimate agents within national politics.

It is not surprising that bodily presentation and the use of certain kinds of clothing are means of making statements regarding the self in a broader political context. This is particularly clear among indigenous groups with a high level of media consciousness and a high level of media presence, such as, in Brazil, the Kayapo and some of the upper Xingú groups. As Beth Conklin has pointed out, those groups who have not presented themselves in quite such striking terms have often lost out in the battle for media attention and hence the ability to put their case to the broader world (Conklin 1997). Hence cashing in on the non-indigenous imagination of what 'real' indigenous people are – or should be – requires the strategic deployment of exotica such as feather headdresses and complex painted designs on the body. It also requires careful assessment of when and for whom it is and is not appropriate to turn out looking either very 'Indian' or very 'White'.[9]

In a similar vein, Turner (1991) argues that Kayapo people's appearance before the media in full body paint and adorned with feathers and beads, where in the 1960s they wore T-shirts and jeans, marks a new level of political self-consciousness where the presentation of an image as a 'really indigenous person' to the outside and the assertion of cultural distinctiveness are politically important strategies.

Clearly, there are situations in which appearing 'really Indian' is advantageous and this appearance is achieved by wearing the attire associated with Indians. It is national society which makes this association but it is indigenous people who, fully cogent of national society's views and expectations, adopt this 'Indian' attire. Thus the Kayapo at their big meeting in Altamira in 1988 when they summoned indigenous people from throughout the region, as well as the national and international media to protest against a planned hydro-electric dam and to discuss issues of

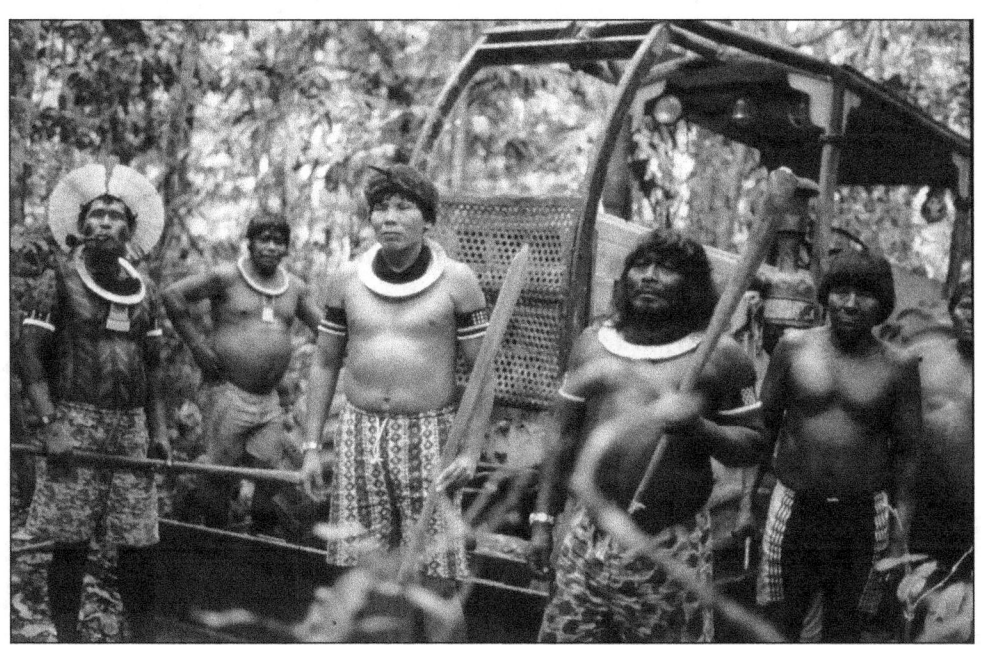

Plate 3.1   *Panará men after capturing machinery from an illegal logging operation, 1998*

environmental and political concern, appeared at the meetings and on TV in full body paint with feather headdresses and carrying war clubs.

However, I wish to suggest that the decisions and choices involved in wearing clothes are not just of a political nature, a self-conscious reflection on how best to manage external expectations of and pressures on one's own self-image. Above I mentioned that the wearing of Western-style clothes, called by the Panará *pe nkâ* (white people's skin) can be understood as a means of acquiring certain attributes and capabilities and is emphatically not about turning oneself permanently or irreversibly into a white person.

When Panará people visit the towns and cities of white people they find very different norms of behaviour. Firstly, they must use Portuguese, pay for food and lodging, and the Panará further maintain that white people routinely pay for sex too. The whole process of acquiring goods – going shopping – requires a string of exchanges, verbal exchanges and exchanges of money for items. If Panará people want to be seen as white people they must adopt their skin, that is wear white people's clothes so that white people will treat them as fully human within their own world. As Viveiros de Castro aptly suggests, we might liken this process to what happens when a diver dons a wet suit. In doing so, he or she is not seeking to turn into a fish but rather to acquire and activate those attributes of fish that allow them to exist under water (Viveiros de Castro 1998:482). Clothing does not conceal a different essence, so a Panará man wearing jeans, sneakers and a shirt is not pretending to be a white man, or hiding his Panará-ness but rather is activating certain attributes of being a white person such as speaking Portuguese, being listened to by other Brazilian people, receiving payments for services and in turn paying for food and drink as you do when you are in the city. Rivière (1994) has suggested that what you see is not what you get and indeed outer appearances can be deceptive. A Panará man in the world of Brazilian national society operates very well – not because he has transformed into a white person but rather because he disposes of the tools, white people's clothes, to operate in white people's worlds.

However, to operate efficiently in the world of white people by modifying one's body appropriately is just one dimension. The other is the necessity to appear 'indigenous' in the eyes of those whites who are involved in acceding to indigenous demands for land, goods, support or whatever the particular issue at hand. It is in this light that we can understand the following: when the Panará go to Brasília on official missions which they have done with some regularity in recent years, during the process of re-claiming and gaining official recognition for the territory they now inhabit, they generally travel in pairs or multiple pairs, one older leader and his younger interpreter. In appearance the elders are quite distinct from their younger companions: the leader leaves the village and meets officials fully painted, with feather headdress and wearing neck and ear ornaments, often bare-chested with jeans or even just shorts. Meanwhile his young interpreter who will be responsible not only for translating during official meetings but also for assisting the leader in his shopping (an important aspect of these trips to the city) will be wearing a clean new pair of jeans, usually brand new shoes and a spotless new T-shirt.

It is as if travelling in pairs these men cover all the aspects of being politically effective as indigenous people. On the one hand they need to assert their indigenousness through their visual appearance before non-indigenous people, meeting the stereotypical expectations and ideas held by large swathes of the Brazilian population about what indigenous people are like. On the other hand, they also need to be able to talk effectively to non-indigenous people in order to see their demands met. Therefore the interpreter at least needs to be seen by government officials as a person who understands the complexities and procedural proprieties of Brazilian indigenous politics. When in the city, young Panará men often also adopt Brazilian names, something older men never do.[10]

Thus a successful mission to the city depends on deploying numerous capabilities: the ability to imagine and correspond to white people's images of what Indians should look like, as well as applying the skills and knowledge of how to be a white person in a white person's world. Travelling in pairs the Panará appear to meet all these requirements, looking on the one hand 'really Indian' and on the other 'just like a white person'.

These trips to the city are not just important in the context of indigenous politics vis-à-vis the Brazilian state. They are also highly significant in terms of internal Panará politics. In this context, the travellers' positions as influential men in their own community rest on their success in persuading non-indigenous people to meet their demands as well as their success in obtaining large quantities of Western trade goods which are in turn highly valued back in the village.

So far I have discussed the way men, and in particular men with a political role vis-à-vis the outside manage their physical appearance. I have suggested that the ways in which they embellish their bodies may be seen to furnish them with certain capabilities that are necessary to operate effectively in particular inter-ethnic situations and contexts.

For women the picture is slightly different in so far as there is a sort of gendered approach to contact with non-indigenous people where men go first and women come after. This temporal order can be seen not just in relations with non-Panará people but also in the order in which people leave the village to go hunting or gathering in the forest, where men walk first and women bring up the rear while the opposite occurs on the way back into the village.

The ideas about who goes first and who encounters non-Panará first and the results of these encounters can be seen as linked to the fact that among the Panará (but also among many other groups) men have started in many ways to look more like non-indigenous people. This is particularly noticeable with regard to their hairstyles. Meanwhile women have also adopted new hairstyles but they tend to be those of women from other indigenous groups as opposed to white women. Thus we find that Panará women today look a lot more like Kayapo or Suya women while Panará men, the younger ones in particular, have adopted the appearance of non-indigenous Brazilians.

There is a further difference between women and men's use of clothing among the Panará. According to their own accounts, Panará people learnt to use clothing from the Suya in the Xingú Indigenous People's park in the late 1970s. As one Panará woman explained to me:

> Kaye (Richard Heelas' wife)[11] brought us cloth and showed us how to sew dresses. The Suya taught us how to sew dresses. They had their own *hipe* (white person) who brought them many things. They told us to look after our *hipe* so that he would bring us many things.

Two things I think are conveyed here. Firstly that the use of clothing was acquired from others, from non-Panará, and secondly that acquiring clothing was closely tied to the importance of maintaining relations with a particular kind of non-Panará other – here white people – in order to maintain access to such items. A further interesting issue raised here, is that these white people's clothes are acquired from white people but this acquisition is mediated and rendered significant by other indigenous people among whom the Panará had only recently started living peacefully.

Earlier in this chapter I described how Panará people came to insert a third category (Indians) into the binary opposition between Panará and non-Panará people (*hipe*). In paying attention to Panará descriptions of how they came to acquire *hipe* clothing, we find that it is from this intermediary category, which is at once different but also similar to Panará people that these items are acquired. In the context of the general relationship of modernity to tradition this clearly raises the question of exactly whose modernity was being acquired here. When Panará women learnt about sewing dresses from Suya women and when they learnt about the importance of cultivating 'their' white person, were they incorporating white people's material culture and knowledge into their repertoire of bodily presentations or was it Suya people's objects and values?

The dresses women refer to when they talk about Suya dresses all follow a single pattern. A relatively tight top is sewn onto a wider skirt. Occasionally a frilly border is also sewn onto the hem. For years this was the only type of dress the Panará wore and they sewed them first by hand and later on sewing machines acquired either in payment for shamanic services to other, more affluent groups, or from a Brazilian non-governmental organisation.

In contrast to the way in which women's clothes were almost always home-made, men never ever wore T-shirts or shorts which were hand-made. However, more recently women too are entering into the ready-made market. In the mid to late 1990s a new style of dress became popular, particularly among women who were not breast-feeding. This is the style of dress worn by Kayapo women and it is quite distinct from the other style. It is straight, with two contrasting coloured vertical bands down either side on the front and often two little pockets on either side. These dresses are not made by the Kayapo but rather are manufactured in the neighbouring towns especially for the Kayapo. I have never seen a non-indigenous person, a white person, wearing such a dress. The Panará get their supply of these dresses from the Kayapo, usually as part of a payment for shamanic curing services or in exchange for peanuts from Panará gardens.

Unlike the men, women very rarely go to the city on missions to negotiate or talk with Brazilians. At most they go when one of their children is ill and needs hospitalisation and they go along to look after the child while in hospital. On such trips they will certainly be accompanied by a husband, or brother who will deal with the white people in the town. While many younger women understand a good amount of Portuguese they consistently refuse to speak in that language. As such, one might say they do not activate any capacities of white people in order to deal with these white people.

In fact, wearing specifically white people's clothes is rather discouraged among women. I remember in particular one men's house debate one warm evening under the stars when several of the men (all of whom use underwear nowadays) made speeches about the disadvantages and dangers of women wearing underpants. These were said to be too tight and would lead to the rotting of vaginas. On the same memorable evening another problem was addressed. Several younger men had allegedly been having sex using condoms which they had picked up in the city on a recent trip. Again, the elders discouraged this in no uncertain terms, suggesting that the condoms would get stuck inside the women's vaginas and would again lead to their rotting.

In both debates, the point was brought home by suggesting that women were not white people and therefore should not wear underpants because that is not what real people, i.e. Panará people do. Likewise, the young men

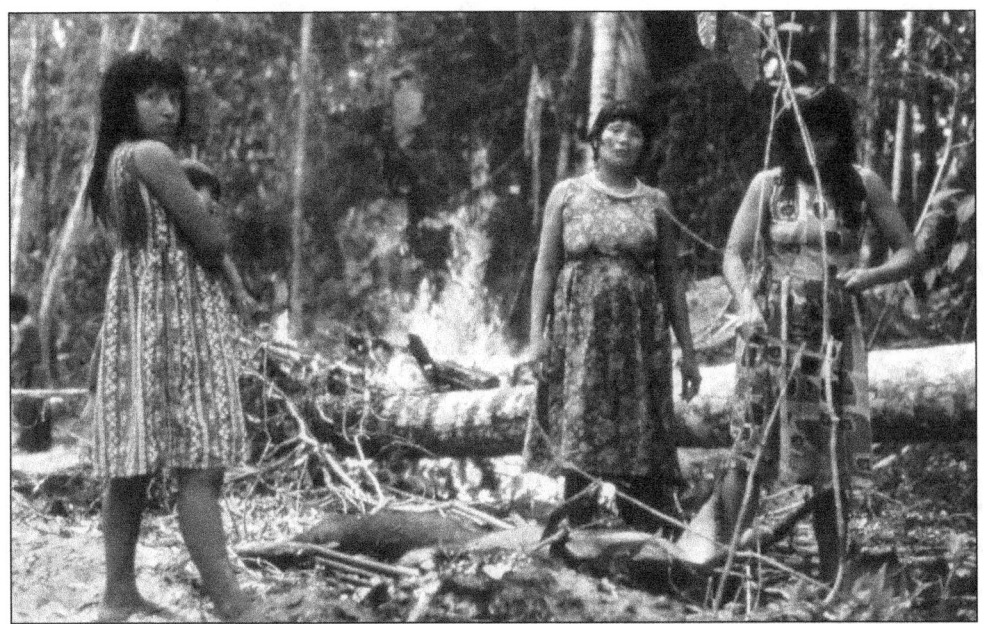

Plate 3.2   *Panará women wearing Suya-style dresses*

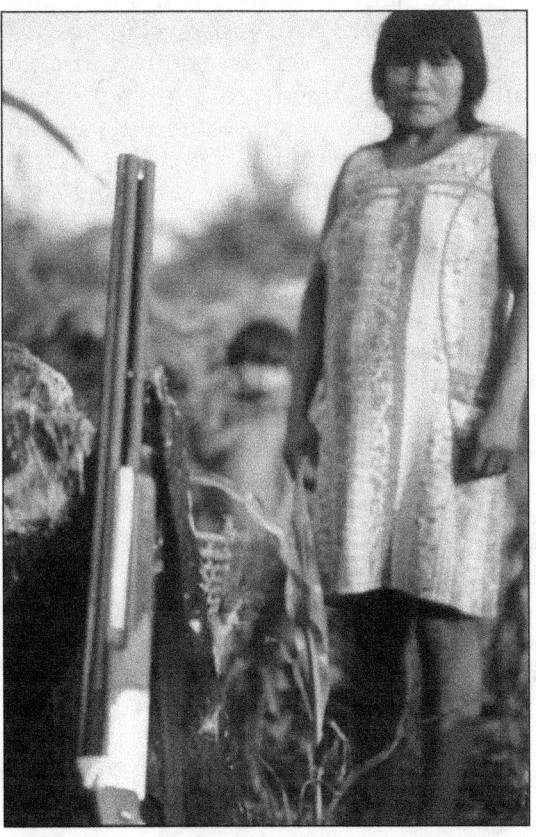

Plate 3.3   *A Kayapo-style dress*

were told: 'Are you white people that you use condoms for sex? No, you are Panará.'

Thus, in spheres, where the attributes and capacities of white people are not desired, particularly in the very Panará domain of conjugal sexual relations with one another (note that the Panará very rarely marry outside their own village) the bodily ornaments of white people such as underpants and condoms are also not considered appropriate. The point here is that whilst the objects and adornments of non-Panará are of interest and use in dealing with non-Panará people, this same paraphernalia is unwelcome if it is seen to be interfering with the nature of human sociality and the social relations that Panará people entertain among themselves. It is not Panará social life that Panará people wish to change in wearing white people's things – or indeed any other people's things – instead, they intend simply to acquire the attire to be able to operate within these distinct social worlds when the need arises to do so. Therefore, the use of white people's clothing effects a temporary transformation rather than contributing to the fabrication of a properly human body.

So in sum, I return to the question of what clothes tell us about the people we study. I suggest they tell us quite a bit, but not simply in the terms illustrated by Veber (1996) where the use of 'traditional' costume manifests ethnic affirmation and claims to authenticity employed in skilful political manipulation. In her argument, clothing reveals much more than it conceals. I suggest that you can see more than just revelation; you can see strategies used in accessing and activating certain bodily capacities on a temporary basis. While in Panará eyes it is perfectly legitimate and even necessary to be able to function like a white person when on a mission to the city, it is totally unacceptable to attempt to activate these kinds of capacities when being Panará among Panará, or rather a human being among human beings, engaging in the highly human exchanges that characterise Panará life, such as sex, marriage or the raising of children.

Likewise, when considering the use of clothing as an aspect of modernity, we do well to examine with some care the gendered dimension of such usage as well as the history of acquiring clothing. By doing so, the Panará case illustrates that what from the outside may well look like a simple case of Panará people becoming more like Brazilian nationals, is in fact far more nuanced, with women and men pursuing differing goals in their use of bodily adornment as well as perceiving the adoption of white people's clothes as not necessarily the bodily adornments of Brazilian national society but rather the adornments of other indigenous groups. It is clear that the Panará attraction to the things of others cannot simply be understood as part of their encounter with a modern world in the recent past. Instead, it seems that, probably like for many peoples around the world, 'traditional' life has depended on innovation and inclusion of new elements from a multitude of sources since long before 'modernity' ever began.

NOTES
1 For examples on the Kayapo see (Lea 1992; Turner 1991; 1995; 1980; 1992b; Verswijver 1996; Vidal 1985; 1992a). For an analysis of body ornamentation among the Suya see Seeger (1975)

2 The term 'ornament' is problematic in so far as it suggests something slightly superfluous, even frivolous while the ethnography on the subject in the region makes it very clear that these objects and practices are key to the making of fully social human beings.

3 Though it was noticeable in 2003 that Panará people were reviving interest in what were identified as Panará songs, dances and body designs. This may well be related to their growing awareness of themselves as a distinct 'ethnic group' as well as the possibilities of promoting 'Panará culture' as a politically useful tool. This in turn can be seen in the context of their successful court case against the Brazilian federal government which resulted in the Panará being granted indemnification for loss of life and land during the contact of the 1970s. This case was unprecedented in the history of Brazil and led to a fair amount of publicity and celebrations in early 2003.

4 In using the term 'white people' I follow Panará usage of the term *hipe* – *branco* in Portuguese – which in the late 1990s referred to all non-indigenous people regardless of skin colour.

5 Historical research suggests that there had been contacts between ancestors of the Panará and Portuguese colonial settlers in the interior of Brazil during the eighteenth and nineteenth centuries but these ancestors, known as the Southern Cayapó subsequently withdrew from the settlers and migrated northwards into the forest see (Giraldin 1997).

6 Today, *hipe* is translated into Portuguese as *branco* (white person) but it may more generally be considered to be the antithetical category to Panará and as such encompasses meanings such as 'enemy/other/non-panará'.

7 Of course, in the late 1990s they were faced with serious problems in terms of territorial management and environmental exploitation as well as being brought into a whole new field of indigenous politics and pressure from surrounding indigenous groups, but that is not the subject of the present chapter.

8 Although in 2003 shop-bought, Brazilian-style skirts and dresses were also quite commonly seen in the village.

9 Hanne Veber for example, discusses the political dimensions of wearing or not wearing indigenous clothes among Asheninka people in eastern Peru (Veber 1996)

10 These Brazilian names are also activated for other white people's activities such as playing football. In 2003 I found that young men employed in jobs such as health monitors or mechanics tended to use Brazilian names while carrying out their duties.

11 Richard Heelas together with his wife, Kaye, was the first to carry out long-term fieldwork with the Panará in the 1970s (Heelas 1979).

Bibliography

Conklin, B.A. (1997) 'Body paint, feathers, and vcrs: aesthetics and authenticity in Amazonian activism', *American Ethnologist* 24: 711–37.

Cowell, A. (1995 [1973]) *The Tribe that Hides From Man*, London: Pimlico.

Fisher, W.H. (2000) *Rain Forest Exchanges: industry and community on an Amazonian frontier*, Washington: Smithsonian Institution.

Giraldin, O. (1997) *Cayapó e Panará: Luta e Sobrevivência de um Povo Jê no Brasil Central*, Campinas: Editora da Unicamp.

Grupioni, L.D.B. and A. Lopes da Silva (eds) (1995) *A Temática Indígena na Escola*, Brasília: MEC/MARI/UNESCO.

Heelas, R.H. (1979) The Social Organisation of the Panará, a Gê Tribe of Central Brazil, unpublished DPhil thesis, University of Oxford

Hugh-Jones, S. (1992) 'Yesterday's luxuries, tomorrow's necessities: business and barter in northwest Amazonia', in C. Humphrey and S. Hugh-

Jones (eds) *Barter, Exchange and Value: an anthropological approach*, Cambridge: Cambridge University Press.

Lea, V. (1992) 'The Houses of the Mebengokre (Kayapo) of Central Brazil – a New Door to their Social Organization', in J. Carsten and S. Hugh-Jones (eds) *About the House*, Cambridge: Cambridge University Press.

Rivière, P. (1994) 'WYSINWYG in Amazonia', *JASO* 25: 255–62.

Seeger, A. (1975) 'The Meaning of Body Ornaments: A Suya Example', *Ethnology* 14: 211–24.

——— (1993) 'Ladrões, Mitos e História: Karl von den Steinen Entre os Suiás – 3 a 6 de Setembro de 1884', in V. Penteado Coelho (ed.) *Karl von den Steinen: Um Século de Antropologia no Xingú*, São Paulo: edusp/FAPESP.

Thomas, N. (1991) *Entangled Objects: exchange, material culture, and colonialism in the Pacific*, Cambridge, Mass.: Harvard University Press.

Turner, T. (1980) 'The Social Skin', in J. Cherfas and R. Lewin (eds) *Not Work Alone: A Cross-Cultural Study of Activities Superfluous to Survival*, London: Temple Smith.

——— (1991) 'Representing, Resisting, Rethinking: Historical Transformations of Kayapo Culture and Anthropological Consciousness', in G. Stocking (ed.) *Colonial Situations: Essays on the Contextualization of Ethnographic Knowledge*, Madison: University of Wisconsin Press.

——— (1992a) 'Os Mebengokre Kayapó: História e Mudança Social: De comunidades autônomas para a coexistência interétnica', in M. Carneiro da Cunha (ed.) *História dos Índios no Brasil*, São Paulo: Companhia das Letras.

——— (1992b) 'Symbolic Language of Bodily Adornment', in G. Verswijver (ed.) *Kaiapó Amazonia*, Tervuren: Royal Museum of Central Africa.

——— (1993) 'De Cosmologia a História: resistência, adaptação e consciência social entre os Kayapo', in E. Viveiros de Castro and M. Carneiro da Cunha (eds) *Amazonia: Etnologia e História Indígena*, São Paulo: NHII/USP/FAPESP.

——— (1995) 'Social Body and Embodied Subject: Bodiliness, Subjectivity, and Sociality among the Kayapo', *Cultural Anthropology* 10: 143–70.

Veber, H. (1996) 'External Inducement and Non-Westernization in the Uses of the Ashéninka Cushma', *Journal of Material Culture* 1: 155–82.

Verswijver, G. (1996) *Mekranoti: Living among the Painted People of the Amazon*, Munich: Prestel.

Vidal, L.B. (1985) 'Ornamentação entre Grupos Indígenas', in FUNARTE (ed.) *Arte e Corpo*, Rio de Janeiro: FUNARTE.

——— (ed.) (1992a) *Grafismo Indígena: Estudos de Antropologia Estética*, São Paulo: Studio Nobel/FAPESP/edusp.

——— (1992b) 'A pintura corporal e a arte gráfica entre os Kayapó-Xikrin do Cateté', in L.B. Vidal (ed.) *Grafismo Indígena*, São Paulo: Livros Studio Nobel.

Vilaça, A. (2005) 'Chronically unstable bodies: reflections on Amazonian corporalities', *Journal of the Royal Anthropological Institute* 11: 445–64.

Viveiros de Castro, E. (1998) 'Cosmological deixis and Amerindian perspectivism', *Journal of the Royal Anthropological Institute* 4: 469–88.

4

Clothing as acculturation in Peruvian Amazonia

Peter Gow

In 1961, the American travel writer Peter Matthiessen descended the Urubamba river in Peruvian Amazonia. Of one place he visited, a major Piro settlement, he wrote the following:

> We arrived at Sepahua ... in the early afternoon and were greeted on the bank by a mixed band of Piros, Amahuacas and Machiguengas. These people were not, alas, in tribal dress and were thus more or less indistinguishable: the place looked less like an Indian village than like a kind of charity fresh-air camp, which of course it is. In saying this I wish to indicate no disapproval of Padre Manuel Diez and his cheerful staff of brothers and sisters, nor of the other good Dominicans who have kept our bodies and souls together for nearly a week: these are all good people doing a good job, however distasteful the effects of that job may appear to people like myself. It is very sad to see that the individual characters of these Indians are disappearing so rapidly into the great blender of the white man, holy or otherwise, no matter how beneficial this may be to the belly and salvation of the individual brave: the people at Sepahua are no longer Indians, but ignorant and indigent Peruvians, and their cousins in the small interior rivers, in their long hair and paint, make a far better appearance. In South America, with few exceptions, the tribe which permits itself to come into complete contact with the white man, on the white man's own terms, has perhaps a half-century of existence left to it. (Matthiessen 1962:211)

Matthiessen's account, however apparently self-evident or banal, belongs to a long and complex intellectual tradition. To paraphrase Gombrich on paintings (1960), travel books owe much more to other travel books than they do to the fact of travelling. In this case, Matthiessen's account belongs to a tradition of thinking about the progress of civilization and its relation to nature, both human and other, that congealed in the USA in the nineteenth century, and then expanded outwards. Central to this tradition was the sense that progress, the expansion of civilization, was necessarily destructive of nature and existent cultural diversity. More culture equalled less nature, and more civilization equalled less cultural diversity. The connection to theories of modernity is obvious.

I must here declare an interest. I agree with Matthiessen, for his aesthetic reaction to visual appearance of the indigenous people of the Bajo Urubamba river was, and to an extent remains, my own. This is almost certainly due to the fact that Matthiessen and myself are products of a shared history, that holds certain aesthetic judgments to be axiomatic. Insofar as we are different, it is because I have spent some twenty-five years of active engagement with the indigenous peoples of this part of Peruvian Amazonia, trying to find out what they think about these things. Matthiessen has spent the same amount of time, and longer, thinking about other, equally important, things.

I would like to contrast the quote from Matthiessen with another, from a myth told twenty-one years later by Artemio Fasabi, leader of Santa Clara village, which lies downstream from Sepahua, and is the community where I did most of my fieldwork. He told me:

Long ago, it is said, there was a man who was the only son of a woman with no husband. To support her, he would go into the forest, take off his *cushma*, and become a jaguar. In this form, he would wander in the forest, killing game. When he was finished he would put on his *cushma* again and become human once more, and take the game back to his mother. He brought her back collared peccary, deer, paca, everything.

Cushma is the Spanish word for what Piro people call *mkalu*, a hand-woven and painted cotton robe. The listing of 'collared peccary, deer, paca, everything' specifies the desirability of the protagonist's hunting prowess from the point-of-view of contemporary Piro people. The myth continues, and recounts the origin of sorcery, in the failure of other long ago people to kill that 'jaguar-man'.

Clearly, for Artemio Fasabi, the narrator of this myth, clothing has another meaning to what it might have for Matthiessen. Fasabi, who was born in 1947, attended secondary school in Sepahua, and is very likely to have been one of that 'mixed band of Piros, Amahuacas and Machiguengas' that greeted Matthiessen on that day. It is the nature of the differences in ideas and practices of clothing between people like Artemio Fasabi and Peter Matthiessen that this paper addresses.

Travel literature

In the travel literature on Amazonia, the transformation in traditional clothing and body art styles among indigenous peoples towards 'Western' style or the use of 'white people's' clothes is asserted as both inevitable and evidence of the 'cultural loss' that attends these people's growing contacts with the civilized world. While ethnographers might not agree with the basic premises of such accounts, they have provided little by way of refuting them. Indeed, most ethnographers have done little more than note the change in clothing, and done very little to analyse it (see Hugh-Jones (1992), Veber (1996), and Ewart and Conklin (this volume)). That indigenous Amazonian people quickly take to wearing Western clothing is therefore an unanalysed banality of the literature. If this process is addressed at all, it is addressed as 'acculturation', imagined as the fragility of indigenous Amazonian cultures in the face of Western expansion. However, a concept like 'acculturation' renders such transformations socially and historically opaque.

As a concept, 'acculturation' covers at least three separable levels of change: (a) a change in *terms* (between traditional modes of body decoration and new and alien ones); (b) a change in *relations between terms* (between traditional meanings of body decoration and modern meanings of body decoration); and a change in *systems of relations between terms* (between systems of meaning production, each conceived of as global and self-sufficient, but also as transformational variations of human potentialities). As such, clothing as acculturation in Peruvian Amazonia might be a fact, but is not an anthropological theory of that fact.

The present essay seeks to investigate this phenomenon by means of an *ethnographic theory*. By this term, which I owe to Marcio Goldman of the Museu Nacional/UFRJ, Brazil (personal communication), I mean the anthropological deployment of the categories used by my Piro informants as the key analytical tools for understanding what they are doing. An ethnographic theory is clearly not a 'cultural account', for it uses local categories in ways that local people would not, or at least do not. Nor is it strictly an anthropological theory, for it necessarily uses categories alien to anthropological thought. Ethnographic theories are especially appropriate in situations like the present one, where the analysts are likely to be so committed to a single version of a phenomenon that they are likely to be seriously misled by their *own* local categories which both interest and discombobulate them.

Theorising clothing change

Piro clothing styles, like their body art styles more generally, can be explored in relation to Viveiros de Castro's concept of *perspectival cosmology* (1998) (see also Rivière 1994; Lima 1999 and Gow 2001). Viveiros de Castro characterises indigenous Amazonian perspectival cosmologies as multinaturalist, and contrasts them to the Western multiculturalist cosmology. Multiculturalist cosmologies assert the unity of bodies (all are constructed of the same things and in the same ways) and the multiplicity of souls, minds or cultures. Multinaturalist cosmologies, such as indigenous Amazonian perspectival cosmologies, by contrast, operate through the unity of the mind or soul of all entities, and the multiplicity of bodies. The body, not the mind, is the source of the differentiation of kinds of entities. The body is a series of its affective apparatuses through which the mind perceives the world. Viveiros de Castro argues that the body in perspectival cosmologies is not a *natural grounding*, as we would find it in multiculturalist cosmology, but something closer to a *mask* or to *clothing*. Viveiros de Castro's argument obviously plays on the meanings that we, as multiculturalists, attribute to minds, bodies, masks and clothing. It cannot carry us directly into the meanings of minds, bodies, masks and clothing for multinaturalists.

For example, in a multiculturalist cosmology, a mask or an article of clothing visually occludes a body, making it look like something other than what it really is – the mask or the article of clothing is expressive of and referable to the multiplicity of the minds or cultures of their wearers. In a multinaturalist cosmology, this cannot happen, for all minds and all cultures are the same. Diversity lies with the body. Here, Viveiros de Castro argues, masks, articles of clothing and bodily attributes must be thought of as more closely related to our category of a *diving suit*: that is, as a tool for moving in a medium alien to our normal one. A diving suit allows humans to operate as aquatic creatures, and to operate with aquatic beings on their own terms. A diving suit literally gives humans the bodily attributes of fish or cetaceans, and Viveiros de Castro argues that the same is true of masks and clothing in multi-naturalist cosmologies.

Perspectivism provides a powerful tool for understanding Piro clothing, in terms of what things look like. Juan Sebastián, recounting the myth of origin of weaving, states:

> Before knowing how to spin, they just beat the cotton balls and then painted the flattened cotton with achiote or with other dye plants. It is said that from a distance, people dressed this way looked as if they had red bodies (*ser-powaa*), but that from close up it looked like cloth, when it was actually just a piece of flattened cotton. (Sebastián Perez *et al.* 1974:119, 126–7)

The issue here is not simply 'what things look like', or of clothing as mask or disguise. The word *ser-powaa*, translated here as 'red body' comes from a root *–powa*, which refers to something that is wrapped in something else (Matteson (1965:328)). The same root generates the word *popowalu* (or *popowlu*) which is defined by the *Diccionario Piro* as 'a dressed person; an animal before it has been skinned or plucked of its feathers' (Nies 1986:176–7). A skinned or plucked game animal is in no sense a purer or better expression of its species than the same animal before it was killed. Similarly, a clothed human is not a disguised or masked human. A clothed human is a complete, fully specified, human.

A phenomenological account of Piro clothing

Viveiros de Castro's analysis cannot be reduced to the opposition or dialectic between an external and deceptive appearance and a hidden but more genuine interior. He has pointed out, in 'GUT feelings about Amazonia' (2001), that the relationship between appearance and what that appearance covers is marked by *perpetual disequilibrium*, a phrase borrowed from Lévi-Strauss (1995). For example, for Piro people, clothing, *mkalu*, can be said to cover the body, *-mane*, but this latter is in turn conceived of as the covering of the usually hidden and interior *samenu*, 'soul'. Further, the soul is in turn the deceptive appearance of the *gipnachri*, 'corpse, bone demon', which can be seen after death and rotting in the grave as a reanimated skeleton with burning eyes. However, drinkers of the very powerful hallucinogen *gayapa* report that they see the *gipnachri* of both living and dead people as young and beautifully attired people. This is the limit to my, and perhaps Piro people's, knowledge of the perpetual disequilibrium of appearance and what that appearance covers, but the regression is potentially infinite.[1] These conceptualisations should be borne in mind in the following discussion.

Contemporary Piro people living on the Bajo Urubamba river all now wear what they call *kajitu mkalu*, 'white people's clothing', or *mkalu potu*, 'real clothing'. This clothing comes in gendered forms: shirts, T-shirts, trousers and shorts for men and boys, and dresses, blouses, T-shirts and skirts or culottes for women and girls. Most clothing is bought in stores in the local towns of Atalaya and Sepahua. Some older women make up their own dresses from store-bought cloth, and a small amount of second-hand clothing from North America or Europe, mainly worn by old people and children, is acquired as gifts from local Catholic missionaries. Such clothing is useful, but not particularly desirable.

There is a strong stress among Piro people that all clothing should be bought. Since most money is earned by men, clothing is either bought by men and gifted to others, or bought by women through cash gifted by men. Money is the exclusive possession of its owner: subsequent claims on that money are couched in terms of 'love' or 'care', but never in terms of multiple modes of ownership. Almost all articles of Piro clothing can be specified in terms of who bought them, who provided the money, and who gave what to whom. Piro clothing is bought with money earned almost exclusively by men, although it is not necessarily men who actually buy it, and given as direct gifts to specific people.

Piro people do not often share clothing even in intimate social relations (between sisters for example), nor do they give clothing to others once it has been worn. Even very young children know which clothing in the household pile belongs to them and will refuse to wear even a same-sex sibling's clothing. Such refusals are respected by adults. Indeed, from talking both to children and to adults, it is clear that clothing is the primary form of the possessed object for Piro people. Clothes are likely to be the only kinds of object actually owned by a small child, and clothing is a key theme in adults' accounts of their earliest memories of care received. And, conversely, at the opposite end of the life cycle, all of a person's clothing is destroyed when they die. In fact, in cases where there is no body to mourn during the night after death (which is quite common in cases of drowning, which in turn are fairly common events), the deceased's clothing can substitute for the body.

This form of clothing is, as I have stated, called *kajitu mkalu*, 'white people's clothing', or *mkalu potu*, 'real clothing'. In Ucayali Spanish it is called *ropa legítima*. The Piro *potu*, like the Ucayali Spanish *legítimo/a*, points towards the 'real-ness' of an object, but this is not a conceptual economy that opposes such 'real-ness' to 'fake-ness'. Something that is 'real' is the best and strongest exemplar of a category. With one very important exception, objects that Piro people consider 'real' are imbued with notions of alienness and supernatural power. Such 'real' things defy Piro people's ability to imagine how they might be made. Contemplating such objects as a wristwatch, a radio or an aeroplane, Piro people are at a loss to understand how such things might be made. The important exception to this pattern is 'humans'. Piro people consider themselves to by *yine potu*, 'real humans', the best and strongest exemplar of the category. The knowledge of how to make *yine potu*, 'real humans' is the everyday knowledge of Piro people.

'White people's clothing' or 'real clothing' is opposed to the clothing forms of older dead generations of Piro people, called *mkalu*, the long woven cotton robe worn by men, and *mkalnama*, 'mouth/vagina robe', the woman's woven cotton skirt. Such clothing is still made, but very seldom worn: most is produced for use in the now rare performances of girl's initiation rituals, or for trading to white people.[2] Old-style clothing may be used in everyday life to keep warm when weather is unduly chilly, or as bed clothing, but wearing it in an everyday setting would elicit unfavourable comment, or ridicule.[3]

Change

What does it mean to Piro people to wear 'white people's clothing'? Does it mean that they are turning into white people? Do they think that they are turning into white people? Do they hope that, by wearing these clothes they might be taken for white people? These are the sorts of questions raised by Matthiessen's accounts, and which also underlay my own initial and continuing aesthetic reaction to the appearance of Piro people.

Firstly, Piro people most assuredly do not wear white people's clothing in order to become white people. The Piro word *kajitutachri*, 'one who habitually acts like a white man' is a very serious insult among Piro people. Piro people fear and despise white people for their anger, violence and meanness. Piro people have no interest in becoming white people, or of absorbing their 'culture' or 'ways of being'.

The core value of Piro people is *gwashata*, 'living well', living in intimate peaceful communities full of kinspeople who generously share food and help. 'Living well' is the collective manifestation of the *nshinikanchi*, 'memory, love, mind, mindfulness' of each co-resident. A person's *nshinikanchi* develops in reciprocation of acts of care given during childhood: a child's mindfulness of others is elicited through gifts of food, attention and good-humoured interaction. *Nshinikanchi* is a specific rather than a general disposition: the care another gives is reciprocated to that other. Piro people feel under no obligation to help unrelated people, and will point out that the Piro are the most mindful and intelligent people in the world because it is habitually other Piro people who are kindest to them. White people, by contrast, are habitually described as *mshinikatu*, 'forgetful, unloving, mindless, thoughtless'. *Kajitutachri*, 'one who habitually acts like a white man', is an insult precisely because it carries that very unpleasant loading.

I should note that Piro people in the past kidnapped or bought children from neighbouring indigenous peoples, and continue to capture and raise the young of wild animals. Carefully cared for, such foreign children or pets manifest growing mindfulness. My own experience of fieldwork suggests that anthropologists fit into the same conceptual frame for Piro people.

Mgenoklu, jaguars

Given the extremely negative association of white people, and the manner in which white people are held to invert core Piro values, and indeed core Piro modes of being, why then do Piro people want to wear white people's clothing? An answer lies in their relationship to what we might call their 'traditional clothing', but which Piro people would be more likely to consider 'ancient people's clothing'. Piro people are actually frightened of their 'traditional clothing', for this clothing, in the eyes of Piro people, made them look like jaguars. As I have discussed elsewhere (Gow 2001), this association between 'traditional clothing' and jaguars is both overt and pervasive in Piro thought.

Piro people fear jaguars for three main reasons: the lethal danger that they pose to people; their awful beauty; and their solitude. Jaguars are highly adapted predators of large ground-dwelling mammals, including humans, and so are just downright dangerous. Jaguars compound their dangerousness with their mesmerizing beauty: Piro people's accounts of encounters with jaguars never fail to mention the aesthetic wonder of their appearance. And finally, jaguars are habitually alone. Jaguars are most frightening when one encounters them alone and unexpectedly, when, for example, one is quietly weeding one's garden. And mythologically, the solitude of jaguars is a precondition of human society. Human sociality emerged out of the destruction of jaguar society, when the creator hero Tsla and his brothers murdered all of the 'group-living jaguars' except for an old and pregnant female.

The style of 'ancient people's clothing', cotton robes and skirts painted with *yonchi* designs, made people look like jaguars (*mgenoklu pixkalutu*). In its strongest form, newly woven and painted 'ancient people's clothing', where the black designs shimmer on the brilliant white background of the freshly woven cotton, was worn only during certain occasions where people were dealing with potentially conflictual relations. The major such occasion was *kigimawlo*, girl's initiation ritual, where all Piro people gathered to celebrate the emergence of a girl into womanhood. This gathering of 'all the Piro people along the river' led to the co-presence of people with a history of bad relations, people connected not by their 'mindfulness' of each other, but by their 'forgetfulness'. Bad relations would range from a sense of abandonment between close kin, through memories of a serious fight, to suspicions or actual accusations of sorcery. In such circumstances, Piro people sought to appear to each other in the form of jaguars.

New 'ancient people's clothing' can be considered as the use of a 'jaguar affect', to borrow Viveiros de Castro's concept. That is, an aspect of what makes a jaguar a jaguar, its visual form, is taken on by a non-jaguar as an intimidatory tool. Hosts and guests see each other as jaguars, and experience the fear that jaguars cause among humans. This fearful appearance is then subverted in the ritual process as the hosts serve the guests 'real food', *nika potu*, that is, cooked game and vegetables and manioc beer, rather than *mgenoklu nika*, 'jaguar food', which is raw meat. Sequentially, the cooked game and vegetables assert that these 'jaguars' are really kinspeople, then the manioc beer subverts this identification by rendering them drunk, and therefore as potential affines. The ritual ends as potential affinity is transformed into real, everyday, affinity in the marriage of the initiated girl.

As events, Piro rituals are marked by the 'new' (*gerotu*). Initiation ritual focuses on the emergence of a 'new woman', and all the ritual paraphernalia, and especially the participants' clothing, is new.

Such novelty is, in the case of both the initiand's appearance and in the participants' clothing, marked by high colour contrast, the jaguar intensity of heightened beauty. The transition between ritual event and everyday life is marked by the process of *gitlika*, 'fading, ripening'. This is most marked in the progressive fading of the participants' *nso* (Latin: *Genipa americana*) facial and body paint over the course of the ritual. Such a 'fading, ripening' parallels the transformation of the initial extreme hostility of guest-host relations into those of intensely respectful everyday affinity. Similarly, newly made ritual clothing 'fades and ripens' with age, vigorous washing and re-dying into the unthreatening 'old and ugly clothing' worn in everyday life.

Everyday life is the product of the successful negotiation of extreme and frightening social difference and its transformation into *gwashata*, 'living well'. The everyday qualities of 'living well' are characterised by complex aesthetic qualities, but not by the visually extreme aesthetic enhancements of 'looking like jaguars'. A jaguar-affect, the use of a jaguar's body parts for instrumental ends, is ritually appropriate, but not appropriate to everyday life. This, I think, is the force of the myth that Artemio told me about the 'jaguar-man'. The problem of the 'jaguar-man' was not that he used jaguar-affect as such, but that he used it in everyday life in such a way as to arouse the jealousy of his co-residents, and thus subvert 'living well'. This jealousy caused those others to seek out the nature of his success, and to expose him as a jaguar. In effect, the 'jaguar-man' treated everyday life the way Piro people treat ritual events: the 'jaguar-man' used Piro clothing, a human-affect to further his everyday relations with his mother the way Piro people use jaguar-affect to further ritual relations with each other.

Artemio's story was an 'ancient people's story', a myth. Viveiros de Castro notes in the conclusion to his exposition of perspectival cosmology that,

> ... Amerindian perspectivism has a vanishing point, as it were, where
> the differences between points of view are at the same time annulled
> and exacerbated: myth, which thus takes on the character of an
> absolute discourse. In myth, every species of being appears to others

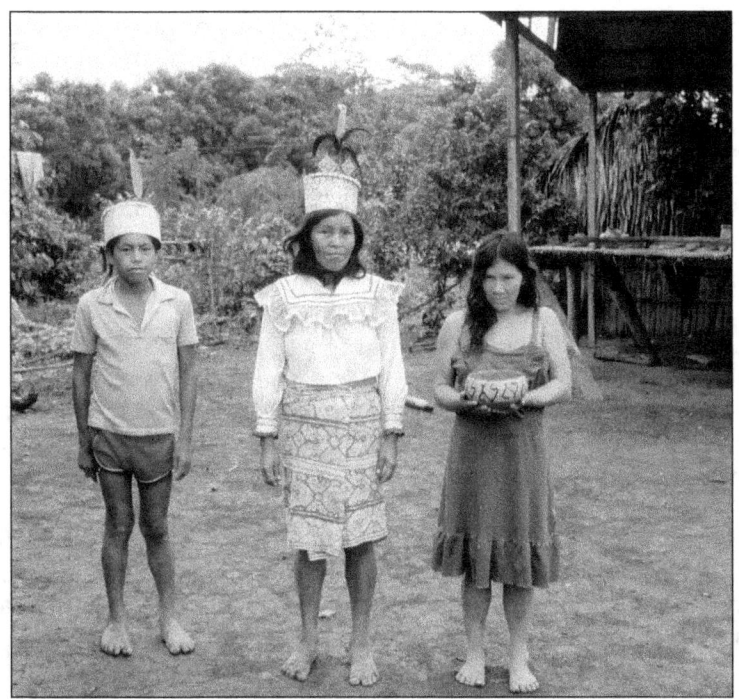

Plate 4.1   *Praga jokingly models her Piro girl's initiation*
outfit, Bufeo Pozo, Bajo Urubamba, 1988

as it appears to itself (as human), while acting as if still showing
its distinctive and definitive nature (as animal, plant or spirit). In a
certain sense, all the beings which people mythology are shamans,
which, indeed is explicitly affirmed by some Amazonian cultures...
Myth speaks of a state of being where bodies and names, souls and
affects, the I and the other interpenetrate, submerged in the same pre-
subjective and pre-objective milieu – a milieu whose end is precisely
what the mythology sets out to tell. (Viveiros de Castro 1998:483–4)

Viveiros de Castro is right here, I think, to address mythic thought through
a spatial metaphor rather than the more habitual temporal one. While it
is true that indigenous Amazonian mythic narratives insistently distance
themselves from everyday life in temporal terms, myths are told and heard
in Piro everyday life, and hence mythic meanings are operative within those
everyday lives (Gow 2001).

    In Artemio's mythic narrative, the central character removes his clothing
and becomes a jaguar. This is because the primary specification of his body
is as a jaguar, which has been secondarily specified as human, through the
wearing of human clothing. As Artemio stated, this myth is the myth of
origin of sorcery. Unlike the 'long ago' people, 'nowadays' people do not
unwittingly share their everyday lives with successful young men who
happen to be jaguars dressed as humans, but they do unquestionably share

their everyday lives with older men who have become jaguars through radical re-specification of their bodies. Such men are powerful shamans.

I mentioned above that the wearing of 'ancient people's clothing' in contemporary Piro settings causes unfavourable comment or ridicule. It is now easier to see why this might be. 'Ancient people's clothing', especially in its strong form of 'new ancient people's clothing' elicits fear, and presumably it always did so. For example, at one girl's initiation ritual I saw, as the fully decorated girls emerged, one young man sniggered and said, 'they look just like Yaminahua women!' The Yaminahua are the local exemplar of 'wild Indians', ignorant, backward and untamed.

At the time, I interpreted this young man's reaction as a sort of racist self-hatred, and that he was imitating the contempt with which he imagined local white people would view this pathetic and backward sight. In hindsight, I realized that this could not be true, for local white people are almost invariably entranced by the aesthetic and erotic power of this moment in Piro ritual performance. I now think that the young man was sniggering in fear at his own reaction to what he saw – his likely future as a young Piro man would lead him deep into the forest as a lumber worker, and might force him into close and solitary contact with real Yaminahua women, and consequently, with their attendant menfolk, people as violent and as unpredictable as jaguars.

Kajine, white people

Once we see that Piro people have, and presumably always had, an ambivalent relationship to what we see as their traditional clothing, we are closer to an explanation of why Piro people wear 'white people's clothing'. Piro people recount their recent history as a history of their decreasing mutual frighteningness. This is the force of Artemio's story, and it is a pervasive theme in Piro people's accounts of the past. Here is Juan Sebastián Perez, an important Piro leader, commenting on the 'present lives of Piro people' in a school primer for Piro children:

> In past times, we Piro people didn't wear clothes like those used by white people, but instead hand-made clothing. The men wore *cushmas* and the women wore skirts, painted just like the men's *cushmas*.
>
> They always hunted animals, birds and fish with arrows. In those times there were men who were naturally good hunters, and others who had learned this skill using herbs. Now in 1968, we are forgetting how to hunt with arrows. We have grown accustomed to using the implements of the white people: the cast-net and shotgun. Good archery has been lost now.
>
> The spiritual life of the Piro people has also changed. Before, the shamans were feared and to children it was said, 'watch out! Don't talk or laugh. Don't make fun of the shaman or he will ensorcell you, and you will die!' But now it isn't the shaman, but God who is feared

and loved. Now only a few people fear shamans. (Sebastián Perez *et al.* 1974:179–85)

For Sebastián, these three changes are tightly interlinked, and they all involve the loss of a powerful form of knowledge (weaving and painting, good archery and sorcery) and its replacement with 'white people's things' (white people's clothing, white people's tools and white people's true knowledge of God). It should be noted that all of these manifestations of 'white people's knowledge' are openly and collectively available to Piro people. This is not true of the knowledge of weaving or of good archery, which Sebastián elsewhere in the same text specifies as knowledge that is both hard to acquire and very unevenly distributed among Piro people. Sorcery knowledge, on which subject Sebastián is silent, follows the same logic.

Central to the meaning of 'white people's clothing' for Piro people in the late twentieth century was their own understanding of the transformation in their relations with white people. Long ago, I was told, the ancient Piro people did not live in villages, but in mutually hostile and endogamous named groups called *neru*, scattered in the forest. 'They lived fighting and hating each other', it is said. Then they were enslaved by the rubber bosses, and came to live on the white people's settlements. There the *neru* came to intermarry and kinship was created. Relations with the bosses were violent and exploitative, but over time they acquired more and more knowledge of how to deal more equally with white people, to the point where, as they say, they 'liberated themselves from slavery', and set up their own independent villages and came to live the sorts of lives described by Sebastián.

A key theme in the history of transforming relations with white people was access to 'white people's clothing'. A constant theme of accounts of former relations of exploitation was the extent to which people had to suffer in order to acquire such clothing. Here is Morán Zumaeta describing, in 1948, his older kinsman Sangama:

Then he announced, 'Look. That's the way we would like to be. I'm like this now. I don't wear trousers, nor shirt. I never do. You've never seen me wearing trousers, white people's trousers or shirts. But I am immensely rich, because I have wealthy children. I always act like a poor person here, wearing these clothes, this *cushma*, this clothing', he said. (Matteson 1965:222–3)

And here, in 1988, is Jorge Manchinari, discussing his early life on the *hacienda* of Sepa:

Vargas treated us very badly, we worked for him the whole time and we never had anything. When I was a youth, my father died and Vargas said that I had to pay off my father's debt. But what debt was that, if he never gave us anything? I ran right away from there, and went downriver to the Bajo Ucayali. Down there, I came to know clothes for the first time. Working there, I became familiar with trousers and shirts. When we lived with Vargas, he never gave us anything!

The earlier problems of acquiring clothing, caused by the meanness of the white bosses, contrast with the current abundance of such clothing. The stores of Sepahua and Atalaya are full of clothing, and the only problem is finding the money to buy it.

But why was it so important for Piro people to acquire clothing from white people? There are two interlinked reasons for this, I think. Firstly, the acquisition of white people's clothing was a very visible manifestation of the state of Piro people's relations with white people. As we have seen, clothing matters to Piro people, and is indeed their prototype of the possessed object. It is therefore not surprising that they should focus, in their transforming relations with white people, on the acquisition of *their* prototypical possessed object, their clothing.

The second reason is in the underlying similarity of 'ancient people's clothing' and 'white people's clothing'. Just as 'ancient people's clothing' is the acquisition of a jaguar-affect, and intimidatory tool, so to is 'white people's clothing'. Like jaguars, white people are violent, dangerous and frightening, such that a white people-affect can perform the same functions that the jaguar-affect of 'ancient people's clothing' once did: the most elaborated forms of 'acting like white people', and the closest approximation to how white people look (*kajitu pixkalutu*) occur during contemporary rituals. People wear their best and newest clothing for rituals, and everyday life is characterized, as before, by a faded version of ritual dress. During rituals, Piro people look and act like white people, but crucially they only do this during rituals. They are not *kajitutachrine*, 'people who habitually act like white people': during everyday life, they look and act like Piro people.

This point leads to another. When you see Piro people going about their everyday lives, you see them in the faded forms of ritual body enhancement. Virtually all the clothing that they wear was bought originally as ritual adornment, and then transformed by usage and vigorous washing into everyday wear. At this point, we might profitably return to Matthiessen's observation. When he visited Sepahua in 1961, he saw Piro people who were 'not, alas, in tribal dress'. In an important sense, Matthiessen was wrong: these people were in tribal dress. Their everyday clothing was the ongoing transformation of ritual events. At most, then, Matthiessen's observations record a transformation in Piro ritual life, from the use of jaguar-affect to that of white people-affect in ritual contexts. The fact that Mathiessen saw Piro people as 'not, alas, in tribal dress' simply records a snap-shot of their current relation to their ritual lives and their other ongoing transformations.

A historical approach to the problem

The approach outlined above is not historical in the conventional sense. At most, I have addressed what Piro people told me about the past, which should not be conflated with what historical research might discover, as I have argued at length elsewhere (Gow 1991, 2001). It is possible to approach the change in Piro clothing from the point of view of the available historical evidence, and then to ask questions about how historical changes might be related to the analysis proffered above.

While Piro people talk about 'white people's clothing' and 'Piro people's clothing', the two styles are historically complex. We can track transformations in Piro clothing style over the nineteenth and twentieth centuries with some precision using the descriptions and drawings or photographs of Piro people provided by missionaries, travellers and anthropologists. I summarise that evidence here.

Until the middle of the nineteenth century, Piro men and women habitually wore the clothing that they call *mkalu*, 'cotton robe' and *mkalnama*, 'vagina robe' (see Marcoy 1875). By the late nineteenth century, they began to adopt a style I will call *cristiano*, 'Christian' style, after an important designation of the people who used it. These were indigenous peoples of northern Peruvian Amazonia who had long been missionised by the Jesuits and the Franciscans, peoples like the Jebero, Cocama-Cocamilla and the Lamista Quechua. Piro people from the Urubamba were coming into increasing contact with these *cristiano* peoples throughout the nineteenth century. Samanez y Ocampo reported of the situation in 1883–4:

> The [Piro men] wear trousers and shirts, or knitted vests; they wear straw hats or caps, which the traders bring them. They also wear the robe, their primitive costume, which they find more comfortable when they work at poling canoes... The women have no other clothing than the *pampanilla* (hand-woven skirt)... Instead of the little shawl they used to wear to cover their backs and sides, they now wear a little jacket or blouse, which only just reaches the waist above the navel. A great belt of innumerable strings of white beads and necklaces of garnets, or of valuables of various colours, combined with good taste, finish their simple dress. The men also wear, as a tie, neckbands of fine beads of various colours, very well woven by the women. (Samanez y Ocampo1980:66–7)

Farabee published photographs of this style taken in 1907 (1922). *Cristiano* clothing style is not, obviously, 'white people's clothing' in Matthiessen's sense. It is a transformational combination of the older style with elements of the new *cristiano* style. It is most certainly not how the white people with whom they were in contact (that is, those people who interacted with Piro people and who would have self-identified as 'white people') dressed. Wealthy white people at this period essentially wore Brazilian-style clothing, that is, clothing brought from Europe.

As is clear from the quote from Samanez y Ocampo and from visual evidence of the time, Piro people adopted *cristiano* style clothing as a transformed combination of their older style and this newer style. The woven cotton robes and skirts continued to be worn on a daily basis, but now combined with trousers and shirts for men, and blouses for women. One feature of *cristiano* style clothing meant that Piro people had to engage in trading for their clothing. Unlike the older style, the men's trousers and shirts and the women's blouses could only be made of commercially produced calico (*tocuyo*). It seems that many items of the older style could have been traded for or stolen in raiding against weaving peoples, but the new style made such acquisition obligatory.

In the 1940s, the *cristiano* style was abandoned, virtually *en masse*, for a new style (see Matteson 1954). I call this new style, *mozo* style. The originators of this style were basically the descendants of the *cristianos*, but they had transformed their self-identifications and clothing style over the intervening period. The major feature of this style is the virtually complete abandonment of hand-woven clothing in favour of clothing made up out of commercially produced and acquired cloth. For men, this involved the abandonment of the cotton robe. For women, the transformation was more dramatic, as they abandoned both woven skirts and calico blouses in favour of cotton print dresses.

This *mozo* style continued until roughly the 1970s and 1980s, when Piro people abandoned it in favour of what I will call *mestizo* style. The *mestizos* were, yet again, basically the *cristianos*-cum-*mozos*, transformed again. *Mestizo* style clothing is based on the purchase of ready made clothing in stores in Atalaya and Sepahua. It essentially consists of shirts and T-shirts with trousers and shorts for men, and blouses and T-shirts with skirts or culottes, and a decline in dress-wearing, for women. Even though the clothing articles themselves are mass-produced in coastal Peru, this *mestizo* style is very distinctive to Peruvian Amazonia, and is not found elsewhere in Peru.[4] And despite the influx of large numbers of Andean migrants into the area, there has been no move to adopt Andean styles. Instead, Andean migrants increasingly use *mestizo* style.

Two points might be made about this historical data. Firstly, the immediate northern neighbours of the Piro, the Conibo people, have followed a very different route. Conibo women, since the 1940s, have pursued a dramatic intensification of *cristiano* style clothing. Hand woven skirts have been abandoned, but replaced by calico wrap-around skirts decorated with elaborate design decoration achieved by rick-rack technique using sewing machines. Simultaneously there has been an explosion of complexity in blouse design and construction.

Given the general similarity between the conditions of both Piro and Conibo people, there is no obvious reason, to me, why they should have pursued such different paths.

Secondly, changes in Piro clothing styles have consistently tracked transformations in the clothing styles of one group of people, the *cristianos*-cum-*mozos*-cum-*mestizos*, who are transforming their self-identifications at the same time. Thus despite what Matthiessen (and, for that matter, myself) think is happening, and despite what Piro people themselves say happened, Piro people do not actually wear 'white people's clothing', in the sense of the clothing worn by local people who would self-identify as 'white people'. They dress in the clothing style of the *cristianos*-cum-*mozos*-cum-*mestizos*, and they do so irrespective of the means by which they acquire their clothes.

In certain circumstances, Piro people do define the *cristianos*-cum-*mozos*-cum-*mestizos*, as *kajine*, 'white people' as opposed to themselves as *yine*, 'humans'. In that sense, Piro people can correctly claim to wear *kajitu mkalu*, 'white people's clothing'. But while the *cristianos*-cum-*mozos*-cum-*mestizos* can be called *kajine*, Piro people do not consider them to be the best or strongest exemplars of the category. *Kajine potu*, 'real white people', are rich white bosses, people who deny any descent from indigenous Amazonian people, and who claim instead to be, or to be descended from, immigrants to the region. When contemporary Piro people talk about the *kajitu mkalu*, 'white people's clothing' that they aspire to own, it is clear that they mean the clothing of such 'real white people', not that of the *cristianos*-cum-*mozos*-cum-*mestizos*. Historically the clothing styles of Piro people have originated from these latter people, but Piro people identify it with 'real white people'.

The pattern of transforming clothing styles described here is probably very ancient. While Piro people have been living on the Bajo Urubamba river for as long as historical records exist, they almost certainly moved there from the east and first acquired their style of clothing when they arrived in the Ucayali basin. It is very likely that the Piro acquired their 'traditional' clothing as they moved into the trading milieu of south-eastern Peru, most likely from the Conibo or Cocama peoples. This hypothesis is supported by two lines of evidence. Firstly, their closest linguistic relatives, the Apurinã of Western Brazil, from whom the ancestral Piro probably separated about eight centuries ago, did not wear such clothing. Secondly, the root of their very word for clothing, *mka-*, is, in related languages, the root for 'to sleep' and 'hammock' (which is also where the English word comes from, *via* the Taino language once spoken in Cuba). I have argued elsewhere that as the ancestral Piro people migrated from the east into what is now Peru, they abandoned hammocks and adopted the clothing style of the local people, and in the process the word for 'hammock' migrated semantically to denote the novel domain of 'clothing' (Gow 2002).

This historical perspective has two important consequences. Firstly, it suggests that the manner in which Piro people think about clothing, as something that points towards alterity (whether that of jaguars or of white people) is historically operant. Piro people do continuously take on the clothing of other beings, even if those other beings are not the jaguars or white people of their conscious categories, but instead their northern neighbours, the Conibo, Cocama and other peoples. Indeed, it might plausibly be argued that the transformation in clothing styles is evidence of a very long process of emulation by Piro people of the Cocama people, historically the most important component population of the transforming *cristianos*-cum-*mozos*-cum-*mestizos* in the region.

Secondly, and of perhaps greater theoretical importance, this analysis suggests that 'acculturation', a phenomenon of such direct and obvious meaning to Western observers like Matthiessen and myself, might well be real, but of a very different order to the one usually supposed. I suggest that 'acculturation' is an indigenous Amazonian understanding of ongoing historical processes. Lévi-Strauss (1976 [orig. 1942]) long ago noted how,

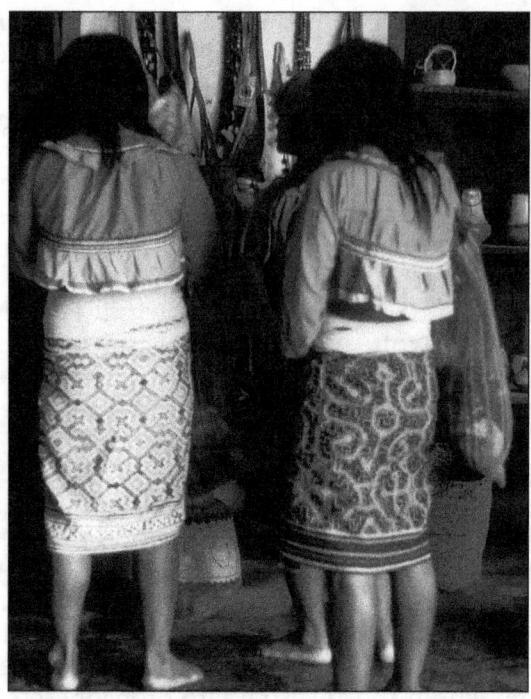

Plate 4.2   *Conibo women, Yarinacocha,*
              1988

for indigenous Amazonian people, war and trade are two sides of the same relation to the other – its violent and peaceful faces, we might say. We should not, therefore, be surprised that peacefulness towards the other is marked by an avid desire to obtain the things and knowledge of the other, for what is at stake here is a social relation (Hugh-Jones 1992). What indigenous Amazonian people are not seeking to acquire is the 'culture' of the other, for 'culture', following Viveiros de Castro, is alien to their perspectival cosmologies. 'Acculturation' is therefore a literally superficial description of perspectival cosmologies in historical action.

Modernity as an Amazonian perspective

In this paper, I have not attempted to set Piro people within modernity, either ethnographically or historically. Instead, I have tried to set a modernist aesthetic response, that of Matthiessen and of myself to the clothing style of Piro people, within a specific ethnographic and historical context. This is, of course, what anthropologists are meant to do, but it inevitably looks totally inadequate. Modernity, as a phenomenon, is not just in Sepahua in 1961, or on the Bajo Urubamba in the 1980's, but *everywhere*. Its local expressions are eclipsed by its ubiquity. In conclusion, I want to return briefly to the ethnographic and historical locality of 'modernity', in the local specificity of the aesthetic reactions of people like Matthiessen and myself.

Modernity, as a concept, necessarily implicates a tradition it is temporally opposed to, and this tradition is necessarily conceived of as traditional. That is, tradition is figured as something that should be passed unchanged down through the generations. Further, such traditions are seen as many, while modernity is conceived of as singular. When Matthiessen describes the indigenous inhabitants of Sepahua, that 'mixed band of Piros, Amahuacas and Machiguengas', he does not need to tell us what their traditional dress might have been. It is enough for Matthiessen, and for his readers, to assert this diversity for it then to be known that they must have, or have had, traditions, and hence traditional forms of dress. Equally, indigenous people living in more remote areas, with 'their long hair and paint', raise no significant historical problems, since they are maintaining both tradition and diversity. Such claims are self-evident, insofar as they are given within a modernist aesthetic.

Such self-evidence begins to break down precisely when we begin to ask what clothing might mean to those indigenous people. As I have shown here, Piro people do not understand their clothing through a notion of traditional diversity opposed to a singular modernity. Perspectival cosmologies do not conceive of 'tradition' in this way. What matters to them is the diversity of perspectives, but perspectives as not traditional, for it makes absolutely no sense to transmit a perspective from one's parents to one's children. Perspectival cosmologies cannot therefore confront modernity as a challenge to tradition, but only as *another* perspective. As such, it is not modernity that interests Piro people, but the fact that modernity interests those they call *kajine*, 'white people'. Piro people look 'modern' to us because they want to look like *kajine*, not because they value modernity or oppose it to a tradition they have abandoned. Indeed, even if we were to set out from the proposition that a 'traditional Piro culture' exists or existed, we would be forced to reach the same conclusions that I have come to here, for we rapidly discover that this 'traditional Piro culture' was made up of all the ideas about perspectives I have set out above.

Finally, I return to the aesthetic reaction with which I started: why is it that, one after another, and with depressing regularity, indigenous Amazonian peoples abandon their traditional body arts for Western clothes? This apparent uniformity does not, I suggest, show the uniform fragility of indigenous Amazonian societies in the presence of modernity. Instead, it records the historically contingent fact that indigenous Amazonian societies are severally dealing with a perspective that imagines itself, quite uniquely, to be a single transferable perspective that anyone can take on. That perspective calls itself 'modernity'. Significantly, however, this same banal phenomenon throughout Amazonia reveals an unexpected feature of that modernity: indigenous Amazonian people can, and do, use modernity to explore the implications and unexpected potentials of perspectivism.

NOTES

Fieldwork on the Bajo Urubamba and in Acre between 1980 and 2001 was funded by the Social Science Research Council, the British Museum, the Nuffield Foundation, the British Academy and the London School of Economics. I thank Michael O'Hanlon and Elizabeth Ewart for their invitation to the conference, and all the participants for their comments on the original version. I also thank Ben Campbell, Jeanette Edwards, Marcio Goldman, Tania Stolze Lima, Maire Mayne, Christina Toren and Eduardo Viveiros de Castro for their questions, comments and suggestions.

1 Viveiros de Castro's account suggests a different conceptual dynamic between Amazonian and Melanesian ideas about deceptive appearance and hidden reality, so well described in the ethnographic literature.

2 Piro women expressed disappointment with the inelastic market for their products among white people, and would undoubtedly produce far more woven clothing if their work was financially rewarding.

3 It should be noted here that most Piro people are in fairly regular contact with Asháninka people who do wear cotton robes as everyday clothing.

4 A major stylistic influence on contemporary clothing styles in Peruvian Amazonia is the clothing style of Brazilian Amazonia.

Bibliography

Farabee, W. C. (1922) *Indian Tribes of Eastern Peru*, Papers of the Peabody Museum of Archaeology and Ethnology, Harvard University, Volume 10, Cambridge Mass.: Harvard University Press.

Gombrich, E. H. (1960) *Art and Illusion: A Study in the Psychology of Pictorial Representation*, Oxford: Phaidon.

Gow, P. (1991) *Of Mixed Blood: Kinship and History in Peruvian Amazonia*, Oxford: Oxford University Press.

_____ (2001) *An Amazonian Myth and its History*, Oxford: Oxford University Press.

_____ (2002) 'Piro, Apurinã and Campa: Social Dissimilation and Assimilation in Southwestern Amazonia' in J. D. Hill and F. Santos-Granero (eds) *Comparative Arawakan Histories: Rethinking Language Family and Culture Area in Amazonia*, Urbana and Chicago: University of Illinois Press.

Hugh-Jones, S. (1992) 'Yesterday's luxuries, tomorrow's necessities; business and barter in northwest Amazonia', in C. Humphrey and S. Hugh-Jones (eds) *Barter, Exchange and Value: An anthropological approach*, Cambridge: Cambridge University Press.

Lévi-Strauss, Claude (1976 [1942]) 'Guerra e comércio entre os índios da América do Sul', in E. Schaden (ed.) *Leituras de Etnologia Brasileira*, São Paulo.

_____ (1995) *The Story of Lynx*, Chicago and London: University of Chicago Press.

Lima, T. Stolze (1999) 'The two and its many: Reflections on perspectivism in a Tupi cosmology', *Ethnos* 64(1):107–31.

Marcoy, P. (1875) *Travels in South America from the Pacific Ocean to the Atlantic Ocean*, (2 Vols.) London: Blackie.

Matteson, E. (1954) 'The Piro of the Urubamba', *Kroeber Anthropological Society Papers* 10: 25–99.

_____ (1965) *The Piro (Arawakan) Language*, Berkeley and Los Angeles: University of California Press.

Matthiessen, P. (1962) *The Cloud Forest: a chronicle of the South American Wilderness*, London: André Deutsch.

Nies, J. (ed.) (1986) *Diccionario Piro (Tokanchi gikshijikowaka-steno)*, Serie Lingüística Peruana 22, Yarinacocha: Ministerio de Educación and Instituto Lingüístico de Verano.

Rivière, P. (1994) 'WYSINWYG in Amazonia', *Journal of the Anthropological Society of Oxford* 25(3):255–62.

Samanez y Ocampo, J. B. (1980) *Exploración de los Ríos Peruanos, Apurímac, Eni, Ucayali y Urubamba, hecho por Samanez y Ocampo en 1883 y 1884*, Lima: privately printed.

Sebastián Pérez E., J., Morán Zumaeta B.; and J. Nies (1974) *Yine pirana 12: Gwacha ginkakle* (Cartilla de lectura 12: Historia de los piros), Lima: Ministerio de Educación.

Veber, Hanne (1996) 'External Inducement and Non-Westernization in the Uses of the Ashéninka Cushma', *The Journal of Material Culture* 1(2): 155–82.

Viveiros de Castro, E. (1998) 'Cosmological Deixis and Amerindian Perspectivism', *Journal of the Royal Anthropological Institute*, (N.S.) 4:469–88.

____ (2001) 'GUT feelings about Amazonia: potential affinity and the construction of sociality', in L. Rival and N. Whitehead (eds) *Beyond the Visible and the Material: The Amerindianization of Society in the work of Peter Rivière*, Oxford: Oxford University Press.

5

Body art and modernity

South-east Nuba

James C. Faris

Introduction

Today, the south-east Nuba body art system, as illustrated in my first book on the south-east Nuba peoples (*Nuba Personal Art*) in 1972 and in Leni Riefenstahl's publication (*The People of Kau*) in 1976 is no longer extant. This is because a severe Islamicist central government came to power in Sudan in the 1980s and established/converted the three villages of the south-east Nuba into 'Peace Villages'. These were to be buffers against the physical and ideological spread of the southern rebel Kush Volcano battalion of the SPLA (Sudanese Peoples Liberation Army) in the Nuba Mountains of south central Sudan. All people but the very young are today dressed, and the ochre decorations of both sexes were subsequently prohibited. Consequent Islamisation – forced or 'voluntary' – has insured that what was illustrated in Faris (1972), and Riefenstahl (1976), no longer exists. Now as targets (involuntarily representing, so to speak, the Sudan Government as they do), however, the villages have illogically been subjected to raids from the rebels, and several of my local friends have been killed by the SPLA attacks.[1] We are talking, then, about most people still living, but with a quite different social and cultural order, certainly regarding the personal art traditions.

While the attention brought to the south-east Nuba by myself – but most especially by the publications and exhibitions of Leni Riefenstahl – may have been a factor in the Sudan Government's choice of the south-east Nuba villages to be 'Peace Villages', their remote location just north of the developing oil fields in Dinka land also made them strategically very important.

On modernity, and modernity and the body.

Let me introduce my discussion of south-east Nuba body art and modernism with comments on the concept of modernism. I want to differentiate two broad forms of modernity: the hard version with the developments after Darwin and Marx and the rise of imperialism – with the rise of rationalism and the emergence of the grand first order truths. Then there is the softer version, commonly later, which questions this development, or at least points out its limits and edges and complications, its contradictions and the subjectivities, and more important politically, the anti-colonial struggles. Both versions involve extensive colonial expansions and the rise of new nationalisms – that is, the global and the varied forms of the local. Modernity inevitably involves the nexus of local/global. Otherwise it has no relevance – there has to be a non-local modern (perhaps metropolitan) place or time, and a local, non-modern (perhaps rural) margin. Later modernity can be viewed then, as an aspect of the expansion of or incorporation to the West and responses.[2] So we are principally concerned here with the extent to which what can be called non-modernist or semi-modernist traditions of other people and their forms of personal art intersect and are blended, blocked, hybridised, syncretised, or coalesce with or are variously replaced by the effluvia and practices and pressures of the modernist West (or other modernist forms, such as the Sudan government).

Modernity and modernism introduce change, direction and a value vocabulary. The notions theoretically imply or at least insinuate a structural contrast, and are basically unable to accept (short of some patronizing 'multiculturalism') others without hierarchy (and make no mistake, these structural contrasts *are* hierarchical – there is little or no 'mediation' or exchange). While the term modernity might entail mediation between structural axes – it is rigidly bound to the old hierarchies, however much its champions would like it to be otherwise. Hybridity and pastiche cannot be terms of anything else. The racist and pernicious evolutionary and power implications of this value nomenclature are clear. Its partisans have attempted to carve out an ostensibly new continent – and make no mistake about the continent-shaking ambitions of its adherents, such as G. Marcus, F. Ginsberg, M. Fischer, etc. But the assumptions of the hierarchies are latent and the power dimensions underemphasized, glossed over, or ignored. The hybridity and pastiche of late modernism differs in not adopting the old romanticist and pastoral nomenclature – authentic/pure *vs.* spoiled/polluted – but its own lexicon of blend is clearly premised on a rationalist continuum and hierarchy.

While there is something unappealing about an entire endeavour focused on the detritus of Western penetration, this does not mean we must focus on the purity/pollution register of this continuum – Riefenstahl's own version of the structural hierarchy. But faced with the hierarchy of tradition and modernity, what advance can we make? The rage for hybridity is in many ways simply the celebration of what Riefenstahl found depressing. The frenzy for pastiche, the syncretic and the associated nomenclatures of mediation and mixing, borders and transgressions has contributed no theoretical advance or innovation – indeed, most analyses founder in a variation of functionalist modernism – a celebration of the quaint charms of global triumph or the appropriation of the world to the West's fickle pleasure, or the adoption and adaptation of the detritus and debris of the West. And rather than consider and contemplate some form of incommensurability or a theory of difference (a genuinely post-modern discourse), we end up with this functionalist nomenclature based upon a set of totalizing notions of local/global. This essentially makes modernity, especially in our focus on the body decorated, the epitome of the colonialist or expansionist capitalism's representational processes.

Body art studies burgeoned with photography. And photography, with its completely dependent heritage of (and confinement to) witness to reality,[3] lent itself to the notion that the photography of others was simply evidential and appropriate. Certainly the commercial success of photography texts of personal art traditions is well attested. Universal photographic access was a non-discursive proposition, and the non-western body decorated was made available to all.[4]

Body art, personal and visual, has become supremely representational and a focus of the application of the notions of modernity – principally photographic – and thus potentially spectacle. That is probably the reason for having the symposium which has resulted in this volume. Benetton could be sponsoring it. We all know that the body and its assorted personal art is the site of the most rigid of attention by all manner of ideological apparatuses. An example: a few years ago the American Museum of Natural History had a major exhibition, *Body Art: Marks of Identity*. The able curator, Enid Schildkraut, tried to emphasize that Western body art was characterised by as much change, exoticism, beauty and the bizarre, as anyone else's, but the administration in the Museum forced alterations so that tattooed and pierced young New Yorkers were not featured, but moved to the rear of the exhibition. It is fine for the body art of brown and black folks to be exhibited, but not that of the kids of the urban West, especially the white ones.

So long as the West could ostensibly celebrate or document – the old modernist project – a catalogue and ordering of the bizarre, the subaltern, that would have seemed fine. But the 'restless drives of the West' (Danto 1989:32) meant this could hardly simply be left alone. At the celebratory or documentary level, other interests took this to greater aims – to a demonstration of one or another theory; in Faris's (1972) case, the old anthropological modernist project – categorizing and museuming and evidencing by way of a virtuoso formalist project with linguistic antecedents. In Riefenstahl's case, it was to insert her specific hierarchies of purity and authenticity, her notions of triumph of the strong and the unpolluted.

South-east Nuba personal art

Nuba Personal Art (Faris 1972)[5] was a description of the local art tradition of males and females in the Chomskyian sense–that a grammar of a language

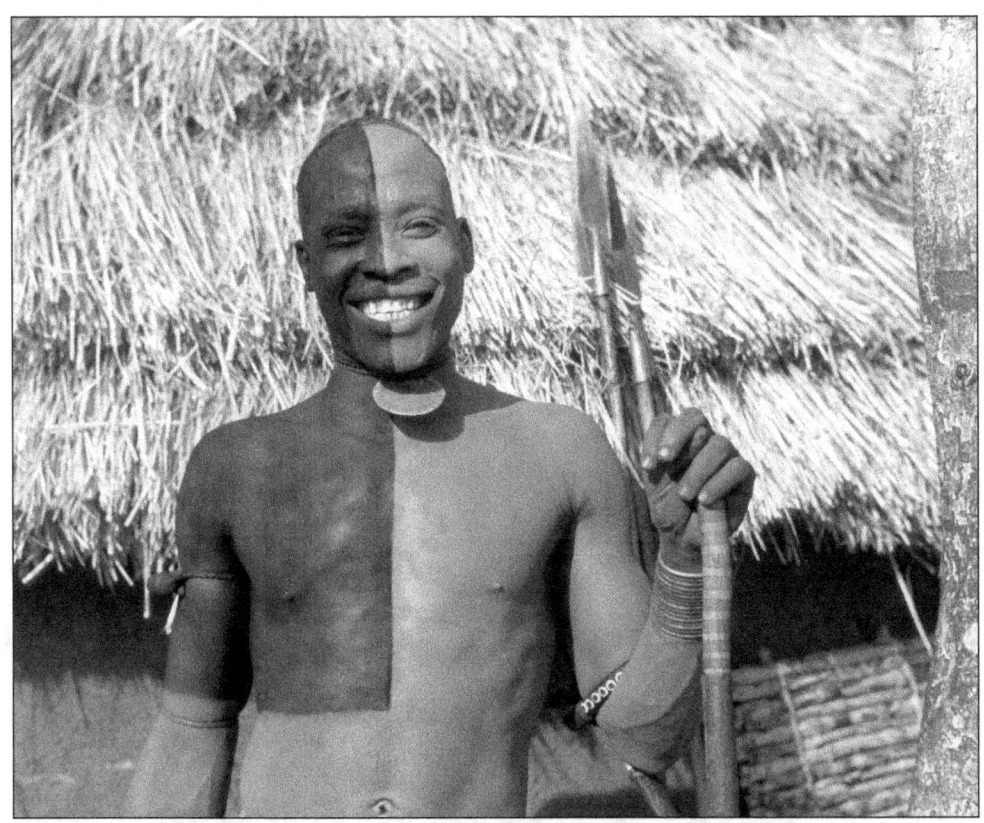

Plate 5.1   *Non-representational male older age grade design. Self-executed by Modu. (Photograph by J. Faris, 1969.)*

is a description of that language. After a general ethnographic description, I specified a series of algorithmic parameters (a morphology) based on some minimal graphics (analogous to phonemes) for the generation of meaningful designs of the young men's personal art universe (see Faris 1972:101ff). Other designs were not representational [Plate 5.1].

And still others of the designs, while meaningful, were unique and particular – what iconicists and linguists refer to as 'supercharges', or those representations not subject to the rules of normal generation – rather like highly particular grammatical idioms [Plate 5.2].

While some critics such as Gombrich, 1972, dismissed the generative algorithms as simply a clever way of specifying the design forms in two-dimensional algebraic formulae, I pushed these resulting morphological expressions to indicate the degree to which all possible permutations were indeed realized with an illustration of a meaningful form – a species or variety of animal. I asked had young south-east Nuba men exhausted in their personal art all possible dimensions available to them? That is, something of all possible phonetic ranges in their coding of natural phenomenon (animals, etc.) – all possible meaningful utterances, to continue the linguistic analogy.

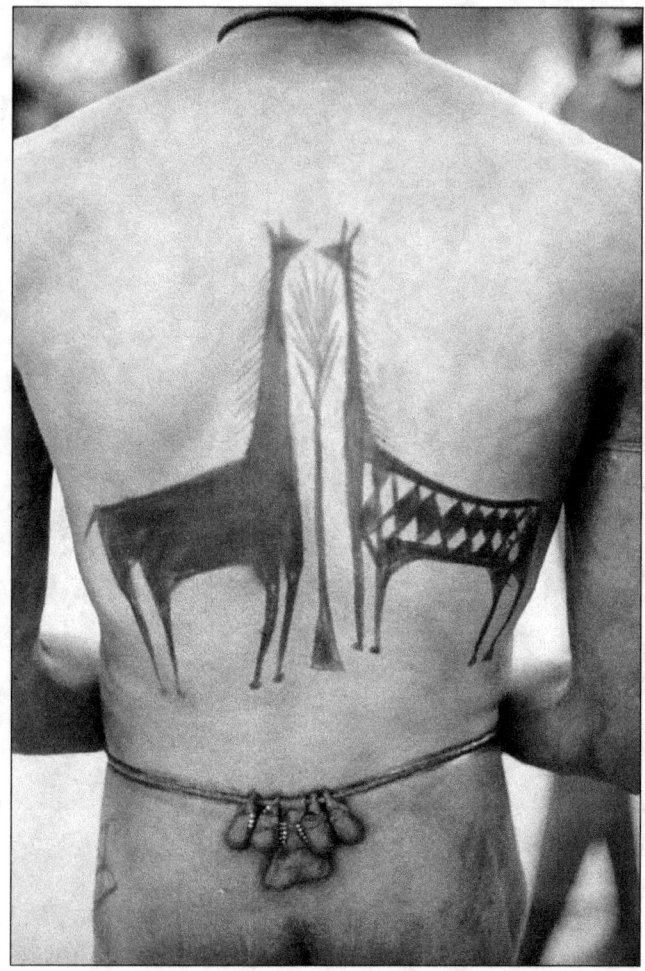

Plate 5.2   *Representational design. Male and*
             female giraffe sp. (dūn). Executed by
             someone other than the person on whose
             body it is. Pouches hanging off the belt
             contain protective and healing herbs and
             roots. (Photograph by J. Faris, 1969.)

This allowed me to speculate about the evolution of the system and its possible directions for change and further elaboration along the same axes (Faris 1972:111).

Now what is interesting about this is that when Riefenstahl arrived in 1973 and began to encourage other expressions of the personal art tradition, introducing new locations, new colours, new designs (of course she doesn't tell us that she chased off and did not photograph the dressed and the aged), the results were inevitably compared to my work. I examined Riefenstahl's

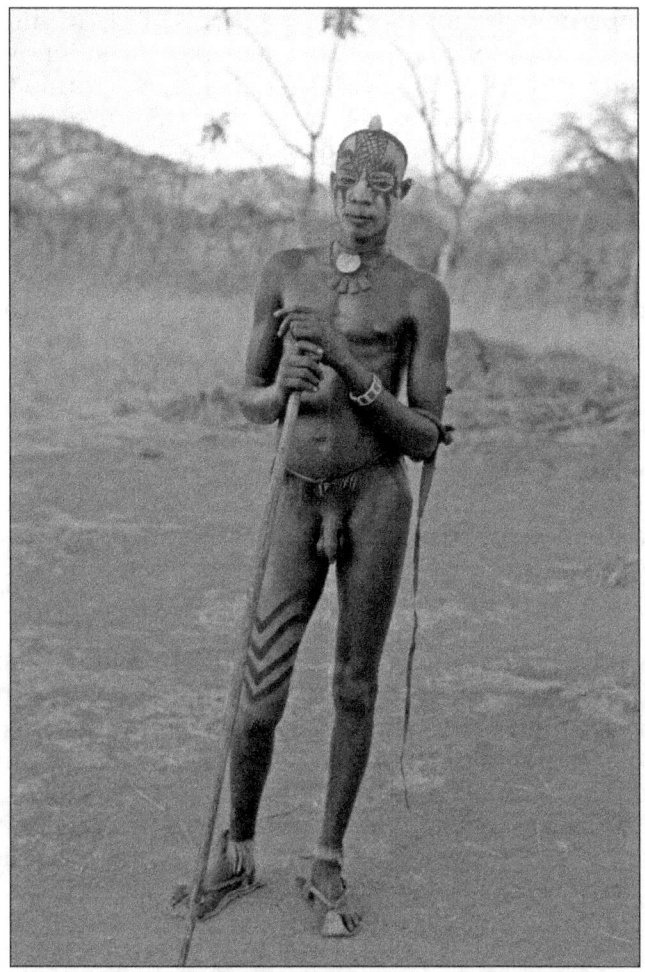

Plate 5.3   *Representational design, wasp. sp. (wēā kōra). Self-executed by Koti, minimal number of times to enable species identification (feature code defined by one finger-sized black stripe on white background). (Photograph by J. Faris, 1968.)*

published photographs (1976) of the young men's designs to see to what extent they were grammatically meaningful and in what ways the art tradition had changed since my initial work several years earlier. I found that Riefenstahl's photographs yielded only the disappointing result that all new designs were indeed 'supercharges' – that is, peculiar and unique – they were not part of the designs using the traditional generative morphology. They could only be traced, or in linguistic terms, re-written in the same register, not subject to any grammatical or morphological declensions. While they may have been representational of actual animals or plants, they did so only as actual *indexes* (in semiotic terms). They may have been innovative, but not within the traditional system of meaning, or better, not within the traditional system of meaningful in a local morphological universe – sort of like Chomsky's grammatically correct but semantically meaningless expression – 'colourless green ideas sleep furiously'. In other words, with Riefenstahl's introductions there was no further evolution of the morphological system of representational conventions along the dimensions of meaning I had earlier specified. The reasons were clear: once the traditional morphological system was executed (usually a minimal number of repeats of at least four times [Plate 5.3]), it required no further decoration – any member of the culture could identify the meaning – the representation intended.

This flew in the face of Riefenstahl's (and those tourists who followed her) request to photograph and photograph and photograph the decorating – which soon required young Nuba males to paint by the hour. To stay within the traditional morphological system, however, soon exhausted the time required, so innovative designs exceeding the time necessary to execute traditional ones began to appear – the 'supercharges' just noted [Plate 5.2], as well as designs without meaning that could be expanded infinitely [Plate 5.4].

I subsequently went further a few years later (Faris 1983, 1988a) to specify and critique the local ideology in south-east Nuba body art with an analysis of its cultural signification. This was more theoretically interesting, for it spelled out the gendering functions and the marking (in the linguistic sense) of such gendering. The art of males is ever elaborated and changing, and personal art of females is simple and unchanging. Yet while the male art is relevant to sport, age, production; female art specifies physiological status, reproductive status, sexual availability and patriclan section membership of both themselves and the patriclan section of their infants (see Faris 1988a:37, figure 10). The cultural significance of the personal art diacritica gendered productive and reproductive activity, with flamboyant elaboration and marking of males and their productive activity, and the denigration of production and unmarking – in the linguistic sense – of females.

Riefenstahl was not, of course, interested in any of this, and she read the signification of south-east Nuba body art of both males and females in Western pastoral racist terms, and as exemplar of the unpolluted, the 'wild and savage'.[6] The source of pollution was for her Islam, schooling, clothing, etc., for these factors had been introduced to the group of Nuba peoples amongst whom she first worked, the Mesakin, a few hundred kilometres to the west of the south-east Nuba. Indeed, on visiting them just prior to her first trip to the south-east Nuba in late 1973, she tells us she cried on finding them in schools and with clothes. The 'pollution' she condemned amongst the Mesakin was from a Semitic source (here Arabs, Islam), an ironic mirror to the pollution from Semites she found in her work for the Third Reich thirty years earlier (there Jews, Judaism).

My own work was never premised on some unchanging traditional system. While I did not introduce more exotic photographic locations,

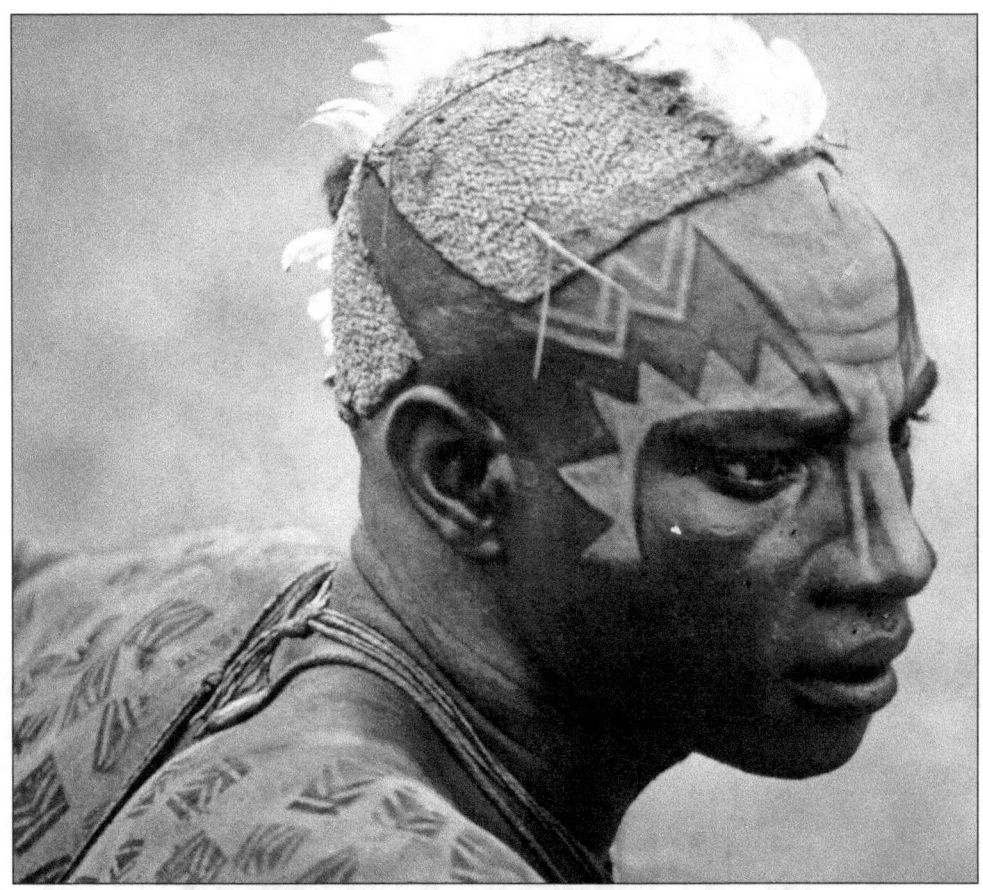

Plate 5.4   *Non-representational ('supercharge') design, both on body and face. Self-executed by Kari on face and front of body, by another person on back. Stamped body design, infinitely expandable. (Photograph by J. Faris, 1969)*

artificial light, new colours, my very presence introduced new inspirations, such as Roman lettering copied off the lettering on a box in my hut, or a young man's name, whom I had taught to read and write in a semi-phonetic manner [Plate 5.5].

And my excessively formalist treatment of the young men's iconic universe at this time was in part to see in what directions change might occur and still stay within the morphologically meaningful corpus of designs. Thus, I was aware change was constant and such change was anticipated and relatively unproblematic. It did not make much sense to me to discriminate between changes my visit introduced – such as Roman lettering – as 'modernist', and a potential expansion within the universe of morphologically specified iconic meaning as 'traditional'. In other words, it was only change, only motion. Riefenstahl herself initiated change (despite her piety about 'corruption', the lack of 'pollution' and the 'unspoiled'). Indeed, as noted, she introduced

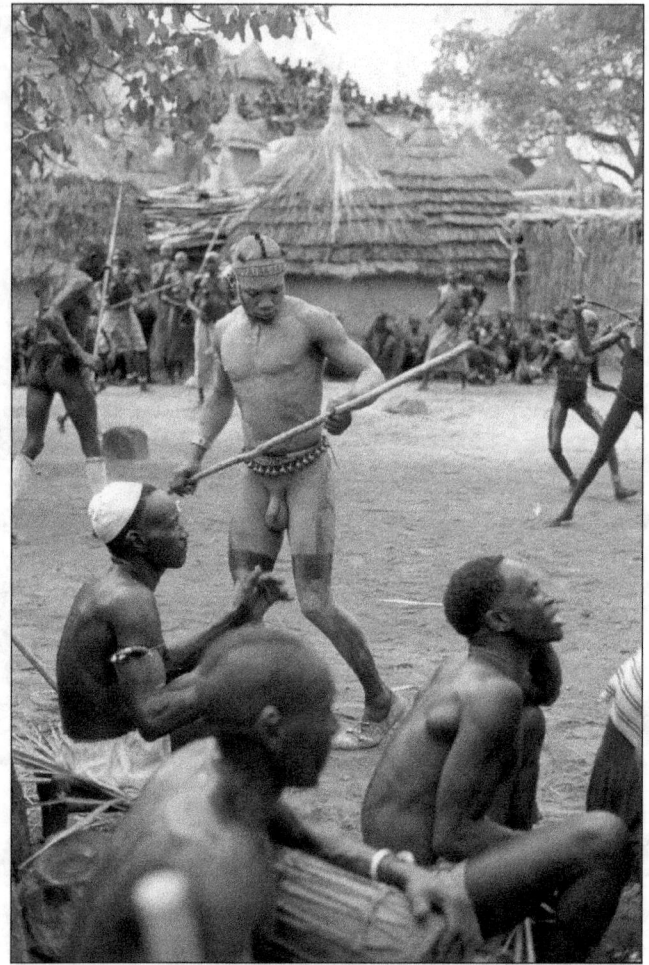

Plate 5.5   *Self-executed forehead design by Poba*
                Aria. This design, the young man's name,
                was executed with a mirror, in which
                case reversals had to be considered in
                its correct application. (Photograph by
                J. Faris, 1969; see also Faris 1972:119,
                note 36.)

new colours, new items of décor, locations she thought more exotic, artificial
light, and too often, herself. I suppose these could be considered exemplars of
pastiche, hybridity and modernism run amok (or perhaps to be celebrated).
But they are just change, such as had happened before and would continue
to happen. As noted above, Riefenstahl's visit, however, had implications for
the art that turned its execution into painting by the hour for the hordes
of European tourists who followed her to capture their own Riefenstahlian
experience – south-east Nuba personal art as capitalist production – or, as
capitalism is wont, overproduction. The designs became ever more bizarre, as

painting by amount of time consumed – art as commodity – supplanted the indigenous feature code system of meaning.[7]

More on Riefenstahl

Let me continue on Riefenstahl, for her financially very successful work helped anchor some of my views on modernism and photographic practice. However much I might like to blame Riefenstahl for everything, it was hardly her that brought an end to the personal art tradition – a tradition essentially doomed in the Sudan civil war that came crashing down on the south-east Nuba.[8] That I might suggest local people liked me better (implied in the disappointing 1982 BBC film, *SOUTHEAST NUBA*), such satisfaction is stupid and facile in the circumstances.

Of course Riefenstahl got the facts all wrong, even when she used my own texts as references. Somehow today, as much as I am outraged at her work and her grotesque use (and misrepresentation) of my published material, this seems less relevant to me now,[9] for any battles between Riefenstahl and myself are certainly of little significance to the south-east Nuba. They didn't care if she was a fascist at worst, a pastoral racist at best, or even that she was a lousy photographer (and I believe she was). Our battles – however much some, indeed, were about the actual facts – were battles between two Westerners, neither of whom could save the south-east Nuba from a more vicious modernity, a national Islamicist system set in a global context.

So while Riefenstahl, having visited such a prurient vision upon the south-east Nuba (as well as earlier on the Mesakin Nuba further west – see Riefenstahl 1974) and having stimulated tourists and others to follow her racist claptrap of purity, aboriginality and savagery, can be argued to have done irreparable harm – that harm was done to anthropological sensitivities and Western perceptions, not significantly, to south-east Nuba personal art systems. It simply changed as it had always been doing. Moral outrage at Riefenstahl over her racism and the directions of the changes she introduced into the art seems somewhat misplaced at this point (though why her vision persists deserves careful attention).

Until her death in the summer of 2003 at the age of almost 101, Riefenstahl lived in luxury outside Munich, in a grand glass house known colloquially as 'the house the Nuba built' (cf. Schiff 1992), a result of the outstanding commercial success of her books on Africans, principally on the two different groups of Nuba peoples, her glossy popular magazine articles and several recent exhibitions of her photographs – usually much larger than life – another reflection of her own narcissism.[10] She certainly made no attempts to share any of her wealth with the communities she photographed. She sold the screen rights to her memoirs (first out in English in the early 1990's) for a reported seven million dollars to a film production of her life starring Jody Foster.[11] It was rumoured that this was to be a 'sympathetic' portrayal – Riefenstahl as the artistic sufferer, the genius stymied, or at least under-appreciated as a consequence of events, poor luck, vindictive and small-minded people.[12] This was pretty much Riefenstahl's own view of herself, save that she persistently claimed her decisions were misunderstood rather than wrong (cf. Riefenstahl 1987, 1992). And despite some court cases and claims, including evidence to the contrary, she continued to insist she 'never knew' about concentration camps.[13] She was rumoured to have been displeased with the Foster production – not so much because it might portray her in poor light – but because she had no editorial role and was not directly involved in the production herself.

Riefenstahl escaped the sanctions that were applied to her after World War II.[14] She then first went to Africa to make a movie in Kenya ostensibly based on the Arab slave trade from the interior to the coast. Those plans came to a halt when she was involved in a serious automobile accident. Riefenstahl seems to have been particularly prone to accidents – she was in a helicopter crash outside El Obied (Sudan) in 2001 on her way to visit 'her' Nuba, which she also survived. Of course she called all this suffering for her great art.

After the collapse of the East African filming experience, Riefenstahl came to Sudan in the 1960's, to film amongst the Mesakin of the south-central Nuba Mountains (having traced them through the work of the British Magnum photographer, George Rodger). This resulted in a volume, *The Last of the Nuba*, which came out in 1974.[15] Her book on the south-east Nuba, the people amongst whom I worked in the 1960's, first came out in 1976, after her first visit to the area in late 1973. She claimed to have learned of the south-east Nuba from a dream, but Faris (1972) (clearly available to her and conspicuous in her bibliography) was complete with maps to the area.

The biographical details are not so important to what I want to say here, however. In my view Riefenstahl's commercially successful photography is quite awful – hackneyed, leaning as it does on the spectacular, with all the apparatuses of long lens, corny posing, artificial lighting, flat flash, etc. Her photography says something about the degree to which these factors have become profoundly absorbed and accepted – the enabling foundations for representational inscriptions so powerful that any alternatives (or critique) are regarded as a kind of Luddite dementia (see, for example, Ruby's (1998) review of Faris 1996). These types of representations are always stubbornly Western,[16] and the photographic objects are commonly people of lesser power. Such photography can be of the humanist sort, which it mostly is these days – grand, (often) colour (and always spectacular) examples of the beauty, the potential contribution, the genius of powerless people, or alternatively, their misery, their fall from grace, their victimhood, their loss – a resurrection of their socio-cultural totalities in the distortions we have seen, perhaps because of the destruction of their previous local totalities.[17] In short, their subjecthood is reinforced, reproduced; their abjection is assumed natural, timeless and outside discourse. Their agency is dismissed. But Riefenstahl's African work reveals a more profoundly disturbing feature characteristic of much modernist Western photographic practice involving non-westerners or any humans of lesser power. That is, there is an assumption, firmly a part of the ideological apparatus (in Althusser's sense) – codified in various national laws of Western countries, and subsequently of ex-colonies – pertaining to subject rights in photography. Priority is given to the camera, or to capital and/or to assumptions of access. Juridical subjection and visualist access is treated as a 'natural' state and therefore as non-discursive.

Riefenstahl's photographic representation of Africans fits the general Western modernist project in a multitude of ways. It is amazing that this photography of subject peoples – a development that enabled and sanctioned complete visual access – came into being at all. Photography might have technically developed in other ways – to portray, for example, the photographer as well as the subject.[18] There is no reason laws could not have developed to protect subjects, rather than allow anything that can be photographed to be photographed. Laws of photographic access in the United States, for example, centre on privacy torts. In public settings, one has no rights to their photographic subjecthood. The law facilitates what should be inhibited – or at least admitted to conditions of litigation.[19]

This Western project is further naturalised by the extraordinarily powerful role of photography in communities of trust in the world today, such as family photos, personal and studio photographs, where photography has a universal acceptance, and where sitters presumably have some control of their image.[20] When this profoundly important use of photography of humans is unproblematically extended outside communities of trust, all access is assumed, commonly as some sort of inherent extension of visual modalities themselves. On the occasion of her ninetieth birthday and the publication of her memoirs in the United States (see Schiff 1992), Riefenstahl pleaded, 'I want to see, that's all. This is my life. I want to see.' The continual problem, in her view, was that the world was not arranged so that she could always see and photograph everything and everybody in every circumstance.

Riefenstahl's work may well have replicated themes she found so successful in her work for the Nazis, but at base her work is part of a long-standing Western aesthetic imperative, and cannot simply be dismissed as fascist (cf. Sontag 1975). In other political circumstances, in other situations, in better hands – those of photographers generally regarded as progressive, for example – made under different political circumstances, we might well embrace other Western photographic projects. In my view, however, this becomes particularly problematic. I have in mind here such work as that of Sebastião Salgado or Susan Meiselas. But that is another entire topic.[21] And this tirade is not to mention the Riefenstahl look-alikes such as Andrea Fisher and Carol Beckwith, with their neo-Riefenstahlian picture books on Africans – each, unfortunately, stupendously successful. Leni Riefenstahl was not at all unique in her photography of Africans. She shared a modernist aesthetic that is not only adored and adopted in the West, but is insulated by law, ideology and philosophy as well as popular assumption. These are simply varieties of the modernist West's project in photography.

Finally, a summary: modernism and modernity conceptually introduce direction, value, a vocabulary of judgment and a structural hierarchy. While it need not be the crude and unsavoury axis of Riefenstahl, it cannot be theoretically discriminated from that. When discussing body art, problems arise stemming from these dimensions of distance, but additional complications are introduced from the current means by which we know such art – photography, and its well-trodden assumptions of access and registers of the spectacular – a problematic that can only be resolved by a rejection of such axes and perhaps renewed attention to a theoretical project of incommensurability. In my view we must argue for such possibilities and against their extinction. The 'traditional' may have been made extinct by late modernist discourses, but I am here speaking not of any preservation notion, but an attitude, an intellectual resistance to rationalist modernism. Since we have as yet no theoretical approach or no access to such a project (a post-modern photography?), we are left only to marvel at the possibilities of its mystery.

NOTES

1 The south-east Nuba 'Peace Villages' are essentially fortified camps, with armed guards – much like the fortified villages introduced by the British in their attempts to contain Mau Mau, or the U.S. attempt to win the hearts and minds of rural people in Vietnam by the same village system – and a severe Islamicist orthodoxy is enforced on everyone. Most combat deaths locally have thus come from attacks by the rebel SPLA on the villages, seen as government outposts. It is thus difficult to share the same unbridled enthusiasm of some of my colleagues for the rebel groups in the overthrow of the current regime. While I certainly advocate the demise of the current Sudan regime, the civil war has cynically hurt those that both antagonists argue they most wish to help. And it should not be forgotten that the National Islamic Front government of Sudan, however unattractive, is not some medieval atavism – it is a local and perhaps inevitable consequence of a specific colonialism. While its vocabulary may sound 11th century, its policies and tactics are thoroughly modernist – i.e. 'peace' villages, helicopter gunships and the like.

Oswald Iten, having visited the south-east Nuba recently (late 2006), informs me that the villages were not technically 'Peace Villages', and inhabitants were not specifically made available as wage labourers on mercantile mechanized agricultural schemes in the Nuba Mountains (the fate of several Nuba 'Peace Villages'). Conflict with nomads today, as in Dar Fur Province, centers about water and gum Arabic gardens, but at least the vicious civil war has now been settled.

2 By West and expansion, of course, I refer to the largely northern hemisphere capitalist nations, in their predation for markets, materials and labour. More recently, we witness expansions in the form of religious traditions, often in the accompaniment of oppressive state forms (e.g., the Taliban of Afghanistan or the National Islamic Front of Sudan). However peculiar it may appear, these too are treated discursively as modernist developments.

3 There is little or no photography that can be described as pre-modernist. Indeed, photography is the archetype gesture of modernism.

4 During my initial research in the mid 1960's, I was also simply naïve and insufficiently reflective in not considering that the publication of south-east Nuba body art photographs in an academic text would stimulate Riefenstahl and hordes of Europeans to visit the area.

5 *Nuba Personal Art* (Faris 1972) – a description of the south-east Nuba body art I documented in the mid 1960s, has been out of print for over twenty-five years now.

6 South-east Nuba males specifically suggest their art is to enhance and beautify the healthy body (the aged and ill do not decorate), while females suggest their body art illustrates physiological and marital status.

7 Apart from the extraordinary expense, obviously none of Riefenstahl's photographs would be allowed by her to be included here.

8 Though I am somewhat embarrassed to bring this up, some may remember my naïve and chilling statement in the preface to Faris (1972:3), to wit:

They [the south-east Nuba] constitute a unique and isolated society, whose traditions, as documented here, will undoubtedly be dead within a generation. I should emphasize that I feel that it is probably not in the national interests of new socialist states that art traditions such as those described in this book survive. That is an issue which must be objectively determined after study. But it is very much in the interests of the State that such traditions of a classless society be documented and analyzed before they die, and this book is offered as a contribution to the rich legacy of the Sudanese people.

9 In Faris 1976, 1988b, 1988c and 1993, I detail some of the errors in her misuses of my material in the art books, and some of the abundant lies and mistruths characteristic of her memoirs (Riefenstahl 1987, 1992).

10 The two Africa books are Riefenstahl 1974 and 1976 (now in their second releases), and there are many adoring picture articles (cf. Beard 1974; Riefenstahl 1979). Exhibitions of her still photographs of Nuba peoples have been held in several parts of the world, including a dramatically successful Japanese show, and more recently, three very controversial exhibitions in Germany itself – Hamburg, Munich, Potsdam (with her Nuba photographs enlarged to much more than life size).

11 There are at least two other films devoted to Riefenstahl that touch on her Nuba photography. These are unfortunate in my view, for they largely present her African photography and ciné work as genius.

12 But it is my latest understanding that the project stirred such irate reaction, that it is now on hold.

13 She was brought to court at least twice – once after the war, and once just a few months prior to her death, the latter based upon a German statute that stated it was illegal to deny the Holocaust.

14 While she was charged with war crimes following World War II, she was ultimately acquitted with the help of powerful friends, primarily in America – amongst them Walt Disney, once chair of the front group of fascist sympathizers, the German–American Friendship Society, and Gary Cooper, a member of the same, who was her official escort on her 1939 trip to America to keep the U.S. out of the war (see Infield 1976).

15 Rodger died a few years ago, bitter to the end by Riefenstahl's use/misuse of his Mesakin photography.

16 'Western' here refers to a disquisition, not necessarily a location or a people. In the context of Africa, it is usually (but not always – witness Japanese) European or European American, usually (but not always – witness the old Soviet Union) capitalist, usually (but not always – witness Riefenstahl) male. It is those with power, those behind the camera, those comfortable with the assumptions, those who accept the law without question. Others, of course, have pointed out the phallic implications of photography.

17 Though certainly not Riefenstahl's specific quest (her emphasis on purity and strength and spectacle is distinctly atavistic – not even rising to the level of pastoral sentimental humanism), this can be seen today in the celebrations and illustrations of *pastiche*, of the blurring and disappearance of boundaries. But for these more recent motions, the epistemology is unchanged – functionalist hierarchies and the assumption of first order totalities and essentialism necessary to posit such functionalism (see also in this regard – and for another specific treatment of Riefenstahl's African photography – Gates 1998).

18 See, for example, Garner 1977

19 And early in photographic history, there *were* legal struggles over the rights of subjects (ironically, in Germany, for example, at the turn of the 20th century), to protect subjects from the rage of the newly available snapshot camera. But these struggles were lost.

20 There are, of course, studio conventions that are outside the control of sitters, or which at least often gender them, or otherwise project other unsavoury hierarchies.

21 In the tenor of this chapter, I would argue we should not necessarily embrace all/any so-called 'progressive' photography, and feel there are particular problems with the work of both these specific individuals. There are now a number of recent critiques of such work. See, for example, Mraz (1998a and b); Binford (1998); Stallabrass (1997).

Extended Bibliography

Anon. (1985) Dispatches. 'West German: Out of the Past', *The Nation* 4 May:520.
BBC. (1982) *Southeast Nuba*, Chris Curling, Producer. James Faris, Anthropologist.
    Hussein Shariffe and Howard Reid, Associate Producers. Roger Deakins,
    Camera. Barry Ackroyd, Assistant Camera. Bruce White, Sound. Ian Pitch,
    Editor. Julian Pettifer, Narration.
Beard, P. (1974) 'A Vision of Primal Man', *Natural History* 83(100):54–63.
Binford, L. (1998) 'Representing Revolution: The Central American War
    Photography of Susan Meiselas and Adam Kufeld', *Estudios Interdisciplinarios
    de América Latina y el Caribe* 9(1):95–109.
Culbert, D. (1993) 'Leni Riefenstahl and the Diaries of Joseph Goebbels', *Historical
    Journal of Film, Radio and Television* 13(1):85–93.
Danto, A. C. (1989) 'Artifact and art', In: *ART/artifact: African Art in
Anthropology Collections*. The Center for African Art, New York.
Deloria, P. J. (1998) *Playing Indian*, New Haven: Yale University Press.
DeVillez, P. (1982) 'Qualifying for a Permit', *Sudanow* 7(3):35–6.
Faris, J. C. (1972) *Nuba Personal Art*, London: Duckworth.
—— (1976) 'Letter: Fascism and Photography', *Newsweek* 88(24) [13 December]:4.
—— (1980) 'Polluted Vision', *Sudanow* 5(5):38.
—— (1983) 'From Form to Content in the Structural Study of Aesthetic Systems',
    in: D. Washburn (ed.) *Structure and Cognition in Art*. Cambridge: Cambridge
    University Press.
—— (1985) 'Nuba', in R. Weekes (ed.) *Muslim Peoples: A World Ethnographic Survey*.
    Westport: Greenwood Press
—— (1988a) 'The Significance of Differences in the Male and Female Personal
    Art of the Southeast Nuba', in A. Rubin (ed.) *Marks of Civilization: Art of the
    Body*, Berkeley: University of California Press.
—— (1988b) 'Southeast Nuba: A Biographical Statement', in J. Rollwagon (ed.)
    Anthropological Filmmaking. New York: Harwood Academic Press.
—— (1988c) 'Some Aspects of Change in Commodity Production in Southeast
    Kordofan', in N. O'Neill and J. O'Brien (eds) *Economy and Class in Sudan*,
    Aldershot: Gower Publishing Company.
—— (1989) 'Southeast Nuba Social Relations' *Monographica* 7, Aachen: Alano
    Verlag.
—— (1992) 'Photography, Power and the Southern Nuba', in E. Edwards (ed.)
    Anthropology and Photography 1860–1920, New Haven: Yale University Press.
—— (1993) 'Review Essay: Leni Riefenstahl and the Nuba Peoples of Kordofan
    Province, Sudan', *Historical Journal of Film, Radio and Television* 13(1):95–7.
—— (1996) *Navajo and Photography: A Critical History of the Representation of an
    American People*, Albuquerque: University of New Mexico Press.
Faris, J. C. and Keo Wutu. (1986) 'Beginning Anthropology: A Review Article',
    Critique of Anthropology 6(2):5–23.
Fenyo, M. (1977) 'A Nubak Foldjen', *Orszag-Vilag* 19:18.
Garner, G. (1977) 'A Psychologist Looks at Photography (interview with Stanley
    Milgram)', *The New Art Examiner* 6–7: 23.
Gates, L. (1998) 'Of Seeing and Otherness: Leni Riefenstahl's African Photographs',
    in S. Friedrichsmeyer, S. Lennox and S. Zantop (eds) *The Imperialist
    Imagination. German Colonialism and Its Legacy*, Ann Arbor: University of
    Michigan Press.
Infield, G. B. (1976) *Leni Riefenstahl. The Fallen Film Goddess,* New York: Thomas B.
    Crowell.
Iten, O. (1977) 'Bilder und Zerrbilder der Nuba', *Tages Anzeiger* 50(17):6.

—— (1979) 'Economic Pressures on Traditional Society', *European University Papers* Vol. 8. Bern: Peter Lang.

Luz, H. and O. Luz. (1966) 'Proud Primitives, the Nuba People', *National Geographic Magazine* 130(5):673–98.

Lutz, C. and J. Collins. (1993) *Reading National Geographic*, Chicago: University of Chicago Press.

Mraz, J. (1998a) 'The New Photojournalism of Mexico: 1976–1998.' *History of Photography* 22(4):313–65.

Mraz, J. (1998b) 'Sebastião Salgado's Latin America', *Estudios Interdisciplinarios de América Latina y el Caribe* 9(1):27–37.

Petley, J. (1979) *Capital and Culture. German Cinema, 1933–45*, London: British Film Institute.

Riefenstahl, L. (1974) *The Last of the Nuba*, New York: Harper and Row.

—— (1976) *The People of Kau*, New York: Harper and Row.

—— (1979) 'Leni Riefenstahl: Portraits of a Masked People', *Modern Photography* 63(9): 104–9.

—— (1987) *Memoiren*, München: Albrecht Knaus.

—— (1992) *The Sieve of Time. The Memoirs of Leni Riefenstahl*, London: Quartet Books.

Rodger, G. (1955) *Le Village des Noubas*, Paris: Achille Weber.

Ruby, J. (1998) 'Review of Navajo and Photography (J. Faris)', *Journal of the Royal Anthropological Institute* 4(2):369–70.

Ryle, J. (1982) 'Invasion of the Body Snatchers', *New Society* 549:54.

Schiff, S. (1992) 'Interview with Leni Riefenstahl', *Vanity Fair* 55(9):252–96.

Sontag, S. (1975) 'Fascinating Fascism', *New York Review of Books* 22(1), reprinted in *Under the Sign of Saturn*, New York: Farrar, Straus, Giroux,. (1980):73–105.

Stallabrass, J. (1997) 'Sebastião Salgado and Fine Arts Journalism', *New Left Review* 223.

Usama, I. (1982) 'The Children of Kau', *Sudanow* 7(3):49.

Zimmerman, P. D. (1976) 'Leni's Triumph of the Will', *Newsweek* 88(22):72–3.

6

From self-decoration to self-fashioning

Orientalism as backward progress among the Gebusi of Papua New Guinea

Bruce M. Knauft

The study of body art has often laboured under separate labels, some associated with indigenous and what were formerly called 'tribal' societies, and others associated with more ostensibly modern ones. Such polar antinomies are easily shredded by the complexities of ethnographic reality. But as Lévi-Strauss might say, oppositions may still persist or be useful to think through for heuristic purposes – or at least to see how their shredding might be a productive process. Further, it is sometimes the case, as in the material I will present shortly, that such dichotomies are clearly expressed by local people themselves, even if they also then dissemble them in fascinating ways.

As an only heuristic point of departure then, we can note that terms such as 'decoration', 'ritual' and the 'collective construction of selfhood' have often been associated with body art in what used to be called tribal societies. These stand in contrast to terms like 'fashion', 'dressing up', 'individual expression', 'choice' and 'lifestyle' often associated with bodily arts in complex and so-called modern societies. If anthropologists used to favour perspectives that were rule-governed, iconographic, or ritualised for the study of body art in pre-state societies, this contrasts with viewpoints for more complex societies that emphasize individualised aspiration and shifting bodily expression in a world of quickly changing styles and statuses. Georg Simmel (1971 [1904]) emphasized the latter perspective for Western fashion. He argued that changing fashion styles reflect the negotiation of status in a context of modern class mobility. More recently, Tseëlon (1992) has attempted to divide fashion into classical, modern and post-modern phases tied to various epochs of Western modernity.[1] These are collectively contrasted with bodily art in societies in which status is not based on personal development along yardsticks of modern progress and perpetual change.[2] This complements views that non-modern body art reflects deeply sedimented if not authentic notions of self and social relations that emerge, for instance, as decorations on the skin.[3] A modern view of fashion, by contrast, emphasises body art as a superficial and individualised covering, shifted at will to reflect the inclinations, styles and fortunes of the present moment.[4] While the first assumes more stable social relations, or at least the attempt to stabilise them, the second reflects if not celebrates the contemporary complexity of what Anthony Giddens (1990 and 1991) calls disembedded social relations.

Though the genealogy of our concepts and the baggage of their legacy in the study of body art can be interesting and important, my present concerns, like those of the Gebusi people I've worked with, race far beyond these constraints (see Knauft 2002a and b; 1996). My present concern is how distinctions that we may be tempted to discard in the dustbin of anthropological history may, as *ideologies*, be adopted, played with, and taken quite seriously by peoples themselves in alternative world areas. This raises a more general problem that anthropology faces today. Anthropologists quite rightly reject simple conceptualizations of development or progress, of modernisation, of individual freedom, of political democratisation, of moral enlightenment, and so on. I agree if not insist that a critical analysis of such concepts is necessary (Knauft 2002c). As ideologies, however, many of these same notions or some refraction of them are quite powerful forces in the non-western world. Nations strive, often with ferocity, to become developed, progressive, or modern in their own sense of these terms. Notions of individual freedom, on the one hand, and those of social and cultural enlightenment, on the other, can be strongly embraced. Though we should certainly not adopt the ideologies of an ostensibly modernising world at face value, neither should we reject the way they have often been ground into very local circumstances.

In the realm of body art, it is now common if not expectable to discover cultural hybridity, a global flow of bodily fashions, creative uses of costuming in a current world, and so on. These portrayals often echo or romanticise the creativity of personal expression and a hopeful modernity-at-large (Appadurai 1996). But it is nonetheless true, as I once heard reported on U.S. National Public Radio, that Avon ladies in canoes up the far reaches of the Amazon sell lipstick, deodorant and make-up to local women at incredibly inflated prices – and make a hefty profit off the local population in the process. Here, the backwardness of the traditional versus the modern body can be ideologically real. The critical edge of decoration under such circumstances resonates with the analysis that researchers such as Timothy Burke makes in his book *Lifebuoy Men, Lux Women: Commodification, Consumption, and Cleanliness in Modern Zimbabwe* (1996).

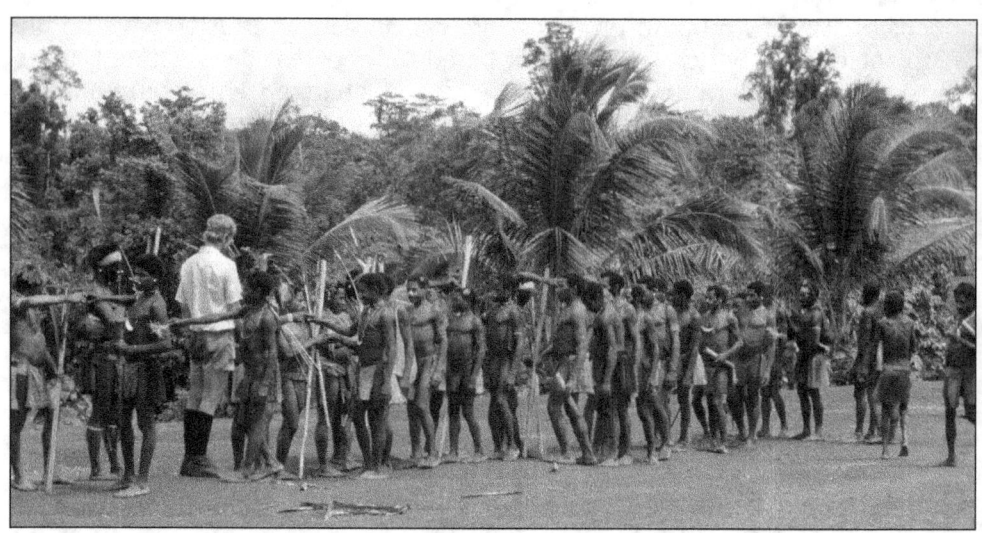

Plate 6.1   *Traditional etiquette: the author snaps fingers in a welcoming line of adult Gebusi men, 1981. (Photo credit: Eileen Knauft)*

Culture, clothing and change among Gebusi

The changing definition of so-called traditional versus modern modes of dress and decoration can be examined in the context of the Gebusi. When I first lived with them in 1980–82, Gebusi were one of the most remote and 'unacculturated' groups in Papua New Guinea. Located in the interior lowland rainforest of the country's expansive Western Province, their population numbered just 450.[5] At the time, Gebusi actively pursued a host of practices that were classic foci in anthropology: shamanism or spirit mediumship; sorcery beliefs and inquisitions; a high level of violence; ornate ritual dances and costuming; elaborate rites of male initiation and male–female fertility; and male sexual practices in which mid- or late teenage initiands manipulated the penises and orally consumed the semen of other males. First contacted in 1962, Gebusi had twenty years later still not been subject to Christianisation, out-migration, significant cash cropping, land alienation, economic development, taxation, or regular government interference in their affairs. The main impact had been the introduction of steel tools and the pacification of their bellicose neighbours, the Bedamini, by Australian patrol officers during the late 1960s and early 1970s. The Australians departed in 1975 when the new nation of Papua New Guinea obtained independence.

Though Western clothes were highly desired, they were seldom available to Gebusi in 1980–82; those specimens that were occasionally worn were usually in tatters or otherwise in an advanced state of disrepair (see Plate 6.1). Most women showed little embarrassment going bare-breasted either during daily activities or when attending major rituals or feasts. At these latter events, bodily adornment with feathers, body paint and various forest-derived decorations was both elaborate and, as far as could be discerned,

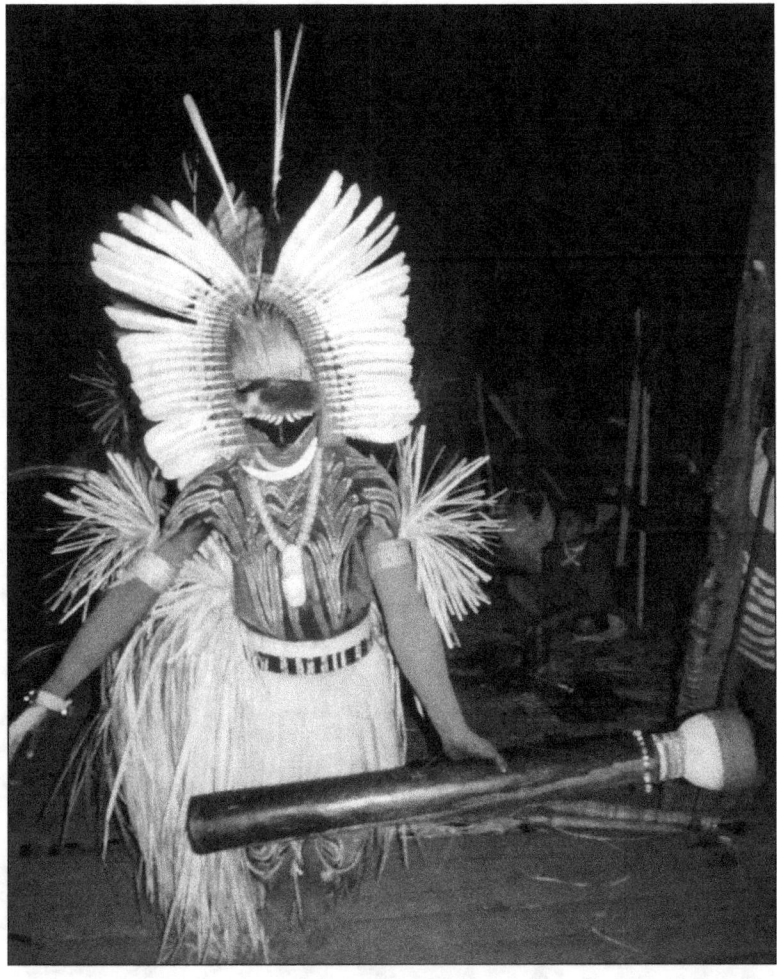

Plate 6.2   *A traditional costumed dancer performs in a village longhouse, 1981. (Photo credit: Eileen Knauft)*

consonant with pre-colonial accoutrements for both men and women. Non-performing visitors and hosts dressed in elaborate but individually variable costumes that included wonderfully diverse arrays of plumage, body painting and other decorations. Ritual dancers were richly clad in costumes that included meticulous and highly standardised arrangements of feathered headdresses, fur, leaves, shell slabs or slivers and body painting, all of which iconised and literally embodied a pantheon of Gebusi spirits (see Plate 6.2).[6] For initiates, the elaborate decorative elements of their climactic costumes indicated both the apotheosis of their youth and fertility as a spiritual 'red bird-of-paradise' and ties of kinship and friendship that bonded them with their initiate sponsors in different Gebusi settlements. The many sponsors of each initiate made and donated specific costume elements that were aesthetically harmonised and integrated with those of others in the initiates'

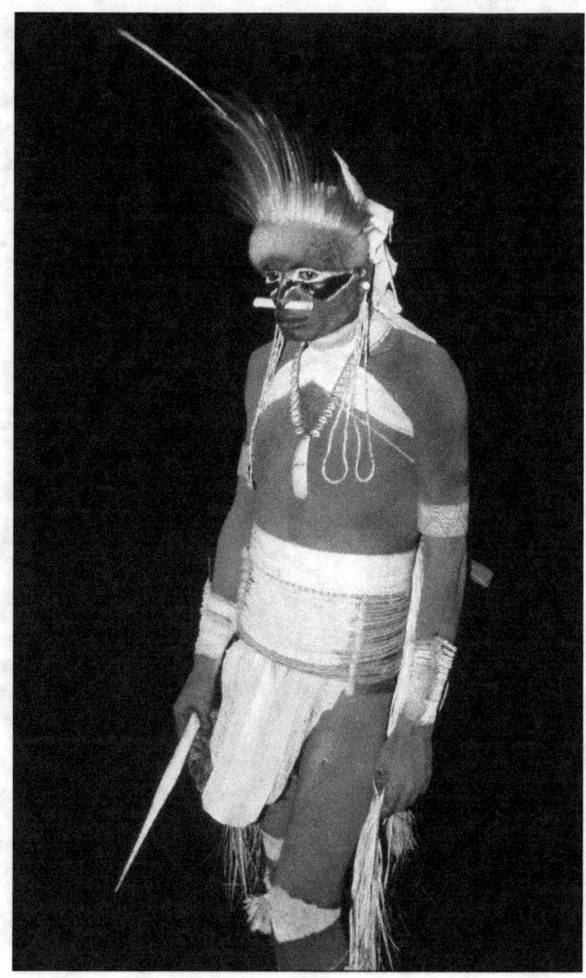

Plate 6.3   *Union of human and spiritual*
beauty, 1981: at the final stage
of the male initiation, an initiand
stands humbly in his completed red
bird-of-paradise costume. (Photo
credit Eileen Knauft)

final body decoration. As such, the initiates' final costuming was a corporeal manifestation of social relations and gift-giving across virtually the entire Gebusi social and spiritual landscape (see Plate 6.3).

Upon returning for a six-month restudy in 1998, I discovered that many aspects of Gebusi life had altered substantially (Knauft 2002a and b, 2003, 2005). The community I had lived with had of their own volition relocated from the deep rainforest to the portion of their land that abuts the Nomad Station. This government outpost boasts an airstrip, a score of administrative staff, a school, police office, several churches and a number of small stores.

It also supports a twice-weekly market, sports league contests on a carefully maintained ballfield, and a range of other government and private activities and events.

The Nomad Station is located at the geographic intersection of several ethnic groups and is the primary point of outside influence and inter-ethnic gathering for some 9,000 persons scattered thinly across 3,500 square miles of lowland rainforest. The Gebusi communities I had previously lived with had re-settled a short twenty-minute walk from this administrative and social centre. In the bargain, Gebusi whom I had known and their descendants had become willing participants in Christian churches, the Nomad sports leagues, the Nomad market and government activities. Their children regularly attended the multiethnic Nomad Community School, where they received instruction by national teachers in the Papua New Guinean dialect of English for a full school day five days a week. Eighty-four percent of adults in the new Gebusi community were baptised members in one of the three local Christian churches – Catholic, Evangelical, or Seventh Day Adventist. All of these denominations were highly fundamentalist in orientation. Amid these changes, Gebusi spirit mediumship had become defunct and male spirit séances – which had previously taken place an average of once every eleven days – were no longer held.

With the decline of traditional spirit mediumship and séances, there was little way Gebusi could communicate with their indigenous spirits. With startling rapidity, Gebusi cosmology had been supplanted by a Christian cosmos of good and evil, sanctity and sin, and heaven and hell (see Knauft 2002a:chs. 6–7; 2005:ch. 8). Initiations were no longer held in my community of residence, and a large cohort of young men had not been initiated and never would be. The ritual dances (*gigobra*) that had accompanied feasts had been largely replaced by 'parties' (*fati*) at which string band or disco music was played. Now living in scattered hamlets rather than in a centralised village, Gebusi resided in individual or extended family houses rather than gathering in a main longhouse. Social life was more differentiated and less exuberant than before.

One of the most immediately visible changes in Gebusi social life was the common presence of Western clothes (see Plate 6.4). Though the paltry local cash economy and lack of economic development or wage labour had stymied many Gebusi material aspirations, enterprising government officials and their affiliates occasionally managed to have cheap bales of Chinese or used Australian shirts and blouses, dresses and pants flown in to the airstrip at Nomad – where they could be quickly and completely sold for a profit even at relatively low prices. As a result, though many aspects of Gebusi economy had not altered significantly, most villagers possessed at least one set of Western clothes for wearing in the village and another set, cleaner and less spotted or torn, for wearing at village feasts or 'parties', at Church and when visiting the Nomad Station. Women invariably wore blouses or dresses – to be seen bare-breasted was highly shameful, even in the village – and men always wore shirts when in church or while visiting the Nomad Station. Traditional female dress of woven grass skirts and male dress of fibre-stripped 'ass-grass'

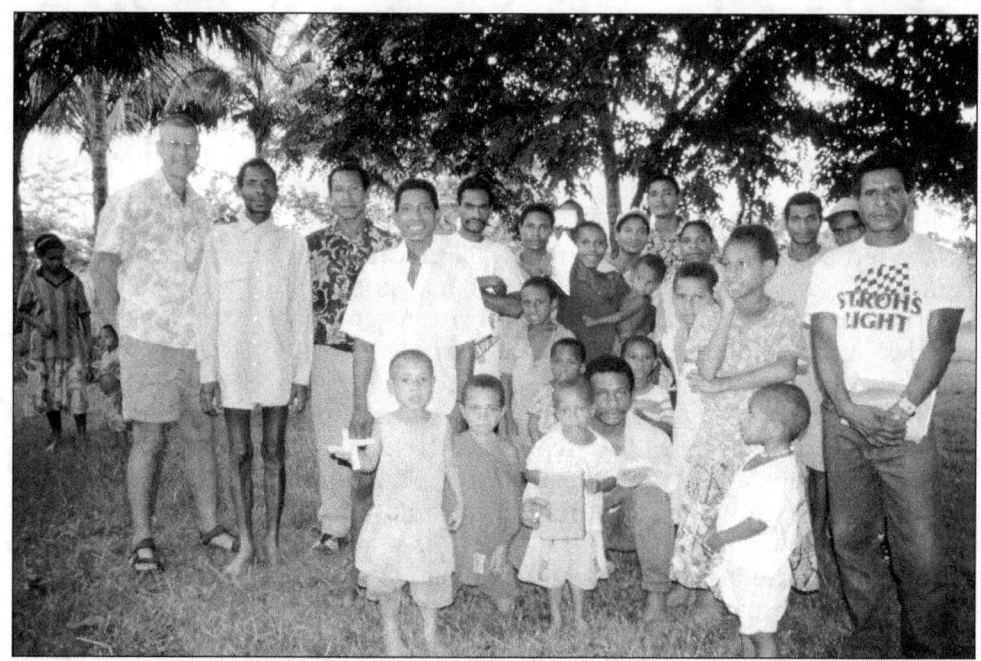

Plate 6.4   *Local parishioners and the author pose for the camera outside the Nomad Catholic church, 1998. (Photo credit: Bruce Knauft, self-timed)*

and loincloths were rarely if ever seen either in daily or ceremonial contexts in the community.

Gebusi practices and attitudes concerning traditional body decoration and dancing were particularly noteworthy (Knauft 2002b). Though the costuming of ritual dancers and initiates had become moribund in most villages – along with the demise of the ceremonies themselves – Gebusi re-staged these processions in full costuming as a kind of folkloric re-enactment for public and multi-ethnic display at the Nomad Station. This was especially the case during the week that surrounded Papua New Guinea National Independence Day on September 16. During this period, the various ethnic groups of the Nomad Sub-District visited and performed in their respective traditional costumes for a collected throng of visitors and government officers on the parade grounds of the government station (see Plate 6.5). These performances were judged by officials, who awarded nominal amounts of prize money to the persons and groups they had rated most highly (see Plate 6.6).

The re-enactment of traditional display was not only for official viewing. Highly talked about and avidly planned for, the folkloric performance of local dances and costuming during the week of Independence Day became an intense focus of community excitement and planning in most villages. The performances were avidly viewed by more than one thousand people, who came from near and far to see the re-display of traditional costumes and dances. In most cases, the performances were undertaken by villagers who

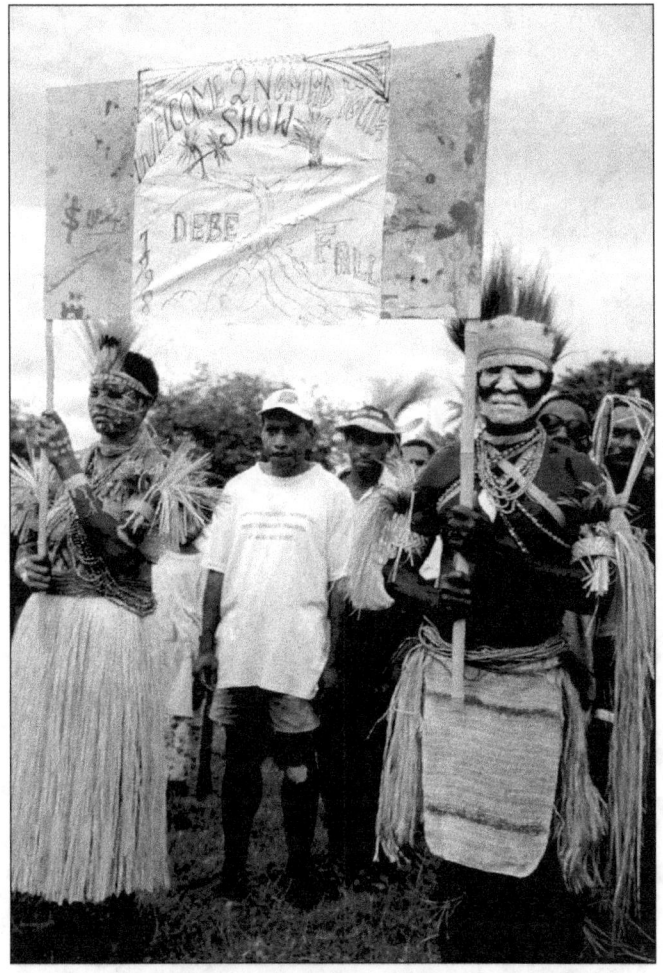

Plate 6.5   *A man and woman in neo-traditional costume introduce their village dances on Independence Day, 1998. The T-shirt of the man standing in the middle reads, 'Compulsive, Antisocial, Manic Depressive, Paranoid, but Basically Happy.' (Photo credit: Bruce Knauft)*

no longer decorated themselves or danced in similar manner in their own villages. Adding to the general splendour of their portrayals, some villages dressed up whole lines of males and females in initiation or traditional dance costumes despite the fact that performers would in all likelihood never be initiated or dance in their own villages (see Plate 6.7). Costume elements were borrowed or lent in ad hoc fashion and typically did not reflect gift-giving, food reciprocity, or enduring ties of ceremonial or spiritual sponsorship that accompanied traditional dances and initiations.

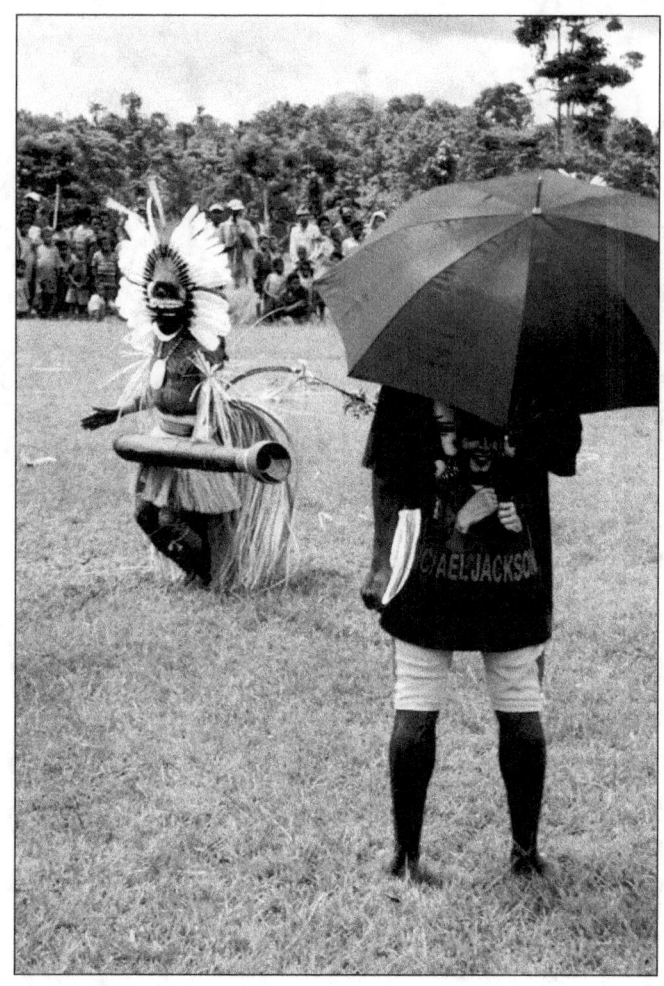

Plate 6.6   *An official wearing a Michael Jackson T-*
            shirt judges a Gebusi dancer during the
            traditional costume competition at Nomad
            on Independence Day, 1998. (Photo credit:
            Bruce Knauft)

Performers in many cases had little ritual or initiatory identification with
the costuming and display they were enacting. Their attitudes concerning
the meanings and beliefs associated with these practices were revealed in an
elaborate series of 'dramas' (*dramas*) that were performed at Nomad at night
during the week of Independence. In these portrayals, performers dressed in
intricate indigenous costumes put on skits that re-enacted traditional social
practices and the spiritual or mythical beliefs with which they had been
associated. In tone and expression, these portrayals were not appreciative;
rather, they were consistently farcical, buffoonish and parodic. In skit after
skit, old costumes, beliefs and ceremonies were served up by villagers in

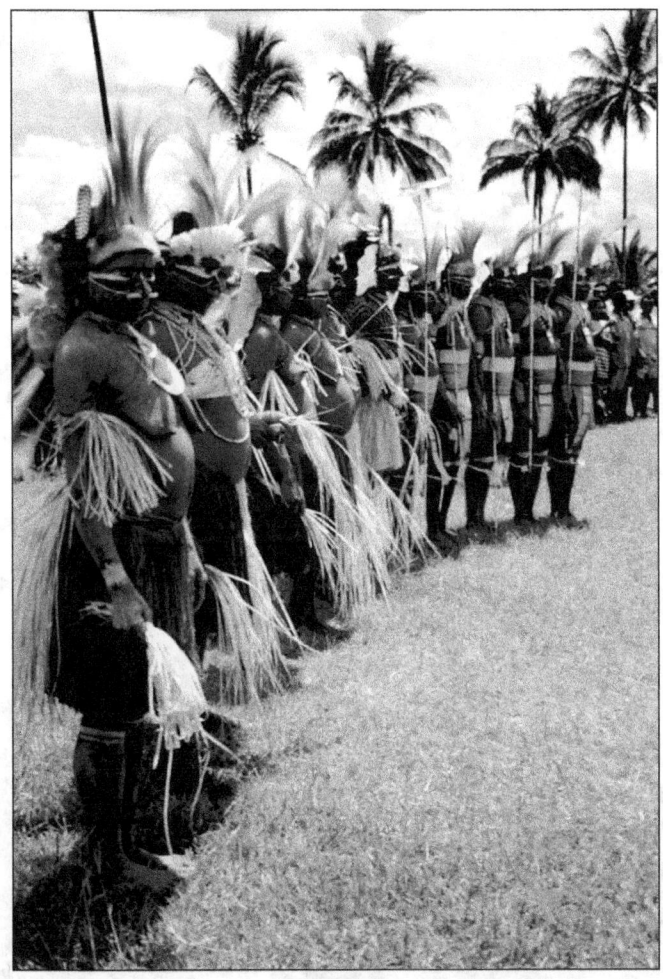

Plate 6.7   *A line of costumed young men pose in initiation costumes at the traditional competition at Nomad on Independence Day, 1998. In some of these displays, performers donned costumes that had traditionally been worn sequentially at difference stages of the initiation, and included boys too young to be initiated. (Photo credit: Bruce Knauft)*

elaborate decorative presentation as ignorant and backward indicators of unenlightened beliefs and practices – to the great enjoyment of the assembled villages from near and far (see Plate 6.8). The exaggerated parody of traditional practices was finely tuned with physical antics, slapstick humour and biting irony that brought roars of appreciative and heartfelt laughter from the large inter-ethnic audience. Among the beliefs and practices made fun of were

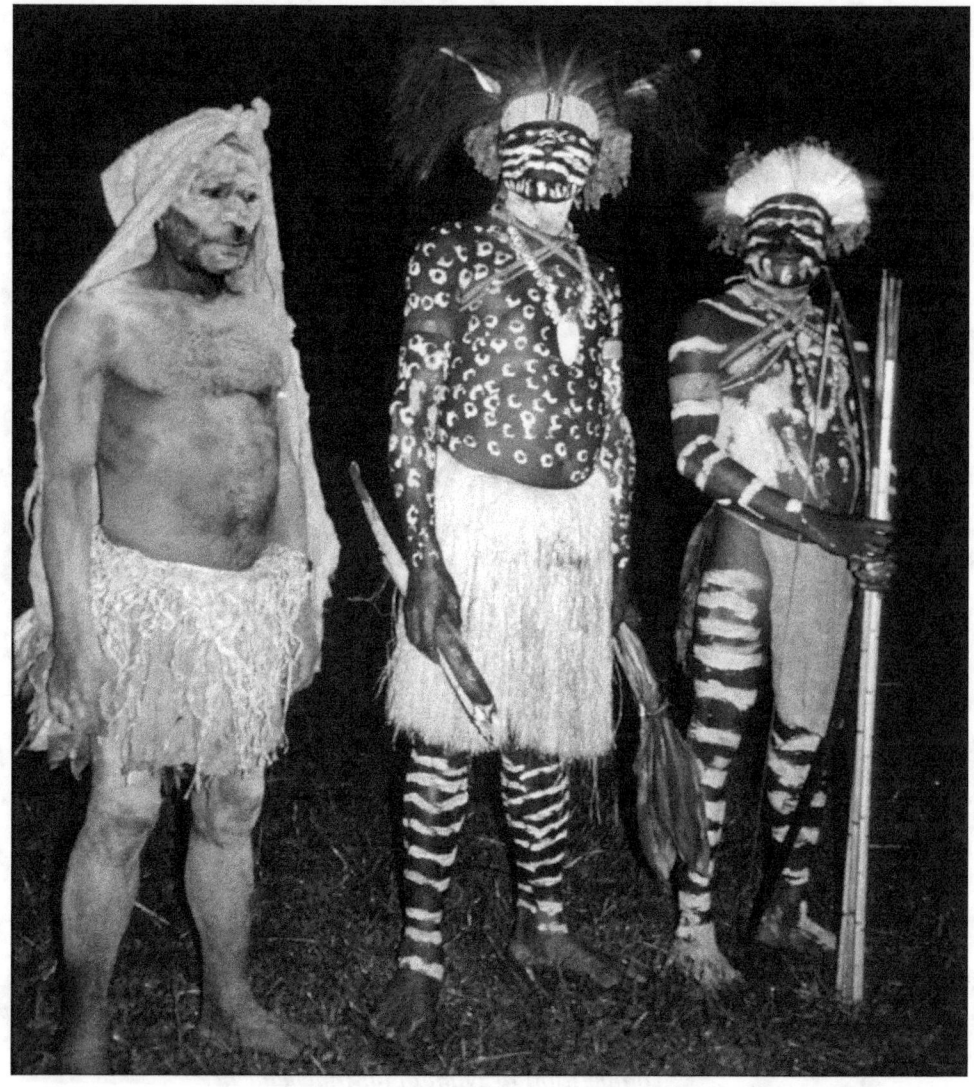

Plate 6.8   *Gebusi performers in mock traditional costume present themselves*
to the evening crowd before performing a drama skit of old-time
customs at the Nomad Independence celebrations, 1998. (Photo
credit: Bruce Knauft)

the difficulty of chopping trees with traditional stone axes; the 'stupidity'
of believing in magical spells and rites; spiritual beliefs concerning physical
affliction and curing; inquests for sorcery; taboos and beliefs that surrounded
fish poisoning; practices of traditional fighting; and indigenous myths and
creation stories.

    These spoofs were in most cases accompanied by an explanation by one
of the lead performers, delivered through a battery-operated bullhorn, that

described in English or in the national lingua franca of *tok pisin* the 'ignorant' traditional practice or belief that was being enacted. The portrayal of traditions was thrown into relief and punctuated by other performances that were staged as Christian morality tales, which were typically accompanied by posters or placards graced with corresponding verses from the Bible. In these skits, those who followed heathen customs invariably became depraved or were struck down while those who followed the dictates of enlightened Christian morality were saved and rewarded.

The general cast of Gebusi 'dramas' can be fleshed out by a few examples. In one common skit, a man in black paint, dark cassowary headdress and wearing an old loincloth groaned buffoonishly as he tried with clumsy and exaggerated effort to hack down a tiny tree by using a traditional stone axe. Every few swings, the stone would fall from the handle and the man would grunt and stumble stupidly while looking for it in the grass. Trying to sharpen the stone proved irritating and ultimately futile. This led to a dispute with an ostensible comrade, who smoked local tobacco from a traditional pipe and refused to help – until the two almost came to blows. The pantomime was enacted with slapstick comedy and rudeness that proved quite funny to the audience.

In another skit, traditional fish poisoning beliefs were lampooned. As I had witnessed in 1980–82, indigenous beliefs led Gebusi to festoon a traditional dancer in full finery so he could conduct a stately dance on the river bank while derris root fish poison was leached into the river. His beauty was thought to woo the fish to the surface and to stun them with his magnificent aura – magnifying the effect of the poison so men could scoop up large numbers of fish into net bags or into their canoes before the effects of the toxin wore off and the fish swam away. In the skit, these beliefs became farcical: men who played 'fish' in the skit snapped at the dancer and scared him so much that he drummed in a frenzy and pranced about wildly – just the opposite of the dignified dance step that was traditionally practiced. The dancer in his awkwardness and uncertainty veered so close to a nearby cooking fire that the extra-long palm leaves at the rear of his costume caught fire. After trying with mock fear to extinguish his own burning tail, the dancer raced in mock terror from the performance area – to the howls of the audience.

For me, the most dramatic skit was a parody of traditional sorcery divination and inquest practices that was performed by some of my close Gebusi friends. The opening performer portrayed a 'sick man'; he was caked in mud and had a huge fake phallus strapped to his waist. He moaned stupidly that he was going to die, to which the 'spirit medium' in the skit responded by yelling loudly directly in his ear, that is, 'to keep his spirit from leaving'. After the man 'died', the spirit medium and his associates sang raucously to contact the spirits for 'guidance'. Eventually, they grabbed a villager and accused him of causing the death through sorcery. In a mock corpse inquest, the sorcery suspect was forced to wail at the corpse of the deceased. (This is a practice I saw practiced very much for real in 1980–82.) At this, the corpse in the skit arched its back and a string was surreptitiously pulled to raise his make-believe phallus high into a large erection. Audience members doubled up with laughter. This 'sign' indicated that the sorcery suspect was guilty. As the suspect was tied up, he whimpered and cried like a baby. He was then intimidated, beaten and eventually 'killed' in buffoonish manner by another man in the skit. Finally, the friends of the murdered man came and, in a farcical battle, 'fought' those who had killed him. The message of the skit was clear: 'in the past we actually thought people could die from sorcery. We followed false beliefs that led us to fight and kill each other for nothing'.

Against such portrayals were enactments of first contact, which featured the proud and disciplined actions of Australian patrol officers – played by villagers. In several of the skits, the officers brandished 'guns' and brought order and peace to villagers, who were portrayed as scared, awkward and prone to needless fighting. One of the favourite skits was of a traditional man who had been given a first tin of fish and bag of rice by a benevolent Australian patrol officer. Uncomprehending, the villager tried to open the can of fish by biting it and then smashing it on a rock. He then built a large bonfire to cook this important but still unopened food. Along with the pulverised tin, he put the unopened bag of rice into a plastic bucket, which he put directly on the fire. The entire assemblage promptly erupted into a ball of flame. The audience convulsed in laughter as the man raced off in mock horror, ending the skit.

Of the forty-two dramas presented, twenty-three were farcical parodies of traditional customs, five were stories of colonial first contact, five were Christian morality tales, four were about modern life, three were song or dance performances, one was a physical drama (men and boys in traditional costume played a game of bounding leapfrog around the performance area) and one was a unique hybrid.

Orientalism revisited

The re-enactment of traditions by Gebusi and other ethnic groups at Nomad – first in decontextualised display during the day and then in parody at night – reflect the notion that indigenous costuming should distance historical meanings, identifications and indigenous forms of social transaction from the present. When indigenous costuming is worn, as the Christian pastors emphasize, it is said that true intentions reside not on the skin but in the innermost heart of the wearer – whether he or she is truly dedicated to God.[7] Under contemporary circumstances, the moral condition of the self is no longer reflected externally; what you see is not necessarily what you will get (cf. O'Hanlon 1995a: 832; 1995b).

Particularly in their 'dramas', Gebusi use of indigenous costuming tends toward what we might call auto-orientalism or self-orientalism, that is, the stigmatised self-attribution of alterity. This notion can be put in larger context by distinguishing auto-orientalism from other species of the genre. In bodily art, we can define orientalism in general as the construction and projection of stigmatised Otherness through the cultural assertion of 'progress' versus 'backwardness' in body decoration and sartorial style. Orientalism in this sense is the visually embodied projection of alterity as stigma across the divide of an imagined rupture of social and moral advancement vis-à-vis the past.

Probably the most generic variety of orientalism, reflected in Edward Said's famous book (1994), is what we might call 'projective' orientalism. This is the outward projection of stigmatised backwardness onto others. By negative contrast, such attributions distinguish and highlight the projecting subject's own superiority and progress.[8]

In contemporary circumstances, orientalist projections across a time-line of supposed progress have several different permutations.[9] In some cases one finds a displacement of orientalising stigma to a sub-population within one's larger group. Here the stigma of being insufficiently modern is displaced from the majority and re-projected onto a minority. This might be termed *internal* orientalism or *sub-orientalism*. In body art, this process is dramatically documented by Louisa Schein (2000) in her book on the cultural politics of the Miao (Hmong) ethnic minority in China. The Miao are just one of many 'primitivised' ethnic groups that provide the alter to dominant Han identity in China; their elaborate traditional costumes and drinking generosity are taken as pre-dynastic relics of Chinese tradition.[10] The costumed folklore of so-designated backward ethnic minorities is large in China, both as foil for national definition and for endo-tourism. Such patterns are common in the nostalgic primitivising of marginal ethnic groups and their elaborate costuming within the larger hegemony of a national imaginary. Such features of backward and yet beautiful ethnicity paraded for the national or international gaze are also marked among Kalasha of north-western Pakistan (Maggi 2001), the Mayan peoples of Guatemala (Nelson 1999) and native American displays in parts of North and South America.

Insofar as it gains media attention and political symbolism, however, internal orientalism is a double-edged sword that can be taken up by performers themselves. As several anthropologists have noted, the self-proclamation of bodily alterity can provide in-your-face resistance to outside standards of progress as moral worth. This is what might be dubbed *counter-orientalism*: the re-appropriation of orientalising images to aggressively assert rather than disparage local styles of clothing and costuming. A poignant example here is Beth Conklin's (1997) trenchant analysis of bodily display in the politics and mass media of Brazilian Indian land and cultural rights.

When Kayapo leader Kube-i arrived at the courthouse to give his deposition, he appeared shirtless, wearing body paint and feathers – for which he was promptly charged with contempt of court. (Conklin 1997:720)

When ordered to show respect by wearing a suit and tie, he replied,

Your Honor, this *is* how we Kayapo show respect. This *is* the Indian's
suit and tie.' Besides, he pointed out, 'When we invite you to our
village, we don't ask you to take off your clothes and paint up like a
Kayapo. (ibid.)

Beyond the Amazon, one can note aspects of counter-orientalism in the increased practice of veiling among educated middle and upper class Islamic women in the mid-East and south-east Asia, including some who were erstwhile feminists. Their point, among others, is that they can reappropriate the erstwhile stigmatising signs of gendered backwardness to demonstrate their equality if not superiority to ostensibly modern sartorial alternatives. One may note a similar theme in the counter-clothing styles of African leaders during the 1980s, when the wearing of Kente cloth was used to assert African sartorial equality, but on their own terms.

Insofar as its value derives from opposition and resistance, however, counter-orientalism flirts with the same oppositions it tries to overcome. In attempting to reverse the terms of stigma, its axes of division can be accepted if not reinforced (see critique by Chakrabarty 2000). Against the standards of so-called modern progress, then, counter-orientalism almost invariably borrows from the essentialism it is trying to reject (this is a point Said himself emphasised in his 'Afterword' to the 1994 edition of *Orientalism*). In terms of body art and sartorial style, counter-orientalism does not return to indigenous styles of clothing or decoration. Rather, it essentialises and reinvents these in ways that are neo-traditional and ethnically modern.[11] This trend dovetails with what Frederick Errington and Deborah Gewertz (2001) call the generification of culture. Conklin's analysis illustrates this generification quite well: certain forms of so-called indigenous decoration are downplayed while others are highlighted and made indigenously generic if not mandatory for political and media consumption. Traditional culture is at once embodied and made iconic as a neo-traditional style of dress and bodily display.[12]

Insofar as counter-orientalist initiatives adopt received lines of group–other opposition (even as they attempt to reverse these) they carry the potential and the threat of reproducing or re-inscribing stigma. This result is highly evident and carried to a self-conscious extreme among Gebusi. Their performative dramas of the past reflect auto-orientalism, that is, the self-projection of stigmatised alterity along a time-line of progress. This disparagement of social and sartorial history is also evident in some other parts of Melanesia. For instance, Errington and Gewertz (1995) describe how Karavar of Manus Province debunk their 'primitive' past in skits that celebrate the arrival of the first white missionary. As among Gebusi, portrayals of indigenous backwardness are contrasted with those of becoming literally enlightened through social and moral progress.

If self-orientalist portrayals are highly evident in historical enactments by peoples such as Gebusi and Karavar, they easily arise as sub-plots in the other types of orientalism mentioned above. In counter-orientalist resistance against stigma, for instance, there often remains suspicion or fear among those resisting that they are, in fact, more backward and undeveloped than they would like to admit. Subverting or denying this stigma is often related to the threat or the reality that it has, in fact, already been internalised. In this respect, groups like Gebusi and Karavar show in a less filtered manner the deeper fears that are common in internal and counter-orientalist initiatives.

Gendered markers?

My final points are more speculative and concern the gendered significance of ethnic-cum-orientalist marking. Though the marking of ethnicity in daily dress may not be explicit for groups as wholes, it often seems to be relatively more pronounced for women than for men. Particularly in Asia, the mid-East and Central America, it is common for women to bear the sartorial marking of ethnicity and/or historical authenticity. For disenfranchised ethnic groups and also for mainstream ones fighting Western stigma, it is often women rather than men who bear the greatest signs of modern alterity in their quotidian appearance. Whether it is an Islamic veil, an Indian sari, a Mayan traje, Kalasha beads, a Miao headdress, or heavy traditional jewellery, women are often icons of contemporary ethnic tradition.[13] These gendered markings are often associated with women's upholding of neo-traditional domestic morality and sexual propriety. While men may also be ethnically marked as Others, they are often at greater liberty, both socially and sartorially, to shift their styles and pass unmarked into more fully modern roles in their daily activities. Insofar as this is true, orientalism can be both displaced and internalised onto a domesticated and neo-traditionalised female sphere. As evident among Gebusi but also more widely, the contextual display of neo-tradition does not prevent someone – but particularly a man – from being superficially costumed in one way at one moment and another the next. Among the Huli of the Southern Highlands, Holly Wardlow (2002), describes how men may wear the famous Huli wig one day only to trade it off for a cowboy hat the next, depending on personal whim. By contrast, Huli women are strongly constrained from wearing Western accoutrements or even from wearing shoes, lest they be seen as sexually loose and immoral. In such cases, the masculine appropriation of contextual neo-tradition as well as modern sartorial style can itself index personal self-fashioning, that is, the notion that modern self-fashioning and the liberties that it entails are masculine prerogatives (cf. Knauft 1999b). From this perspective, the double standard whereby men can disembed and reimbed themselves into neo-tradition more flexibly than women is consistent with sexual double standards that are frequently indexed by corresponding differences in modern and neo-traditional sartorial marking.

Lastly and on a yet larger scale, it can be noted that the shift from so-called decoration to so-called fashion has its own gendered component. Though the global fashion industry certainly includes clothing for men, *haute couture* is overwhelmingly objectified on and in the context of the young female body. This may be one reason why the masculine tribal chic rarely exceeds a national boundary even though the masculine dimension of indigenous costuming has been historically prominent if not pre-eminent in world areas such as Melanesia (e.g., Strathern and Strathern 1971; Kirk 1981; O'Hanlon 1989).

Consonant with these general trends, indigenous patterns of Gebusi costuming may be at once a dying breed and an apt commentary on larger patterns – the owl of Minerva in the heart of modern clothing.

NOTES

I heartily extend thanks to Michael O'Hanlon for inviting me and enabling my participation at the 'Body Arts and Modernity' conference, held in Oxford on June 27–9, 2002, at which the initial version of this paper was presented. Comments on this conference presentation as well as on its written version are very gratefully acknowledged from Michael O'Hanlon, Elizabeth Ewart and several of the conference participants.

1 See Entwistle 2000:43–8.

2 See Blumer 1968 and 1995; Sellerberg 2001; Entwistle 2000; contrast Brydon and Niessen 1998; cf., Greenblatt's (1980) analysis of self-fashioning as an emergent form of modern subjectivity during the European Renaissance.

3 E.g., Strathern and Strathern 1971; M. Strathern 1979; Turner 1980; O'Hanlon 1989; Knauft 1999a; Johnson 2001.

4 E.g. the journal *Fashion Theory* and books on fashion published by Berg Press.

5 Concerning Gebusi in 1980–82, see Knauft 1985a and b, 1986, 1987a and b, 1989a and b, 1996: ch.6; 2002a, 2005a:chs 1–6.

6 Concerning indigenous Gebusi costuming, see Knauft 1989b; 1999a:78–80 and photos 1–12, 14 therein; see also Knauft 1985b:257–60.

7 It is for this very reason that the evangelical pastor disparaged costume elements such as the red bird-of-paradise – not because he found them ugly, but because they confused a glossy surface appearance with an inner individual state.

8 For sake of argument, it may be asserted that orientalism in general and projective orientalism in particular are distinctively modern forms of ethnocentrism. Ethnocentrism in general does not require a sense of being modern or a time-line of progress to effect stigma. When in early colonial Papua New Guinea the Etoro peoples disparaged the Kaluli as disgusting because they inseminated their initiates anally rather than orally; when the Kaluli returned the slur; and when the Onabasulu thought that both groups were depraved by forcing semen into the body of initiates rather than coating it on their skin (see Kelly 1977:chapter 1), they were all being ethnocentric but not orientalist. Their mutual disparagement was based on what Theodore Schwartz (1975) called ethnic totemism; it did not draw on notions of historical development based on collective and individual progress. That is, assertions of being 'better' did not in these cases depend on a sense of having 'gone ahead' or having 'become more developed' over time.

9 I thank Carla Jones (pers. comm.) for her insights concerning orientalism – though she bears no responsibility for the coarseness of my own distinctions. Jones and Ann Marie Leshkowich have recently elaborated a nuanced notion of self-orientalism in the context of contemporary Asian fashion (Leshkowich and Jones 2003).

10 The projection of Otherness has strongly affected Miao themselves, many of whom displace this ethnic attribution onto others who they claim to be yet more 'authentic' Miao – and hence more distant, remote and 'backward' – than themselves. More diffusely reckoned, however, Miao are typically considered to be China's largest ethnic minority.

11 Strictly speaking, this is not the invention of tradition as much as it is the re-appropriation and re-definition of tradition as a self-conscious and more generic form of bodily presentation in the explicit context of modern cultural politics.

12 Over time, this process can become recursive: ethnic or tribal styles find their way into wider fields of representation and even into fields of national or international fashion. Conversely, local couture may assert self-representation in ever more ethnic-modern guises. In the fashion world, one sees this tendency in the production of 'ethnic chic', for instance, the selective appropriation of Banana Republic ethnicity as a marker of *haute couture*. Middle Eastern veils, Rastafarian dreadlocks, Indian saris, tribalising feathers and beads – all are fair game in the hunt for next season's newer-than-new fashion line-up. In their book *Re-orienting Fashion*, Niessen, Leshkowich and Jones (2003) analyze how east and south-east Asian clothing designers are both complicit and subversive in this process, that is, they strive to reassert the difference and distinctiveness of Asian styles of dress while linking these with symbolic and commercial success in a wider world of fashion (see also Kondo 1997). In the process, sartorial identity is inextricably intertwined with rather than resistant to the market-driven terms of capitalist production, distribution, advertising and consumption.

13 Counterexamples could also be noted, including the wearing of turbans by Sikh men and highly distinctive hairstyles and black hats worn by Jewish men.

Bibliography

Appadurai, A. (1996) *Modernity at Large: Cultural Dimensions of Globalization*, Minneapolis: University of Minnesota Press.

Blumer, H. G. (1968) 'Fashion', in D. L. Sills (ed.) *International Encyclopedia of the Social Sciences, vol. 5*, New York: Macmillan.

—— (1995) 'Fashion: From Class Differentiation to Collective Selection', in M. E. Roach-Higgins, J. B. Eicher and K. K. P. Johnson (eds) *Dress and Identity*, New York: Fairchild.

Brydon, A. and S. Niessen (eds) (1998) *Consuming Fashion: Adorning the Transnational Body*, Oxford: Berg.

Burke, T. (1996) *Lifebuoy Men, Lux Women: Commodification, Consumption, and Cleanliness in Modern Zimbabwe*, Durham, NC: Duke University Press.

Chakrabarty, D. (2000) *Provincializing Europe: Postcolonial Thought and Historical Difference*, Princeton, NJ: Princeton University Press.

Conklin, B. A. (1997) 'Body Paint, Feathers, and VCRs: Aesthetics and Authenticity in Amazonian Activism', *American Ethnologist* 24(4):711–37.

Entwistle, J. (2000) *The Fashioned Body: Fashion, Dress, and Modern Social Theory*, Cambridge: Polity Press.

Errington, F. and D. Gewertz (1995) *Articulating Change in the "Last Unknown"*, Boulder, CO: Westview Press.

—— (2001) 'On the Generification of Culture: From Blow Fish to Melanesian', *Journal of the Royal Anthropological Institute* 7(3):509–25.

Giddens, A. (1990) *The Consequences of Modernity*, Cambridge: Polity Press.

—— (1991) *Modernity and Self-Identity: Self and Society in the Late Modern Age*, Stanford: Stanford University Press.

Greenblatt, S. J. (1980) *Renaissance Self-Fashioning: From More to Shakespeare*, Chicago: University of Chicago Press.

Johnson, R. (2001) 'The Anthropological Study of Body Decoration as Art: Collective Representations and the Somatization Affect', *Fashion Theory* 5(4):417–34.

Jones, C. and A. M. Leshkowich (2003) 'Introduction: The Globalization of Asian Dress: Re-Orienting Fashion or Re-Orientalizing Asia?', in A. M. Leshkowich and C. Jones (eds) *Re-orienting Fashion: The Globalization of Asian Dress*, Oxford: Berg Press.

Kelly, R. C. (1977) *Etoro Social Structure: A Study in Structural Contradiction*, Ann Arbor: University of Michigan Press.

Kirk, M. [with A. J. Strathern] (1981) *Man As Art: New Guinea*, New York: Viking.

Knauft, B. M. (1985a) 'Ritual Form and Permutation in New Guinea: Implications for Socio-Political Evolution', *American Ethnologist* 12:321–40.

—— (1985b) *Good Company and Violence: Sorcery and Social Action in a Lowland New Guinea Society*, Berkeley: University of California Press.

—— (1986) 'Text and Social Practice: Narrative "Longing" and Bisexuality among the Gebusi of New Guinea', *Ethos* 14:252–81.

—— (1987a) 'Reconsidering Violence in Simple Human Societies: Homicide among the Gebusi of Papua New Guinea', *Current Anthropology* 28:457–500.

—— (1987b) 'Homosexuality in Melanesia', *The Journal of Psychoanalytic Anthropology* 10:155–91.

—— (1989a) 'Imagery, Pronouncement, and the Aesthetics of Reception in Gebusi Spirit Mediumship', in Herdt, G. H. and M. Stephen (eds) *The Religious Imagination in New Guinea*, New Brunswick, NJ: Rutgers University Press.

—— (1989b) 'Bodily Images in Melanesia: Cultural Substances and Natural Metaphors', in Feher, M., R. Naddaff and N. Tazi (eds) *Fragments for a History of the Human Body, Part Three*, New York: Urzone.

—— (1996) *Genealogies for the Present in Cultural Anthropology*, New York: Routledge.

—— (1999a) 'Bodily Images in Melanesia: Cultural Substances and Natural Metaphors', in Knauft, B., *From Primitive to Postcolonial in Melanesia and Anthropology*, Ann Arbor: University of Michigan Press.

—— (1999b) 'Gender and Modernity in Melanesia and Amazonia', in Knauft, B., *From Primitive to Postcolonial in Melanesia and Anthropology*, Ann Arbor: University of Michigan Press.

—— (2002a) *Exchanging the Past: A Rainforest World of Before and After*, Chicago: University of Chicago Press.

—— (2002b) 'Trials of the Oxymodern: Public Practice at Nomad Station', in *Critically Modern: Alternatives, Alterities, Anthropologies*, Knauft, B. M. (ed.), Bloomington: Indiana University Press.

—— (2002c) (ed.) *Critically Modern: Alternatives, Alterities, Anthropologies*, Bloomington, IN: Indiana University Press.

—— (2003) 'What Ever Happened to Ritualized Homosexuality?: Modern Sexual Subjects in Melanesia and Elsewhere', *Annual Review of Sexuality Research* 14:137–59.

—— (2005) *The Gebusi: Lives Transformed in a Rainforest World*, New York: McGraw-Hill.

Kondo, D. (1997) *About Face: Performing Race in Fashion and Theater*, New York: Routledge.

Leshkowich, A.M. and C. Jones (2003) 'What Happens When Asian Chic Becomes Chic in Asia?', *Fashion Theory* 7 (3/4): 281–300.

Maggi, W. R. (2001) *Our Women are Free: Gender and Ethnicity in the Hindukush*, Ann Arbor, MI: University of Michigan Press.

Nelson, D. M. (1999) *A Finger in the Wound: Body Politics in Quincentennial Guatemala*, Durham, NC: Duke University Press.

Niessen, S., A.M. Leshkowich and C. Jones (eds) (2003) *Re-orienting Fashion: The Globalization of Asian Dress*, New York: Berg.

O'Hanlon, M. (1989) *Reading the Skin: Adornment, Display, and Society among the Wahgi*, London: British Museum; Bathurst, Australia: Crawford House Press.

—— (1995a) 'WYSISWYG: What You See is <u>Sometimes</u> What You Get; And Some Further Thoughts on the Skin, the Body and Decoration in Melanesia', *Journal of the Anthropological Society of Oxford* 26(2):155–62.

—— (1995b) 'Communication and Affect in New Guinea Art', *Journal of the Royal Anthropological Institute* 1:832–4.

Said, E. W. (1994) *Orientalism*, New York: Vintage.

Schein, L. (2000) *Minority Rules: The Miao and the Feminine in China's Cultural Politics*, Durham, NC: Duke University Press.

Sellerberg, A-M. (2001) 'Fashion, Sociology of', in N. J. Smelser and P. B. Baltes (eds) *International Encyclopedia of the Social and Behavioral Sciences, vol 8*, Amsterdam: Elsevier.

Schwartz, T. (1975) 'Cultural Totemism: Ethnic Identity, Primitive and Modern', in G. DeVos and L. Romanucci-Ross (eds) *Ethnic Identity: Cultural Continuities and Change*, Palo Alto, CA: Mayfield.

Simmel, G. (1971 [1904]) 'Fashion', in D. Levine (ed.) *On Individuality and Social Forms*, Chicago: University of Chicago Press.

Strathern, A. J. and M. Strathern (1971) *Self-decoration in Mount Hagen*, London: Duckworth.

Strathern, M. (1979) 'The Self in Self-Decoration', *Oceania* 49(4):241–57.

Tseëlon, E. (1992) 'Fashion and the Signification of Social Order', *Semiotica* 91:1–14.

Turner, T. S. (1980) 'The Social Skin', in J. Cherfas and R. Lewin (eds) *Not Work Alone: A Cross-cultural View of Activities Superfluous to Survival*, Beverly Hills: Sage.

Wardlow, H. (2002) '"Hands Up"-ing Buses and Harvesting Cheese-Pops: Gendered Mediation of Modern Disjunction in Melanesia', in B. M. Knauft (ed.) *Critically Modern: Alternatives, Alterities, Anthropologies*, Bloomington: Indiana University Press.

7

Lipsticked brides and powdered children

Cosmetics and the allure of modernity in an eastern Indonesian village

Catherine Allerton

In much of the comparative literature on body arts, a general contrast can be noted between anthropological examinations of various forms of 'tribal' body decoration, and a more eclectic series of writings, from sociology and cultural studies, on Western fashion and cosmetics. Throughout this literature, the argument is repeatedly made that these two phenomena cannot be easily compared, since they may express quite different notions concerning the individual and society, the body and the self, as well as conceptions of gender and sexuality. For example, Turner's famous work on Kayapo 'beauty' as 'an ideal expression of society itself' (1980:135) or arguments that Melanesian body decoration celebrates 'social and cultural vitality' (Knauft 1989:254) can be contrasted with descriptions of how Western women achieve an individual 'look' through the use of cosmetics (Rudd 1997:68) or must 'put their face on' in order to signify 'femininity' (Craik 1989:18). More generally, poststructuralist theories of 'masquerade' have contrasted Western cosmetics, which are required to accurately represent an 'inner' self, with tribal body markings that are not necessarily premised on a belief in the unity and integrity of the ego (Negrin 2000:85–6). In other words, whilst anthropological writings focus on the social aspects of body decoration, sociological work on cosmetics focuses on ideas of individual choice and expression, apparently reflecting the disembedded nature of social relations in Western societies.

This distinction between two quite different ways of decorating the body can of course be criticised for being somewhat over-drawn. After all, neither 'tribal decoration' nor 'Western cosmetics' could be said to be unitary categories. The latter, in particular, refers to a range of different phenomena that in some accounts includes cosmetic surgery (Negrin 2000:97). Nevertheless, whilst acknowledging the slightly false nature of this dichotomy, it is also important to appreciate its value as a heuristic device. Perhaps the most well-known anthropological work that builds on this contrast is Marilyn Strathern's article on 'self-decoration' among Hageners (1979). Strathern introduces the notion of the 'cosmetic paradox', by which she refers to Western processes of beautification that, whilst ideally aiming at individual enhancement, may actually and paradoxically end up detracting from a person's individuality. Strathern argues that this 'cosmetic paradox' is also apparent to Hageners who, through their heavy body decorations, precisely aim to achieve this deflection of attention away from the person. However, this is because bodily decoration in Hagen should ideally reveal the inner qualities possessed by the group as a whole. Whilst feminists may argue that Western cosmetics *disguise* the individual by objectifying their face, disguise for Hageners is *the* mechanism for revealing the inner self (Strathern 1979:249).

In Strathern's article, the contrast between Western cosmetic practice and local traditions of body decoration is put to an interesting analytical use. However, in situations where a rural, non-western society with relatively underdeveloped 'traditions' of body decoration has embraced the 'modern' cosmetics of face powder, lipstick and rouge, such a contrast is more difficult to sustain. The Manggarai, who inhabit the far west of the Indonesian island of Flores, are one such society. Primarily subsistence cultivators of rice, corn and various tubers, they are increasingly focusing on production of cash crops such as coffee, vanilla and candlenut. As the Manggarai economy becomes increasingly monetised, villagers have growing access to a range of consumer goods focused on decorating the body in new and prestigious ways. These include hair-clips, T-shirts, earrings, watches, lipstick and other cosmetics and toiletries. In this chapter, I focus on two emerging 'icons' of cosmetic decoration – the bride and the young child – in order to explore what this distinctively modern 'body art' might mean to Manggarai villagers.

Notions of 'tradition' and 'modernity' are of course extremely problematic within both anthropology and social theory. In using them here, I am building on recent work that questions viewing modernity as a 'singular or coherent development' (Knauft 2002:2), and instead sees modernity as 'regional, multiple, vernacular, or "other" in character' (*ibid*: 1). The Manggarai people who I describe here are, in their daily lives, and in their reflections on these lives, concerned with the characteristics of what they call *tana maju*, 'modern/ developed lands'. However, the notion of the modern or *maju*[1] is constructed with reference to a specifically Indonesian set of discourses on 'tradition' (*tradisi*) and the 'authentic' (*asli*), particularly the significance of *adat*, a term generally translated as 'custom'. Under the cultural policies of the New Order state, Indonesian *adat* tended to lose its broad holistic meaning and became instead a primarily aesthetic category to describe clothing, houses and other 'objects' (Acciaioli 1985:152–3; Kipp 1993:111–13). In Manggarai, notions of 'modernity' (the *maju*) and 'tradition' (*adat*) are mutually constitutive. Moreover, as notions that constantly shift and change they are, as I shall describe, constituted and negotiated through *performance* (Schein 1999:361).

Powder, body decoration and two icons of beauty

Traditionally in Manggarai, houses and textiles have been the most significant art forms, with relatively scant attention paid to the living body. Past practices of teeth-filing and blackening were, as elsewhere in south-east Asia, aimed primarily at reducing the 'animal-like' appearance of human teeth (Blanc-Szanton 1990:365), but the Manggarai do not appear to have otherwise socialised the body through painting or tattooing. Woven sarongs were once the only form of clothing for both sexes and, despite the wearing of T-shirts, shorts and skirts, remain the common way to clothe the body in villages. However, despite the complexity of some woven patterns, sarongs are primarily significant as containers of bodies and their substances, rather than a form of decoration to be 'read' or interpreted by others. Sarongs are a comforting, second skin, used to cradle children, to absorb rain, dirt, blood and sweat, and, when pulled up over one's shoulders or head during illness or emotional upset, to block out the outside world (Allerton 2007). This is not to deny that woven textiles may sometimes, particularly on ceremonial occasions, be worn as 'body art', but simply to stress the everyday importance of sarongs as three-dimensional, highly sensual objects.

In more recent years, Manggarai interest in forms of body decoration has grown. This interest is directly connected to the increasing availability of consumer goods and the cash with which to purchase them. Indeed, the link between cash and toiletries can be seen in the way that small sums of money, such as those sought by people selling a few mugs of coffee beans, or those given by adults to children, are almost always described as 'money to buy soap' (*séng kudut weli sabun*). In the southern Manggarai community with which I am most familiar, villagers have access to modern 'body goods' through a range of outlets. A small kiosk in the highland village sells the cheapest brands of soap and toothpaste, whilst a wider range of toiletries can be found at the lowland, Chinese-run store. At the weekly coastal market, people purchase body powder, lotion, lipstick, perfumed sprays, hair dye, shampoo, clothes and the popular medicinal balm known as *rémason*. Clothes and linen are also sold by travelling pedlars (*ata dagang*), who are particularly popular with older inhabitants of remote villages. However, for one-off purchases of items such as watches or gold jewellery, people travel by truck to the regional town of Ruteng, where stores offer a dazzling array of more expensive consumer goods.

Body powder, although not considered as essential as soap, has become a key toiletry in Manggarai – one that is thought to have both medicinal and cosmetic benefits. The Johnson's baby powder that appears to be so ubiquitous in Melanesia (Liep 1994) has made relatively few inroads into eastern Indonesia, and the brands available tend to be Indonesian or Chinese, sold in tins or plastic containers. Although adults often use the white, scented powder on their bodies, it is particularly associated with babies and young

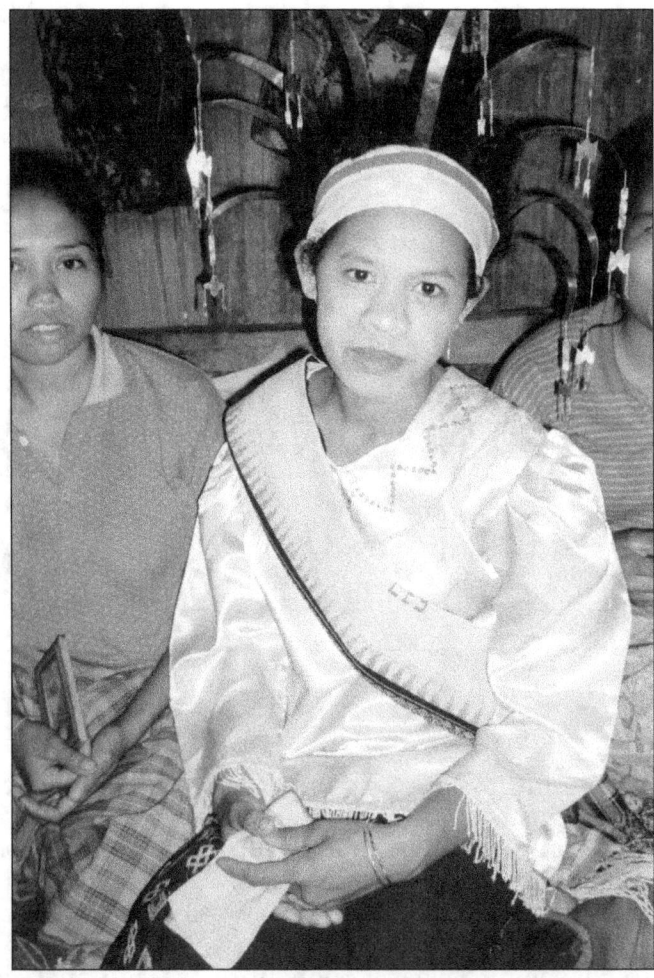

Plate 7.1   *A Manggarai bride wearing white powder,*
lipstick and bali-bélo headdress for her
village marriage ritual

children, who are liberally dusted with it after bathing. In addition, and as part of powder's general association with youth and beauty (Liep 1994:70), it is also used as a facial powder, particularly by young women who team it with red lipstick and other make-up. This cosmetic use of body powder to eliminate natural shine and create a pale, smooth face, reaches its pinnacle in the decoration of young brides, who have become a key icon of 'beauty' in present-day Manggarai.

The process of Manggarai marriage is a rather lengthy affair, involving a sequence of ritual events in the bride's home, as well as numerous procedures required by the Catholic church (Allerton 2004). The final, effervescent occasions in this process are the church wedding, possibly followed by a party or *pésta*, and the traditional marriage ritual known as the *wagal*. For each of these occasions, the bride (and, to a lesser extent, the groom) will

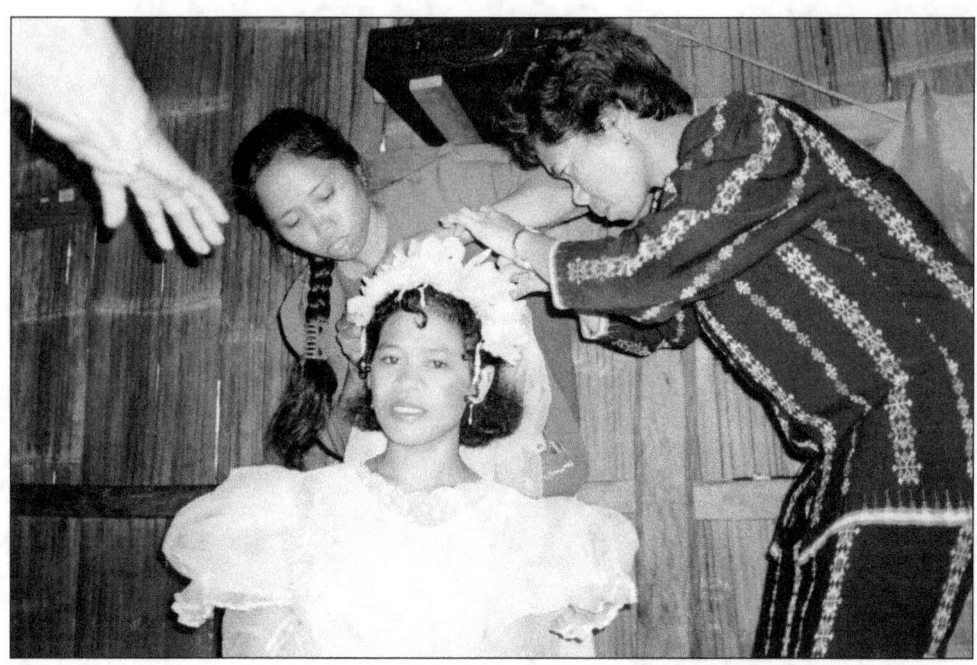

Plate 7.2   *The bride is dressed and made up prior to her church wedding*

be elaborately costumed in the appropriate clothing, and decorated with a large amount of make-up. As elsewhere in south-east Asia, weddings in Indonesia can be considered to be 'flash points of argument about the past and the present' (Kendall 1996:ix), and such arguments frequently focus on body decoration. For at least the past twenty years, Manggarai brides have been increasingly opting to marry in white, Western-style wedding dresses, and to change into what is thought of as traditional, *adat* costume (a blouse, woven sarong and headdress known as a *bali-bélo*) for the *wagal* ritual. This is undoubtedly a result of early missionary emphasis on a 'clean marriage' (*kawin bersih*) symbolised by a white dress and veil. However, a minority of Manggarai people are starting to express resentment at the idea that wearing traditional costume in church signifies a 'dirty marriage' (*kawin kotor*). These arguments are backed up by the views of some priests, who are showing increasing dismay at the 'inauthentic' consumption of Western-style weddings.[2]

At the church weddings that I attended during fieldwork, the majority of brides wore white wedding dresses with veils, stockings and lacy gloves, whilst grooms wore rather ill-fitting suits, shoes and white gloves. On the morning of their wedding, brides are dressed and made-up by a group of female friends and relatives. These decorative procedures are not surrounded by the kind of superstitious secrecy common in Britain or America, but are relatively public events attracting the attention of curious children, concerned mothers and nosy neighbours.

In the village where I lived, brides had their hair oiled and arranged, and their faces heavily powdered, before lipstick, rouge and eye shadow were applied using a communal box of make-up. Although this make-up is always applied by the woman considered to be most experienced at the job, it has no subtlety, with round, rosy cheeks painted onto the densely powdered skin of the bride. This often reflects the quality, age and range of cosmetics available, since lipstick may have to double as rouge, and vice versa.

These relatively recent decorative practices, which are unanimously declared to have made the bride 'beautiful' (*molas*), directly copy styles of dress and make-up found in the town. Town weddings are displays of social status through individual consumption, with brides buying wedding items from a specialist bridal boutique, and visiting beauty parlours to have their hair and make-up styled. However, for village weddings, the experience of 'modernity' is one mediated less through individual consumption than through sharing practices and a widespread and somewhat ironic mimicry of 'city people' (*ata kota*). At each wedding, the same box of old cosmetics appears, to be shared with the village's newest bride – a process similar to that of poor Bicolanos in the Philippines 'passing round the powder-puff or a piece of scented soap between households' (Cannell 1999:207). In addition, the wedding dress itself (an extremely costly item to purchase) may be hired, for a small fee, from another woman. One married woman I knew had lost count of the number of times she had hired out her old wedding dress and bridal accessories. Unlike American brides, those in Manggarai do not hope to express their individuality through their choice of wedding dress (Friese 1997:53). Nobody expects a wedding dress to fit perfectly: what is important is that, as with all those women who have worn the dress before, one looks the part of a bride.

A second major icon of modern body decoration is the young child. Both male and female children are on certain occasions – for a 'party' or ceremonial event, in preparation for a photograph, or in order to attend church – dressed up in smart clothes and decorated with face powder, lipstick and rouge. Whilst the slightly garish appearance of these children may be found comical, it is also considered extremely endearing.

When mothers who have left this decoration to younger women finally behold their transformed offspring, they may let out a shriek of delight, or good-humouredly castigate the aunt for making the child appear ridiculous. Decorated girls are dressed in shiny, frilly dresses, whilst boys wear smarter T-shirts and shorts. In the year 2000, a number of pyjama-type tops and bottoms depicting such characters as the Indonesian Millennial super-hero 'Panji' were sold to villagers, and many of my most recent fieldwork photos show children in these two-piece outfits. As in the case of the bridal couple, many of these decorative practices involve a rather ironic mimicry of city life. Indeed, as I shall describe, this irony is particularly strong in the case of children.

Although babies do not have make-up applied to their faces, they are particularly associated with scented soap and powder, and mothers may buy a special pack of Lux soap to be used only on their young infant. This

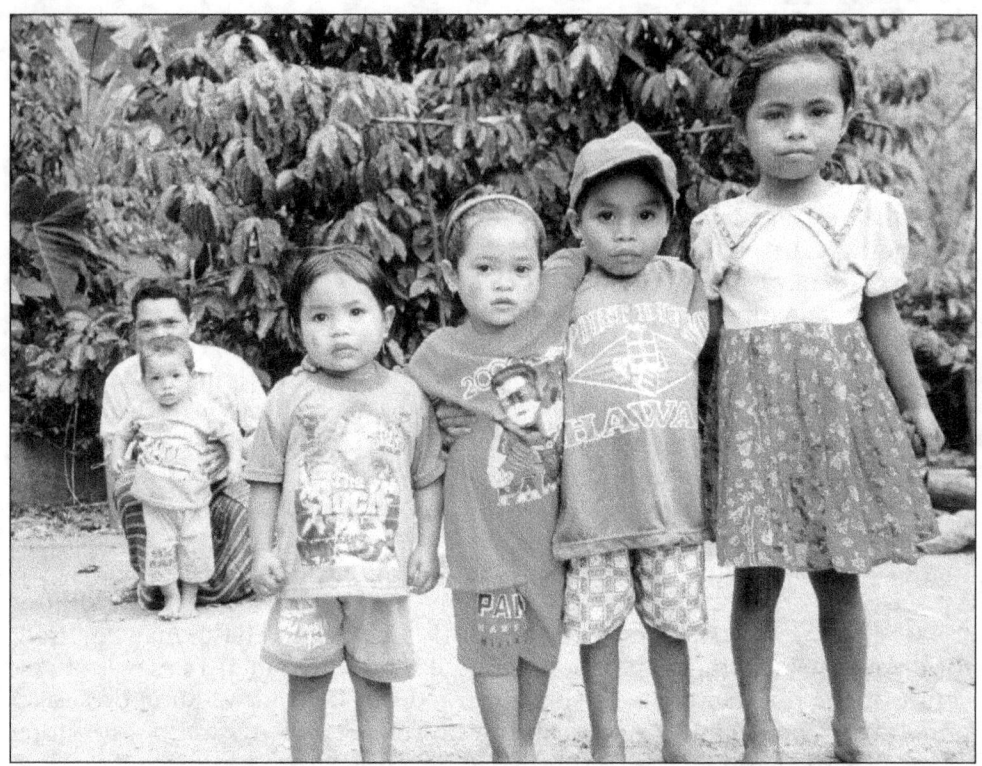

Plate 7.3   *Children with powdered faces and rouged cheeks for a photo requested by their parents*

association of perfumed toiletries with babies becomes particularly poignant in the sad event of an infant death. The bodies of babies and young children will be very carefully washed, powdered and dressed in their finest clothes, and tins of powder and small bottles of oil will be buried with the child, together with extra clothes and sarongs used as baby-slings. After the death of one baby, her grandparents told me that they continued to smell the oil and powder used on her during her life, particularly after a meal or when going to pray at her grave. This recalls Gell's comments on the connection between perfume and the transcendent since, as he argues, the 'disembodiedness of smells.... makes them the model for the ideal which hovers on the edge of actualisation' (1977:29–30). Since repeated intimate acts of care had associated the baby with the scent of dusting powder, the grandparents interpreted their continued awareness of this smell as evidence that the soul of the deceased child was still close to them.

Sources of modern body images

How are we to interpret these cosmetic practices, or to explain the iconic significance of brides and young children in connection with modern body arts? In Manggarai, a range of interconnected forces of 'modernity', all of which are associated with 'outsiders' (*ata pé'ang*), have influenced ideas about body decoration and the evaluation of beauty. In the first place, the preference for pale, powdered faces must be clearly linked to Dutch colonialism and perceptions of the power of Europeans. The Dutch saw Flores as an 'unprofitable' island and adopted a strategy of 'non-interference' up until the establishment of their 'Ethical Policy' in 1907 (Dietrich 1983). Thus, most Manggarai people had little awareness of Europeans until the arrival of colonial administrators and Catholic missionaries in the 1910s and 20s. Of these, it was undoubtedly the missionaries who had most impact on perceptions of the power of 'outsiders', although older villagers also remember the occupation of Flores by Japanese troops during the Second World War.

Such perceptions of 'people from outside' have long been merged with ideas about various categories of supernatural beings, known collectively as 'people on the other side' (*ata palé-sina*). For example, spirits of the forest called *darat* are one rather ambiguous category of spirit that is likened to Europeans. *Darat* are thought to be like strangely beautiful (*molas*) humans, with very pale skin and long, dark hair, but possessing twelve fingers and twelve toes. Although *darat* are thought to live in wild places uninhabitable to humans – cliffs, thick forests, the bottom of the ocean – they are also represented as living in cities, near to good roads, with all manner of modern (*maju*) conveniences. Images of *darat* domestic places represent a modern ideal of all-concrete 'luxury houses' (*mbaru lux*), with bright electric lights and television sets. Perhaps most significantly, pale and beautiful female *darat* are thought to try to marry human men by appearing to them in their dreams – a process that can cause the death of a human who chooses to embrace 'the other side'.

Like many postcolonial societies, Indonesians continue to link status and beauty with a pale skin colour. Moreover, however uncomfortable I may have felt seeing women powder their faces chalky white, eastern Indonesians have yet to be politicised to the extent of those Zimbabweans who, during the 1970s, began to refer to the users of skin lightening cosmetics as 'Fanta faces with Coca-Cola legs' (Burke 1996:190). Nevertheless, ideas about the rather supernatural power of Europeans, or the perceived 'beauty' of white skin and European features such as 'long noses', do not mean that all Europeans are uncritically found attractive. The community in which I worked has occasionally received visits from tourists, drawn to the highland village's isolated position and traditional housing. Informants were very fond of telling me stories about these tourists, and revelled in scandalous tales of European women who didn't wear bras or comb their hair neatly, and whose skin turned bright red as they struggled up the mountainside. Such tales remind us that the ideal of the smooth, pale face with straight black hair and neat clothes is primarily a look filtered through images of Jakarta and other modern Indonesian cities. It is also important to stress the local connection of such body images with Chinese-Indonesian shopkeepers. Although Chinese-Indonesians face much prejudice within the country, and suffered terrible violence during the riots of 1998, they remain a potent image of 'modernity' to most Manggarai villagers.

In the absence of magazines or other forms of advertising, villagers' perceptions of pan-Indonesian 'beauty' or modernity are formed on trips to the town, as well as during visits home by those working away from the village. Manggarai people speak of this specifically Indonesian modernity by drawing a contrast between (modern) town-life and (traditional) country-life, between the lives of 'village people' (*ata kampong*) and *pegawai*, a term meaning 'state official' but used to refer to all salaried workers and their families. Interestingly, children figure strongly in this contrast. When one man, who was working as a tax official in West Timor, returned to the village, he brought photos of his family, including one of his baby son all wrapped up in frilly white clothes. An old villager shook his head and chuckled as he looked at this photo, remarking to a child sitting near him, 'oooh, that's certainly the child of a *pegawai*!'. Similarly, when parents in the village buy smart clothes or little shoes for their children, others will remark that they have become 'children of *pegawai*' rather than 'village children' (*anak kampong*). Of course, these comments also contain an ironic awareness that village children have quite different lives to children in the town. People will often humorously address children as 'teacher' (*guru*) or 'nurse' (*bidan*), and when one mother was sewing a zip back onto her son's ragged pair of shorts, his father joked that they were 'soldier's shorts' (*déko tentara*).

As I have described, both church weddings and the parties that follow them involve a quite conscious copying of styles of dress, dancing and food that have been glimpsed in the town. Not all couples will hold a party (*pésta*) after the wedding, but those with relatives living in the town are more likely to do so. These town-dwellers take charge of the proceedings, making-up the bride, ensuring continual amplified music, calling on various worthies to give speeches and organising group dances. Thus, within the context of a life involving hard agricultural work, weddings and receptions have become a key way in which villagers 'perform' modernity (see Schein 1999). The same is true of the wearing of watches or shoes by men, or the use of cosmetics by women. However, this performance is hedged with anxiety since it may be rejected by those of higher status, dissolved in ironic comedy or perceived as transgressing village notions of propriety.

In contexts where an elite freely connect their own consumer needs with their social status, there may be a deep-rooted desire to protect the boundaries of consumption, and with them social distinctions (Burke 1996:104). When I took bright hair-clips or earrings as presents for villagers, I occasionally got the impression that my town-dweller friends thought them rather inappropriate. These friends also noted (rather disparagingly) the garishness of the make-up in photographs of weddings. Indeed, when village women 'perform modernity' by wearing body powder to whiten their faces, they mark themselves *as* villagers to women in the town, who have access to 'proper' face powder. However, town-dwellers may be unable to read the irony that is often at play in such performances. Cannell argues that Bicolano attitudes to 'beauty' are 'an ironic but genuinely funny comedy, a play on the gap between heartfelt consumer aspiration and the limits of possible achievement' (1999:207). Such comic irony is a constant refrain of Manggarai village life. Just as children are addressed as 'teacher' or 'nurse', so I was told that a village healer was a 'healthworker' (*menteri*), chewing up dried coconut to put on one's hair was 'shampoo', and eating cassava was 'medicine' (*rewos*).[3] However, such irony is not always at play in the attempted performance of modernity. At the end of my first period of fieldwork, my adoptive father accompanied me to the local town, in order that I might transfer my post office box and key to his name. For our visit to the post office (*kantor pos*), he dressed in a way I had never seen him do before, wearing a black *peci* hat and the kind of patterned shirt worn in banks and state offices. His intention in doing so was perfectly serious, but the assumption of such formal 'office clothes' (*baju kantor*) for a relatively informal visit made this an uneasy performance to witness.

One factor which complicates the modern town/ traditional village contrast is that not all 'town' looks are thought desirable. For example, women in the village value very long hair, and disapprove of the short haircuts worn by women returning from living in town. People also thought that older women in the town dressed and behaved too much like young, unmarried women, wearing excessive lipstick and taking part in the dances at wedding parties. A further area of tension revolves around the issue of spending too much money on appearance. Before a wedding, and as one of a number of named sums of money given by the groom's side to the bride's, the bride receives 'shopping money' (*séng belanjar*), also known as 'money for clothes' (*séng pakaian*). Although part of this money is supposed to be spent on kitchen equipment for the new household, it is largely used to buy gold jewellery for the bride and rather impractical (in the tropical heat) shiny bedclothes that are blessed with holy water during the church ceremony. The spending of this money is creating a number of new tensions between brides and their mothers-in-law, who say they would prefer saucepans.

A further source of ideas about body decoration is the Catholic church. Whilst Christian moralists in the West may have been concerned about the vanity and vice represented by cosmetics,[4] Christianity in Manggarai has been deeply implicated in the creation of glamorous body images. As I described earlier, Christianity came to Manggarai through the missionary activities of Europeans and remains, in the eyes of villagers, profoundly associated with the power of 'the outside'. Attending a *pésta* and attending church are the pre-eminently 'modern' activities in rural areas, and large parish churches offer uniquely visible spaces in which people can view and be viewed. Cannell has argued that for Bicolanos, a well-dressed appearance offers a kind of protective layer to a person sent out into the world (1999:207). Similarly, Manggarai villagers dress for church mindful of the public gaze, and keen to escape censure for being either too poorly or too frivolously dressed. Indeed, most people are rather nervous about attracting too much attention, particularly given rumours of sorcerers who practice magic to make trousers and skirts fall down in church, or cause a bride to begin menstruating as she stands in her white wedding dress.

In the days before Christmas and Easter, there is much talk about and preparation of 'Mass clothes' (*baju misa*). Particularly on these occasions, but also on ordinary Sundays, people seem to be attending church as much for an outing in their finery, and to view the finery of others, as to pray and receive communion. Older men and women wear smart blouses and shirts with their best sarong worn down to their ankles. Young men wear long trousers and collared shirts, ideally with shoes, and splash themselves with cologne. Young women wear matching nylon blouses and skirts, preferably with embroidered details and fancy buttons. They carefully oil and comb their hair, wearing it loose or accessorising it with bright head-bands and clips, and make their faces up with powder and lipstick. Indeed, if one is specifically wearing an outfit to attend church, it is possible to get away with something – a shorter skirt or a lace-effect blouse – that would be considered outrageous in a village setting. This is particularly the case with those of higher socio-economic status, such as the families of teachers and healthworkers. One Christmas, people exchanged nudges and whispers as the very glamorously dressed family of the local truck 'boss' paraded up the aisle of the church. On this occasion, villagers did not need to travel to the town to sniff the heady perfume of Indonesian modernity.

Photography and ideal images of modernity

One extremely popular development in Manggarai that is closely connected with 'performing' a modern identity, and that further explains why brides and young children are such central icons of body decoration, is photography. Kathy Peiss (1996) has linked the legitimation of cosmetic use in late nineteenth and early twentieth century America with the rise of photographic portrait taking. As 'factual' representations of appearance, she argues, photographs 'measured the distance between ideal beauty and reality', a tension which led most women to demand to have their faces made up for the camera (*ibid*: 321). Similarly, photography in Manggarai can be seen to have created a highly formal style of body decoration, allowing men and women to make themselves and their children over into a new social image. Photographs are often displayed on house walls, particularly the very modern images sent by migrant workers or children who have become *pegawai*. For example, the walls of one woman's house were covered with photographs of her long-absent brother and his house in Jakarta, since he was the only person connected with the family who possessed a camera.

During the 1970s, photography was mainly introduced by studios in town, where people could pose in front of stylised backdrops depicting waterfalls or flower gardens. Gradually, people with cameras also came from the town to villages, charging for photographic services at weddings, deaths and other rituals. The fact that, whether in studios or rural areas, people were paying for individual images, meant that Manggarai people preferred formal, posed shots with little facial expression. Indeed, throughout my fieldwork, and despite my own interest in taking informal shots in everyday settings, I was continually asked to take these kinds of photographs. Christopher Pinney has similarly commented on how, during fieldwork in central India, he found himself taking two different types of photographs: his own 'candid, revealing' shots, and the posed portraits requested by villagers, inevitably involving elaborate decoration of the body (1997:8–9). Like Pinney, I initially felt rather ambivalent about these formal portraits, feeling that they 'extinguished' the everyday quality of village life. However, in the course of writing this paper, I have come to see them as more intriguing, ethnographically speaking. This process by which photographs become 'ethnographic' has been nicely described by Elizabeth Edwards, who notes that '..... "ethnographicness" resides in the absorption and consumption of images within specific discourses, rather than in the intention of the images at their inscription' (2001:15).

Pinney argues that photography is prized in India for its capacity to 'construct the world in a more perfect form than is possible to achieve in the hectic flow of the everyday' (1997:149). The photographic studio, in particular, is a creative space for the 'transcendence and parody of social roles' (*ibid*: 178). These descriptions apply equally well to Manggarai, where photography seems to offer similar possibilities for modernity-play and ironic transformation. For example, Amé Huber, an elderly man who lived in the house next to mine, once asked to have his photograph taken with his radio, a modern possession of which he was extremely proud. For this, his daughters dressed him up in long trousers, a white shirt, jacket and Indonesian *peci* hat. Since he normally wore a sarong or shorts with a T-shirt, this was something of a transformation, and I commented that he looked quite the *pegawai*. His family were delighted, laughing that Amé Huber was normally to be found guarding his crops from monkeys, and now here he was, all dressed up and looking like an 'office head' (*kepala kantor*). As with other performances of modernity, this kind of gentle teasing was not meant to poke fun at Amé Huber, but to reflect on the disparity between his life and the way he had been decorated.

Amé Huber's *pegawai*-style transformation was unusual since, in general, it is younger villagers who 'perform' modernity, whilst the elderly are more often presented in self-consciously 'traditional', *adat*-style. For example, during my first fieldwork, the local government sponsored the rebuilding of the village's communal 'drum house'.[5] At numerous sacrificial rituals held in connection with this rebuilding, the young man responsible for liaising with the government insisted that the male elders should remove all T-shirts, sweatshirts and woolly hats. In their place they should wear only white shirts and batik headscarves, with Manggarai scarves and sarongs. Despite some criticism, this ritual 'uniform' was insisted on, so that photographs of the rituals would show the elders in an 'authentic' (*asli*) identical costume. It is interesting that, as elsewhere on Flores, the negative valuation of modern dress in ritual contexts is more a concern of state officials than villagers (Molnar 1998:41). Like other situations in which 'authenticity' is expressed by body decoration, this apparently 'traditional' uniform was seen not merely as costuming, but as an expression of 'spiritual and cultural roots' (Conklin 1997:725).

If the old are, through their ritual responsibilities, more associated with 'tradition', the only image suitable for children is that of modern youth. Parents are always keen to have pictures of their children looking clean, well-dressed and endearing, and were annoyed when I snapped kids covered in mud and dressed in old and dirty clothes. Images of children with powdered faces, wearing colourful new clothes, represent an ideal image of modern childhood. Similarly, the bodies of the deceased may be dressed up in their finest clothes, their faces powdered, before photographs are taken to record a last, idealised image. When visiting different houses, I was often shown such images. I also frequently asked to look at any wedding photographs, a process that inevitably led the bride, now a mother of several children, to sigh over the powdered image of her past self, declaring that she had been very *bakok* or 'white' then. However, although photos of the church wedding should represent an ideal image of the bride and groom as an attractive, modern couple, they are also likely to be photographed in more 'traditional' clothing for village-based marriage rituals.[6] Indeed, young women of marriageable age frequently asked me to take two photographs of them – one in 'modern' dress of T-shirt and trousers, and one in *adat* costume of blouse, sarong and *bali-belo*. This further demonstrates how in Manggarai, the construction of modernity and tradition through performance is a dialectic process.

The body, health and youth

Although the forces described above have had an extremely powerful impact on Manggarai ideas about dress, propriety and beauty, they cannot on their own account for the significance of brides and young children as icons of cosmetic decoration. To this end, I want to briefly consider some common ideas about the body and its health, particularly in relation to the stresses and strains caused by agricultural work and reproduction. Within the village, and as a continuation of contrasts between those who work with their hands in the fields and those who work in offices, it is felt that the body of any adult is bound to become thin and 'hardened', and to suffer from various aches and pains. By contrast, *pegawai* and others who live in towns are more likely to have attractive 'big bodies' (*weki méhé*) and to have hands and feet that are *ngoél* or 'new' like those of babies. The sense that village life affects all bodies in some way can be seen in local ideas about healing and massage. If a person is suffering from a particular ailment, a healer will silently 'blow' (*pur*) a healing prayer into some ginger, or other hot or bitter roots to be eaten. However, these roots are also used as preventative medicines, chewed up to bolster immunity to supernatural and other dangers. Similarly, massage (*kedur*) is practised on the sick, but also on the apparently healthy, whose bodies are bound to be a little 'damaged/ broken' (*rusak*) somewhere, bearing physical memories of a childhood fall or the repetitive strain of carrying an overloaded basket.

This sense that even apparently healthy bodies will inevitably carry some signs of 'damage' may have been one of the reasons why Manggarai people historically devoted little attention to the exterior of the body. However, a more significant influence may have been a set of ideas concerning blood. Local notions of 'fate' are expressed by the phrase *dara-weki*, which literally means 'blood of one's body'. Despite their Catholic faith, people believe that one's actions in life do not entirely shape this fate, which may be affected by the actions of others, or follow an apparently random and cruel path. For example, the fate of one man, who had eight daughters but no sons, was thought to have been influenced by the actions of his father, who had murdered another man in the village. Murder is the kind of violent death that creates green or 'unripe' blood (*dara ta'a*), and this was believed to have entered the blood of the murderer's family, curbing their ability to produce sons. Ideas about blood were also seen in people's worries about the spells made by sorcerers. I was told that if the blood of your body was 'bitter' (pa'it) then such sorcery would not affect you, whereas if it was 'sweet' (minsé), you would fall ill and even die. What is interesting about this 'blood of one's body' is that it only reveals its nature *after* events, and cannot be shaped by or known from one's appearance.[7]

Although Manggarai villagers have a strong sense of the frailty of human bodies, there is nevertheless a distinction made between those who are older and have children, and those who are young and unmarried. The latter are thought to have a kind of plump, blossoming energy, and this should be exemplified by the appearance of a bride and groom. The inevitable attractiveness of youth is revealed in language: unmarried women are referred to as *ata molas* or 'beautiful people', whilst unmarried men are called *ata reba* or 'handsome people'. Indeed, during wedding events, these terms are used to refer to the bride and groom, as in the ritual called *suru molas* or 'meeting the beautiful person', when the bride first enters her new husband's village. One reason for the attractiveness and vitality of young, unmarried adults is that they are thought to have 'full blood' (*dara penuh*), as compared with older people who may have 'tired blood' (*dara kamar*) or 'cooked blood' (*dara mamé*). Moreover, the contemporary significance of unmarried adults as a group is also related to social changes in Manggarai, since young people tend to have more independence, and to remain single for longer, than in the past. They are also seen as a distinctive group by the church, which organises activities and work parties for *muda mudi*, an Indonesian term meaning 'youngsters'.

After marriage, the appearance and energy of young people is thought to inevitably fade and the health of their bodies will instead become assessed in terms of the number of children they produce. This further accounts for the significance of wedding photos as a symbol of diminished physical beauty. Moreover, the connection between an adult body's vitality and the number of children it produces is seen in the common belief that Manggarai people were bigger, more healthy and thus more fertile in the past (see Clark 1989). People said that women had more children, and menstruated for longer, in the past, and that it was only because of newly introduced family planning that women's menstrual blood now dried up early, making them thin.

Although they are, in many respects, considered to be more vulnerable than unmarried adults, young children are also thought to possess a kind of bodily purity, untouched by the illness or hard work that marks the bodies of adults. Adults always comment on the paler skin of babies and toddlers, and tell their children off for spending too much time out in the sun. In his descriptions of Kayapo body painting, Turner describes how the painting of children is more elaborate than that of adults, reflecting the process of socialisation that the child is undergoing (1980:124). In Manggarai, the decoration of children serves quite a different purpose. Rather than reflecting socialisation, applying cosmetics to the faces of young children seems to be aimed at producing a kind of perfect, ideal child, to be preserved in a photograph as something separate from physical labour and village living conditions. This picture of the ideal, decorated child also connects with pan-Indonesian images of cutely dressed kids whose faces are enhanced with make-up. Indonesian TV, for example, features a very distinctive genre of pop videos, with oddly professional, fashionably dressed children singing in high-pitched voices whilst dancing against psychedelic backgrounds.

Cosmetic decoration and gendered propriety

In conclusion, I would like to outline some of the limits of this modern aesthetic of cosmetic decoration, and to return to the question of what similarities it may or may not share with 'Western make-up'. In my description of the symbolic distinctions between town and village, I noted that villagers did not value all aspects of town-style body decoration, particularly as regards hair and the appearance of older women. Although the embracing of cosmetics by young women does not meet with any kind of moral disapproval, and although adults of all ages may sometimes use body powder, there is a definite sense that, once married with children, a person should not pay too much attention to their exterior appearance. Mothers should of course have neat hair and relatively formal clothes when they attend church, but the use of cosmetics would be considered inappropriate. Indeed, whilst the beauty and appearance of unmarried women, particularly prospective brides, is freely discussed, it is taboo to 'praise' (naring) the body of a woman who is a mother. This is one of the reasons why people become very embarrassed when older, town women take part in the dances at wedding pésta, joking that they are 'looking for another husband' (kawé rona kolé). The only older women who may legitimately dress glamorously and make up their faces with cosmetics are female schoolteachers, whose salaried position exempts them from an all-consuming 'motherhood', and connects them with town propriety.

In addition to mothers, the second category of females who are expected to suppress the desire to decorate themselves are schoolgirls. All children attend the local primary school from the age of seven, wearing the standard Indonesian school uniform of white shirts and red shorts or skirts. Such children may often appear dirty and unkempt at home, but will generally have clean faces and combed hair for school. This is largely a result of the efforts of schoolteachers, who devote much time and energy to stressing the need for a good appearance. Indeed, such bodily discipline is perhaps largely what school is *about* in rural areas. Every morning, the children line up for exercises on the school-yard, where they may be inspected by the headteacher. On one occasion, he lectured them on discipline and cleanliness, telling them to mend ripped and button-less shirts, to brush their teeth, wash their faces with soap and to blow their noses. However, whilst the boys were only included in this general advice, the girls were singled out for attention, as the headteacher declared 'Girls may not have long hair. Don't wear hair bands! Starting today, don't wear powder. Cut your long hair. Take out all of your hair bands. Don't wear lipstick.' Similarly, on another occasion, the teacher of class six told the girls that they should cut their hair at the end of each month since 'that is called being a schoolchild. If you don't do this, you are already a young woman (gadis)[8] in the village. School children may not follow that model.' What is intriguing about this interest in the appropriate appearance of schoolgirls is that, although girls *do* like having long hair and wearing clips and hair-bands, I have *never* known them to show interest in wearing lipstick or powder to school. Instead, and in order to encourage a mental separation between being a 'villager' (*ata kampong*) and a 'school-person' (*ata sekolah*), teachers exaggeratedly stress the dangers of cosmetic decoration for a serious, hard-working female pupil.

This latter point connects rather interestingly with themes in the discussion of Western 'make-up'. I have argued in this paper that cosmetic decoration in present-day Manggarai is an explicitly modern innovation that does not continue or transform any earlier styles of body art. Where this decoration does intersect with more traditional notions concerning the body is in relation to the status of brides and young children as iconic images of beauty. However, many of the specific discourses surrounding body decoration that are now starting to appear in Manggarai bear some comparison with those surrounding Western cosmetics. For example, although both bride and groom may wear powder to whiten their face, and although both male and female children are decorated with lipstick, tensions surrounding the appearance of both mothers and schoolgirls suggest that cosmetics are beginning to raise a series of issues concerning feminine propriety. Similarly, many early Western discourses on cosmetics identified them with disrepute and deceit (Peiss 1996:316) and although people in Manggarai do not concern themselves too much with the 'problem' of female sexuality, there is a definite sense that cosmetics are most appropriate for young women who have left school but not yet married and had children.

However, despite the common links between this Manggarai concern with female propriety, and Western moral criticism of cosmetics, not all analyses of Western cosmetics are appropriate to the Manggarai case. For example, Manggarai women do not have a 'deeply personal relationship with cosmetics' (Rudd 1997:64), but rather share them between households. In the West, religious and other critics of cosmetics have argued that they are an instrument of 'the ubiquitous modern drive for conformity, in which all persons must look alike and act alike' (Wax 1957:589). A second strand of criticism objects to the way in which cosmetics conceal a 'true' self behind a 'false' mask, whilst poststructuralist writers on 'masquerade' argue that the self is actually constituted by the masks one assumes (Negrin 2000:83–4). Interesting as these ideas might be, they cannot account for both the irony and idealism at play in Manggarai cosmetic decoration. Brides and other 'beautiful people' who wear make-up absolutely *do* hope to 'conform' to an ideal modern image, which is valued precisely because it is different to their everyday self. However, they are not worried about whether this image is 'true' or 'false'; what matters is that they can temporarily, and possibly ironically, escape to a fantasy far removed from the toil of rural village life. Whilst Strathern's well-known article on 'self-decoration' (1979) argues that the decorations of a Hagen dancer should deflect attention away from the individual to the group, the decorations of a Manggarai bride or young child should deflect attention from the everyday 'damage' of the human body to an ideal image of modern beauty.

NOTES

I would like to thank Mike O'Hanlon, Elizabeth Ewart and other participants at the Oxford Body Arts colloquium, particularly Bruce Knauft, who suggested some pertinent references. Doctoral fieldwork in Manggarai was carried out between 1997 and 1999, under the sponsorship of the Indonesian Institute of Sciences (LIPI) and Universitas Nusa Cendana, Kupang. Financial support came from an ESRC Research Studentship. Two subsequent trips to Manggarai, between March and August 2001, were funded by the British Academy's Fund for South-east Asian Studies, with the support of a Junior Research Fellowship from Wolfson College, Oxford. In Manggarai, I am indebted to the residents of Waé Rebo-Kombo, who have generously welcomed me into their homes and lives. I would particularly like to thank 'Edis' for letting me tag along and photograph her wedding, as well as the many beautified children whose portraits I have gladly taken.

1 On the use of the term *maju* elsewhere in Indonesia, on the island of Sulawesi, see Schrauwers (2000:141).

2 See Kendall (1996:52–3) on a somewhat different backlash against 'Western-style' weddings in Korea.

3 My over-enthusiastic research response to the idea that cassava was medicine – 'medicine for what?' – led the man I was talking with to roar with laughter as he exclaimed 'medicine against hunger!'

4 On this issue see Wax (1957:589) and compare with Burke (1996:198) on Zimbabwe.

5 For more on the implications of this rebuilding, see Allerton (2003).

6 Kendall describes how Korean brides who marry in antique dress have the 'added option' of being photographed in a white dress and veil (1996:67).

7 Interestingly, fears about sorcerers also lie behind some people's nervousness about *appearing* to be too healthy or attractive. Since sorcerers are often motivated by jealousy, it may not be prudent to dress oneself in the visible signs of wealth, such as watches, gold jewellery and fine clothing.

8 The implication of being called a *gadis* rather than a schoolgirl is that one is almost ready for marriage.

Bibliography

Acciaioli, G. (1985) 'Culture as art: from practice to spectacle in Indonesia', *Canberra Anthropology* 8: 148–72.

Allerton, C. (2003) 'Authentic housing, authentic culture? Transforming a village into a 'tourist site' in Manggarai, eastern Indonesia', in M. Hitchcock and V.T. King (eds) *Indonesia and the Malay world*. Special issue on Tourism and Heritage in Southeast Asia 89: 119–28.

—— (2004) 'The path of marriage: journeys and transformation in Manggarai, eastern Indonesia', *Bijdragen tot de Taal-, Land- en Volkenkunde (BKI)* 160(2/3): 339-62.

—— (2007) 'The secret life of sarongs: Manggarai textiles as super-skins', *Journal of Material Culture* 12(1): 22-46.

Blanc-Szanton, C. (1990) 'Collision of cultures: historical reformulations of gender in the lowland Visayas, Philippines', in J.M. Atkinson and S. Errington (eds) *Power and difference: gender in island Southeast Asia*, Stanford: Stanford University Press, 345–84.

Burke, T. (1996) *Lifebuoy men, lux women: commodification, consumption and cleanliness in modern Zimbabwe*, London: Leicester University Press.

Cannell, F. (1999) *Power and intimacy in the Christian Philippines*, Cambridge: Cambridge University Press.

Clark, J. (1989) 'The incredible shrinking men: male ideology and development in a Southern Highlands society', *Canberra Anthropology* 12(1and2): 120–43.

Conklin, B. A. (1997) 'Body paint, feathers and vcrs: aesthetics and authenticity in Amazonian activism', *American Ethnologist* 24(4): 711–37.

Craik, J. (1989) '"I must put my face on": making up the body and marking out the feminine', *Cultural Studies* 3(1): 1–24.

Dietrich, S. (1983) 'Flores in the 19th century: aspects of Dutch colonialism on a non-profitable island', *Indonesia Circle* 31: 39–58.

Edwards, E. (2001) *Raw histories: photographs, anthropology and museums.* Oxford: Berg.

Friese, S. (1997) 'A consumer good in the ritual process: the case of the wedding dress', *Journal of Ritual Studies* 11(2): 47–58.

Gell, A. (1977) 'Magic, perfume, dream....', in I. Lewis (ed.) *Symbols and sentiments: cross-cultural studies in symbolism*, London: Academic Press.

Kendall, L. (1996) *Getting married in Korea: of gender, morality and modernity*, Berkeley: University of California Press.

Kipp, R.S. (1993) *Dissociated identities: ethnicity, religion and class in an Indonesian society*, Ann Arbor: University of Michigan Press.

Knauft, B. M. (1989) 'Bodily images in Melanesia: cultural substances and natural metaphors', in M. Feher (ed.) *Fragments for a history of the human body*, New York: Zone.

——— (2002) 'Critically modern: an introduction'. In B. M. Knauft (ed.) *Critically modern: alternatives, alterities, anthropologies*, Bloomington: Indiana University Press.

Liep, J. (1994) 'Recontextualization of a consumer good: the ritual use of Johnson's baby powder in Melanesia', in T. van Meijk and P. van der Grijp (eds) *European imagery and colonial history in the Pacific*, Germany: Saarbrücken.

Molnar, A. K. (1998) 'Transformations in the use of traditional textiles in Ngada (western Flores, eastern Indonesia): commercialization, fashion and ethnicity, in A. Brydon and S. Niessen (eds) *Consuming fashion: adorning the transnational body*, Oxford: Berg.

Negrin, L. (2000) 'Cosmetics and the female body: a critical appraisal of poststructuralist theories of masquerade', *European Journal of Cultural Studies* 3(1): 83–101.

Peiss, K. (1996) 'Making up, making over: cosmetics, consumer culture and women's identity', in V. de Grazia and E. Furlough (eds) *The sex of things: gender and consumption in historical perspective*, Berkeley: University of California Press.

Pinney, C. (1997) *Camera Indica: the social life of Indian photographs*, London: Reaktion Books.

Rudd, N. A. (1997) 'Cosmetics consumption and use among women: ritualized activities that construct and transform the self', *Journal of Ritual Studies* 11(2): 59–77.

Schein, L. (1999) 'Performing modernity', *Cultural Anthropology* 14(3): 361–95.

Schrauwers, A. (2000) *Colonial 'reformation' in the highlands of Central Sulawesi, Indonesia, 1892–1995*, Toronto: University of Toronto Press.

Strathern, M. (1979) 'The self in self-decoration', *Oceania* 49(4): 241–57.

Turner, T. S. (1980) 'The social skin', in J. Cherfas and R. Lewin (eds) *Not work alone: a cross-cultural view of activities superfluous to survival*, London: Temple Smith.

Wax, M. (1957) 'Themes in cosmetics and grooming', *American Journal of Sociology* 62(6): 588–93.

8

Encounters on the surface of life

T-shirts and visual analogy in South Auckland

Chloe Colchester

Introduction

This chapter describes a genre of humorous T-shirt art that has been developed by New Zealand-born Pacific Islanders living in South Auckland. The T-shirt designs synthesise and develop a number of foreign, modern genres of graphic humour, related to identity politics and the subversion of commercial art, which emerged in Honolulu and in other cities along the West Coast of America in the seventies and which have subsequently gone on to become a ubiquitous, and it must be admitted now a rather tired, form of modern counter-cultural expression. T-shirt artists working in South Auckland, however, have significantly reworked these genres so as to address their own more specific and local concerns about their relationship to the islands, to different Polynesian communities and to mainstream modernist culture. This chapter will focus upon the way that graphic humour has been developed in response to – and as a way of mediating and changing – the conflicts that have arisen as Pacific Islanders attempt to find a way of living in the midst of this bi-cultural nation.

Polynesian T-shirt art has enjoyed a relatively recent efflorescence. Over the past four years Auckland has witnessed the emergence of a number of independent T-shirt artists, the majority of whom identify as being Samoan. They all sell T-shirts at Otara Market, a popular Polynesian market that is held in a remote industrial suburb of South Auckland. In many ways the market is an unlikely venue for the emergence of a youth-cultural form. For one thing it opens at five on a Saturday morning closing at mid-day, for another it is a place where South Auckland's mixed community of whites and Polynesians comes together. It is this mix which seems to have contributed to the development of T-shirt graphics. 'The designs are about these people, these people here' was how one designer put it.

A variety of food and clothing is for sale. Food bargains are a big attraction. There are stalls selling off-cuts of New Zealand lamb from the local freezing plants and stalls selling fruit and taro from the islands. Maoris sell cress and other vegetables grown on their farms. Women from the Cook Islands sell huge family sacks of doughnuts. The market also offers a variety of clothing. Poorer members of the white and Asian communities sell cheap foreign clothing, including counterfeits of known brands like USA Athletic. There are stalls run by Fiji-Indians which are full of 'island prints'; versions of Pacific *tapa* and former colonial fabrics designed for the Pacific market that are printed in acrid colours: acid yellow, maroon, ochre, viridian green and black. Also, because the market is held on a Saturday, the older Pacific mamas can also run stalls without fear of missing church. In fact, many of the hand made textiles they sell reveal the legacy of colonial and missionary influence upon indigenous cloth traditions. For example, the long lengths of Tongan–style barkcloth, which the Tongan women sell, have either the Tongan royal seal or images of doves printed upon them. Women from Niue sell pillowcases that have been embroidered by hand. The market resonates to a mixed cacophony of sound, Pacific and Maori hip-hop and island tunes mingling with the sound of church choirs, an appeal for funds for a local school and political canvassing.

Because my original intention in coming to Auckland was to compare the contemporary uses of traditional indigenous cloth wealth (like barkcloth) at family gatherings with what I knew of their exchange in the islands I was interested to hear that T-shirts were typically presented as gifts (either birthday or Christmas presents, or as souvenirs). Designers told me that they could sell close to a thousand T-shirts in the run up to Christmas. Pacific expatriates who had moved on from Auckland to Sydney or Los Angeles (where it has been hard for Pacific expatriates to achieve this degree of interaction because the pattern of settlement is much more dispersed) also bought T-shirts when they returned to Auckland to visit family and friends.

Yet the market offered T-shirt makers the opportunity to put their work and concerns on display. Here, the designers competed for attention through the topicality of their cultural references and wit. Even in mid-winter, market-goers gathered round the stalls to read the designs. One of the designers called this his 'market research', however many people just stopped to look at the designs and another designer said ' that's enough for me, to see that they are interested and get a laugh out of the jokes' all the designers watch the visitors carefully studying people's reactions to their designs.

Here is the first example of their work that caught my attention (Plate 8.1: Samoan Express T-shirt by Pacific Apparel). It shows how a particular humorous device – the use of a visual pun – has been used to reveal a surprising connection between Samoan indigenous religious imagery and American commercial art. In this case the similarity between contrastive pattern on Samoan barkcloth and on the background of an American Express

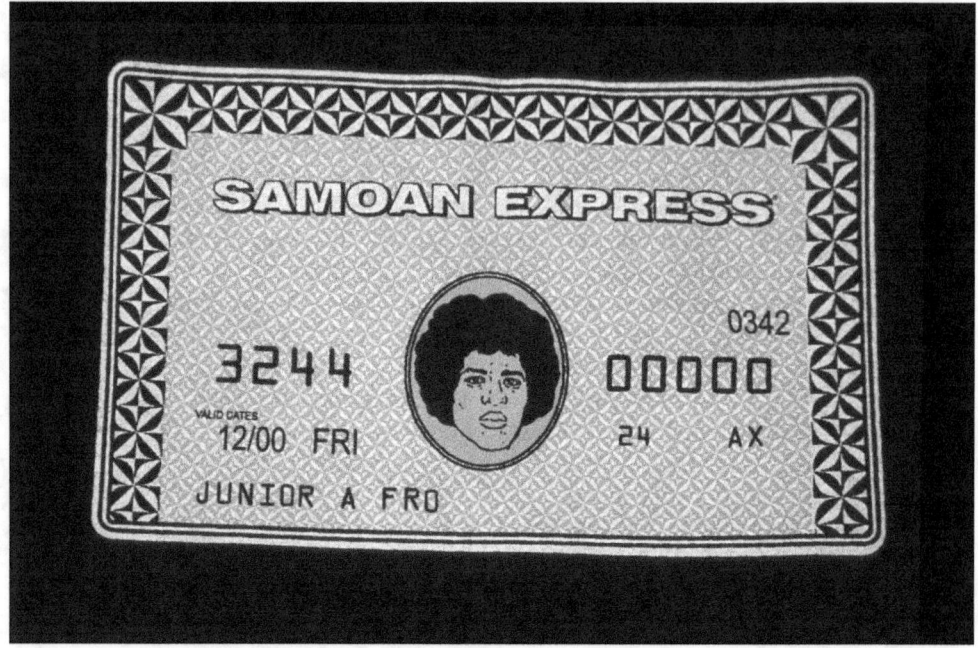

Plate 8.1   *Samoan Express T-shirt by Pacific Apparel*

card, has been selected because it sets off stereotypical oppositions between Samoan and Western ways of life to comic effect. I would suggest that it is the surprising nature of this analogy – as well as its perceived relevance in addressing the tensions posed by social and economic assimilation – which makes it funny and which would seem to encourage people to shift the contexts of their thought. It is a good example of the 'found connections' that have allowed the pressures of social change to be brought up to the surface and turned into a visible feature of people's behaviour.

The problem

'Clothing', as Anne Hollander, the curator of a recent exhibition called *Fabric Visions* has put it, 'is a verb, not an object'. She was referring to one's experience of the movement of cloth and clothing, to its use in gesture (wiping a child's mouth, draping the head, sweeping out of a room disdainfully) as well as to the depiction of drapery as a quasi-animate entity in European conventions of painting and sculpture. T-shirt art is active in a different sense, in so far as the nature of its activity, or agency, emerges through the demonstration that Polynesian religious art and Western commercial art are connected by surprising specific, and visual, points of resemblance. I would like to suggest that these connections provide an interesting example of how 'people's relationships to words and things are shaped by the demands, dynamics, and risks of interaction with others' (Keane 1997:224). More specifically, I want to raise some questions about what Alfred Gell has called the 'relations between relations', that is, the nature of the connections involved in T-shirt graphics and their effects – both in response to and in changing – specifically local situations of social interaction.

Here I have to confess, that ever since reading Alfred Gell's *Art and Agency* when I was studying Fijian barkcloth I have been fascinated by his hypothesis that the relationship between things, or on another level the relationship between motifs, may be shown as having an 'elective affinity' with specific situations of social interaction. You may recall that he outlined this problem in his chapter on Marquesan ornament, which he suggested had become more elaborate and compelling during a period of profound social upheaval, which presaged the collapse of the Marquesan ritual hierarchy. Perhaps you may also recall that he extended this hypothesis in his discussion of the development of collaborative genres of public art, such as Maori meeting houses, and how they make manifest specific relations between cultural anticipation and remembering through time (Gell 1998).

I have been driven to think about cultural expectation by the slight jolt that T-shirt designs produce. For I think it shows how the familiar forms of logos, which one has learnt to recognise without reading, sets up a field of expectation, which is then subverted by the pun. They make one notice that, as Bartlett put it long ago, 'a great amount of what goes under the name of perception is recall' (Bartlett 1932:66). As Bartlett demonstrated, most perception involves quite cursory scanning, which is supplemented with detail from the imagination; it is an imaginative reconstruction.

> Some scene is presented for observation, and a little of it is actually perceived... but the observer reports much more than this. He fills up the gaps of his perception by aid of what he has experienced before in similar situations or... by describing what he takes to be fit or suitable, to such a situation. (Bartlett 1932:67)

What seems significant, then, is that T-shirt designs make social change visible by making people more aware (more self-conscious) of the relationship between recall, imagination and perception.

This seems important to emphasise at the outset because, as Nicholas Thomas has pointed out, much of the literature regarding the indigenous appropriation of foreign or consumer goods (that emerged in the wake of Appadurai's influential publication, Appadurai: 1986) has reinforced the very thing that it sought to break down: the simple opposition between descriptions of modern and traditional culture. That is to say, descriptions of the indigenous appropriation of unfamiliar foreign goods, or their response to historical happenings have often suggested that the process of appropriation/interpretation is governed by a largely conservative and unreflective attitude (Thomas 2003:94). The kind of imagery that is found on T-shirt art is problematic for theories of recontextualisation which posit the substitution of one interpretive scheme for another indigenous one, because it provokes what Arthur Koestler has described as an essential ingredient of humour: bi-sociative thought. That is, it encourages people to see an object (or situation) in different ways, causing an abrupt transfer of the chain of thought from one associative context to another (c.f. Koestler 1989:95).

Gell did not specifically address the kind of art which emerges in the wake of cross-cultural interaction, yet I have found his interest in 'the nature of the connections' in Pacific pattern useful because it raises the issue of whether the kinds of conjunctions found in T-shirt humour are altogether foreign, or whether they have to some degree been immanent within traditional Pacific ritual forms. Of course, commercial and religious art share certain formulaic qualities of format and inscription in common that are characteristic of all indirect, non-personalised, forms of expression. But what seems to be significant here is that the highly formalised registers of speech and image – or pattern – making that are characteristic of Oceanic ritual oratory and art have been shown to coincide with a relatively high density of metaphor (see for example Kaeppler 2002), which is said to be compelling in contemporary contexts because it provokes interpretation, and not simply social consensus (Keane 1997; McKellin 1990).

Furthermore, given the importance of cloth in Polynesian religious art the choice of clothing as a medium for analogical thinking seems significant. One reason for this is that surface coverings have been shown to play a central role in Polynesian conventions of image-making, of describing likenesses. For example, as Babadzan's historical analysis of Tahitian ritual art during the period of contact has indicated, wrappings of diverse kinds were elevated to the status of religious relics (that is, they were imbued with *mana* or efficacious power) through performances which developed their analogy to ancestral skin (Babadzan [1993] 2003). More generally however, the choice of clothing seems significant because it brings the (often highly oppressive and contentious) issues of adaptation and change to the surface where they matter, that is directly in the scenes of social encounter, and in the midst of a new kind of gift exchange (Plate 8.2).

The Pacific diaspora in Auckland

Auckland has now become the largest Polynesian city in the world. Half of New Zealand's population of Pacific Islanders (roughly 200,000 people of Pacific descent were recorded in the 1996 census) is based there. Polynesians from islands under New Zealand administration such as Western Samoa, the Cook Islands, Niue, as well as other islands within the Tokelau group came to New Zealand during the post-war boom in manufacturing and agriculture in the 1950s and 1960s. These early migrations set up a chain reaction. During the 1970s and 1980s other islanders came to join their relations, and many of them chose to stay in spite of the imposition of tougher immigration laws.

The coming together of communities of Pacific islanders, after an interval of nearly two thousand years, coincided with significant changes in the New Zealand economy as well as in cultural politics throughout the region. The mid to late 1970s witnessed the relocation of more than half the Pacific community to a newly built city suburb, called Manukau, which grew from a settlement used by the Polynesian builders who worked on the construction of Auckland's main power station. The economic fall-out prompted by

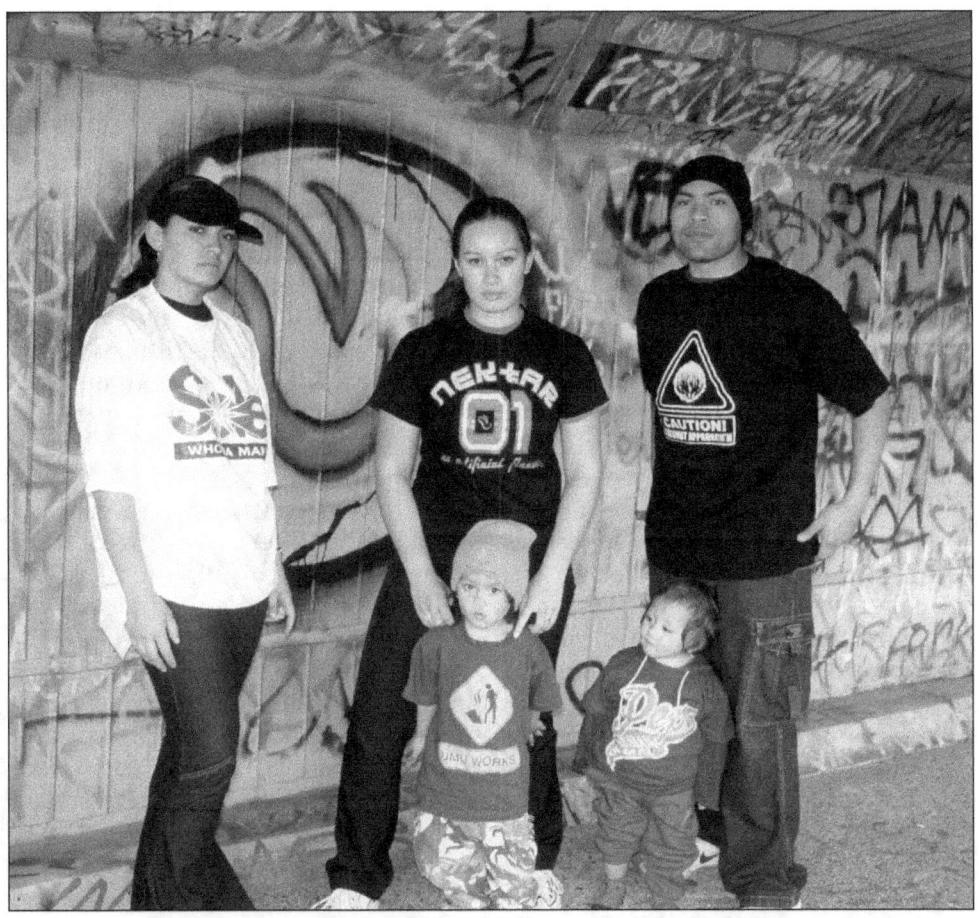

Plate 8.2   *Dean Purcell wearing one of his own designs, Coconut Approachin',*
under Mangare Bridge, August 2001

the formation of the European Common Market, the deregulation of the economy and the downturn in manufacture, combined with a rapidly growing migrant population meant that the area achieved some notoriety for inter-community violence as unemployment soared. The imposition of spot checks and dawn raids by the police to locate and deport illegal migrants added to a sense of embattlement. As intercommunity relations worsened, gang violence between different Pacific communities increased. Tyrone Laurenson, a New Zealand born Samoan who served as a detective superintendent/chief constable with the Auckland City police for most of the 1990s, has described how historical rivalries between Samoans and Tongans became re-expressed through gang violence, which he believed required culturally aware police-work that was sensitive to Samoan and Tongan cultural differences (Laurenson pers. comm. 2002).

Due to gang violence the southern suburbs of Auckland began to be viewed as the 'Badlands', a ghetto characterised by inter-community strife; they were also called 'Southside' after downtown Los Angeles. Both on the street, in the dole queues and at school Pacific migrants and their offspring were laughed at and called names such as 'Overstayer', 'Coconut', 'Freshy' or 'FOB' (as in fresh off the boat) or 'Bunga' – all of which suggested that they were too provincial, too 'out there' and 'back then', too passionate, violent, and too slow-moving a people to fit into life in the fast lane.

The legacy of nineteenth century evangelism remained a defining point of identification until relatively recently. Up until the 1980s, sport and the Church were the lynch pins of tightly knit enclaves that circumscribed Samoan, Tongan and Cook Islander's separate social worlds. These communities remained largely oriented to the islands – home was elsewhere – and links to it were maintained through fundraising schemes, family gatherings at marriages and funerals and the return of remittances.

As the status quo has begun to change, it has contributed to growing tensions between different generations of Pacific islanders. Sociologists have noted how for second or third generation New Zealand born Pacific Islanders, affiliation to their home-islands have started to be replaced by stronger attachment to place and an increasingly international, or cosmopolitan outlook. New ideologies of education (which encourage children to speak out, to express cultural criticism and debate, for example), the weakening of church based enclaves due to the growing influence of secularism, and a rise in inter-community marriages have accompanied the decline in the gerontocracies' control of indigenous cultural forms. So too has welfare provision, which enables young Samoan couples to live apart from their families.

Nevertheless it is no coincidence T-shirt art has been largely pioneered by New Zealand-born Samoans. For in spite of these intergenerational tensions, the distinctive features of Pacific Island practice continue to reflect specific histories of engagement with discreet phases of modernity. Thus the formative influence of nineteenth century Protestant evangelism and British imperialism on Tongan indigenous cloth and codes of appearance and conduct continues to make its presence felt, as does Samoans' strong identification with American culture (and to American products such as corn beef), which dates back to the use of the islands as an American military base during the Second World War. It should also be noted that several T-shirt artists had some affiliation with the Mormon Church, which meant that they had gained direct experience of American culture through studying in Hawai'i and visiting relatives in Los Angeles. Here it may be worth adding that members of the Mormon Church eschew aspects of traditional family ceremonial involving the exchange of cloth and food that are condoned by other Christian denominations in Samoa, indicating how the place of artefacts in cultural (or rather religious) practice remains a subject of debate in the islands.

In fact, there is a substantial difference between the degree of cultural disruption that Maori and Pacific Islanders have experienced due to foreign encroachment. For many Maori the experience of being in a minority within a larger white settler community (an experience which was compounded by years of enforced cultural assimilation) has meant that many have experienced a profound degree of rupture with the past. By contrast (and in spite of the dramatic changes in religious practice and belief which accompanied conversion or colonial intrusion) different island nations have developed practices of ceremonial exchange that typically involve the display and transaction of cloth and food which recall many features of pre-colonial religious practice.

Maori anger, caused by the experience of cultural alienation has recently found expression in growing concerns over cultural representation through the display of Maori artefacts in museums. The critical acclaim with which *Te Maori,* a blockbuster exhibition of largely traditional Maori art and culture, in which the Maori community had some degree of involvement, was greeted in the United States encouraged the redefinition of New Zealand as Aotearoa, a bi-cultural Pacific Island nation. Nevertheless, Aotearea–New Zealand's new status as a bi-cultural, as opposed to a multi-cultural, nation has in certain ways made it harder for newer migrant populations to find a public voice through the display of their own traditions. It is perhaps due to these difficulties that young Samoan artists have started to develop new kinds of cultural practice that are more cosmopolitan in character and which enable them to articulate a sense of place within the diaspora.

New Zealand born Pacific peoples are acutely sensitive to their status as visitors in the homelands of the Maori, and the fact that their distance from their own homelands – and the land in particular – is undermining the authority of traditional cultural practice in everyday life. There is a growing sense of separation between the forms of cultural resistance and experimentation in the islands with that of their diaspora. For example, the cultural opposition between tradition and modernity, and between a rural self-sufficient life style, and 'the way of money' and growing economic dependency that is often evoked by neo-traditionalists is difficult for urban-based Pacific expatriates to identify with. The difficulties that expatriates and people of mixed parentage face in fitting back in to life in the homelands has been a recurrent theme of the novelist Albert Wendt, who has wryly remarked that its only in New Zealand that he's called a Samoan Islander. I believe that these difficulties are enabling Maori and whites to overcome the differences that have stemmed from their different historical experiences of modernity. Through openly articulating such difficulties in T-shirt design Samoan T-shirt makers seem to be sketching out points of commonality and difference with other Polynesian communities.

T-shirt graphics

As Lissant Bolton notes in her contribution to this volume, visitors to the Pacific are often struck by the way that Island women's dress seems fixed in the nineteenth century, indicating how powerfully the long reach of Victorian evangelist missionary influence stretches into the present. Yet the spread of T-shirts has been no less extensive (a recent estimate suggests that two billion T-shirts are now sold worldwide each year). In many islands in the Pacific the combination of a T-shirt and a sarong, or *lavalava*, has become the accepted and traditional form of informal attire in rural areas. Thus one needs to be wary of assuming that T-shirts have served to import the physical expression of American liberalism into the midst of Pacific cultural life.

Charlotte Brunel has recently provided us with an overview of the development of American T-shirt graphics. Her book examines how T-shirts became a central to a new phenomenon – American youth culture – at the beginning of the Cold War when, as she puts it, 'Europe and the rest of the World were watching America develop a new economic and cultural model': consumer culture (Brunel 2002:52). One of the most appealing aspects of her account is that it reveals how T-shirt graphic genres evolved as they passed back and forth from one section of the American population to another. For example, T-shirts were printed with slogans in US presidential campaigns in the late 1940s, such as the (unsuccessful) 'Dew it with Dewey' campaign. Soon afterwards, civil rights protesters and political activists started to print their T-shirts with their own slogans.

The use of T-shirts to carry advertising slogans followed a similar trajectory. In the 1960s, T-shirts printed with commercial logos brought advertising into the midst of people's lives, carried on their personal belongings. This set up a chain reaction – once started, personalising logos would prove impossible to stop. By the 1970s logo subversion was rife. T-shirt makers hijacked the graphics of well-known commercial brands and twisted their slogans: 'Enjoy Coca Cola' was rendered 'Enjoy Cocaine'; 'Heineken' was transformed into 'High Again'; 'Rice Crispies' became 'Nice Tripsies'; and so on.

These trajectories also played their part in the development of T-shirt graphics in the Pacific. In the late 1970s T-shirt graphics began to be used to express Hawai'ian cultural pride by surfers on the beach. Samoan students studying at Brigham Young, the University funded by the Church of the Latter Day Saints in Honolulu were inspired to develop their own T-shirt designs. Some of the T-shirts bore Samoan catchphrases, others had slogans that were intended to convey a sense of collective cultural pride with expressions such as 'Polynesian Strength' or, 'Don't Mistake our Quiet Ways for Weakness', or 'Samoan Built to Last'. A design bearing the legend 'Super Samoan', using the superman lettering, underlines the way in which collective affirmation began to be expressed through appropriating icons of American popular culture. This graphic genre reached New Zealand in the mid-1990s through trans-national networks linking the Samoan diaspora.

Many T-shirt designs draw upon the cultural stereotypes that were used against Pacific Islanders in Auckland in the 1970s and 80s as inter-community relations worsened. They use a device that developed in counter-cultural strategies in hip-hop and the gay pride movements where terms of abuse are re-appropriated and their meanings altered, 'turning the negative positive' as one designer put it. For example, Dawn Raid and Pacific Gear make T-shirts printed with the words Overstayer, South Side, Coconut, Dawnraid and Bungas Worldwide.

A second genre that has been developed by the T-shirt artists is logo subversion. In the hands of the T-shirt designers in Auckland logo subversion

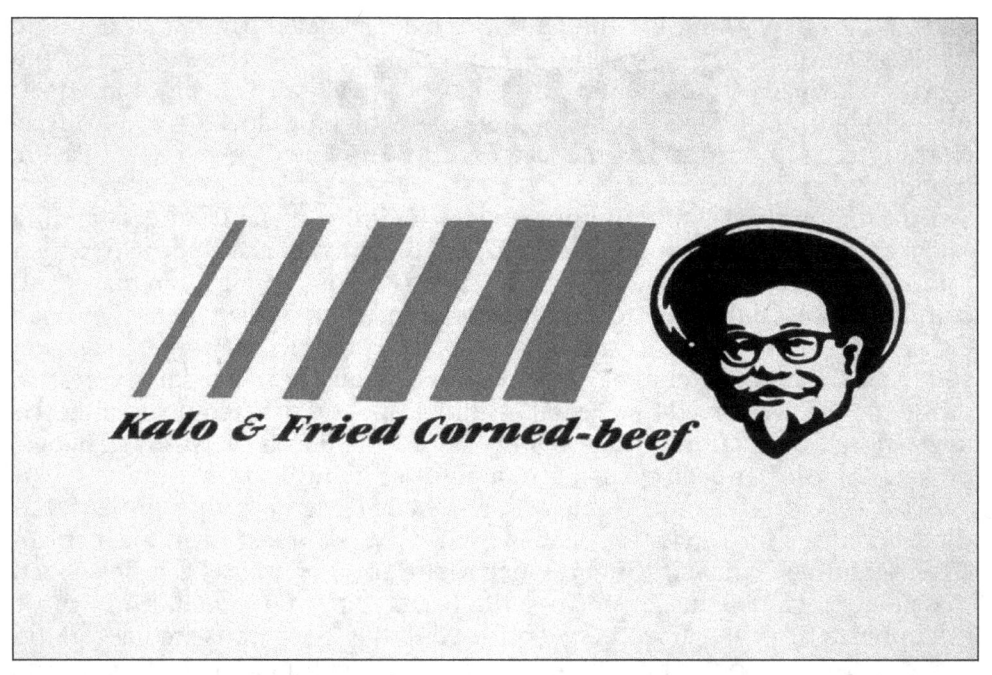

Plate 8.3   *Kalo and Fried Corned-beef. Photo: Seliga Setoga for Popo Hardwear, 2000.*

has been developed to comment on cultural stereotypes and the relationship between indigenous material culture and multinational brands. Thus well-known slogans such as 'Coca-Cola, the Real Thing' have been wittily changed into the new slogan 'Coco-Nuts Harder than the Real Thing'. KFC (Kentucky Fried Chicken) has been translated as Kalo and Fried Corn, a reference to the progressive incorporation of foreign goods such as corn beef and even Kentucky Fried chicken within the spheres of Samoan exchange. Logos have also been localised, designers will typically reference brands to which Pacific Islanders' are attached such as Kentucky Fried Chicken and Milo. New Zealand government-issue signage has also been used in this way.

The obligation to eat well at family gatherings at which the exchange of food is an important component of the ceremony has meant that clothing is an area where the difficulties of 'fitting in' have been directly experienced and where tensions regarding cultural assimilation and differentiation are made manifest. Up until the late 1980s many second generation Samoans wanted the latest American sports-gear, and patronised recent arrivals from the islands wearing vivid island prints. Since then island style prints, worn on shirts, bandanas and even lavalavas (sarongs) have begun to emerge on the streets and in the clubs. Certain T-shirt designs comment on this, for example in a design by Nektar the USA Athletic logo has been translated as, USO Crazy (uso is the Samoan term for brother).

T-shirt designs also draw upon the graphics of successful street-wear brands that emerged from the surfing, skateboarding and rap scenes in the States. Here it should be noted how graphic humour seems to achieve a highly localised in-joke, alongside the empowerment achieved through extending the local through the expansion of terms of reference. For example, in the design that reads 'FOBU XXXL' the logo of a well-known, hip-hop street-wear producer, FUBU (For Us by Us Clothing) which produces baggy, oversize clothing for rap enthusiasts has been wittily subverted to reference Pacific Islanders' concerns.

Another genre of graphic humour references Samoan's faulty understanding of English. Self-deprecating and self-parodying comic sketches in which Samoans ridicule their own attempts to assimilate foreign language and culture are an established form of humour in the islands, where they may either be used to reference oppression or cultural affirmation (Sinavaiana 1995). Such comic sketches have shown how language can become expressive of the tensions involved in cultural assimilation, and of attempts to alter the negative self-evaluation it may involve. Yet in the hands of T-shirt designers broken English has been turned into a point of identification.

The 'O is for Awesome' found on one T-shirt design cites a comment that the Samoan boxer David Tua made when he was a guest on the American TV Programme, *Wheel of Fortune*. Once again, this genre has been developed to change slogans. Thus Fresh Up, a local sickly, fruit-flavoured drink whose catchphrase runs 'Its got to be good for you!' has been translated as 'Freshy I'm got to be good for you!' Another salient cultural opposition is the distinction between oral tradition and literacy. The authority of foreign, (often anthropological) descriptions of Samoan culture has been a source of contention in cross-cultural relations in the past. One T-shirt designer has developed the genre of humour by producing designs that explore people's relationship to academic text, and to the socially distancing idiom of formal academic expression, by inventing an entry in an imaginary dictionary of slang. His design reads 'Freshy n. derived from the abbreviated expression f.o.b. – fresh off the boat, a term given to Polynesian natives. The expression must only be used in a light humorous manner as this fob may perceive your humorous intentions derogatory and bust you in the eye' (Plate 8.4).

It is a good example of the way in which T-shirts can make the wearer more threatening, by clothing him in subsidiary spirit selves that reference the cumulative effects of cultural experience through time.

The sense of mediated agency is also conveyed because it is often difficult to know where the designers' sympathies and intentions lie. T-shirt designs that address the apparent simplicity of the material culture of the islands all show this through the complex devices that they use to frame iconic cultural elements. For example, in his design 'Bump n' Grind' Dean Purcell has set a series of grainy black and white photos (in a style redolent of the kind of modernist material culture ethnography that was preoccupied with technical process) showing the different stages of preparing coconut milk within highly contemporary chromium plated frames which are set, in turn, against a textured graphic background that is now a ubiquitous feature of Pacific Island websites: the pandanus mat.

The use of cultural icons, like the coconut, which traditionally carries sexual associations in many different Pacific island cultures, reveals an attempt to develop in-jokes that can be shared by Maori and Pacific islanders

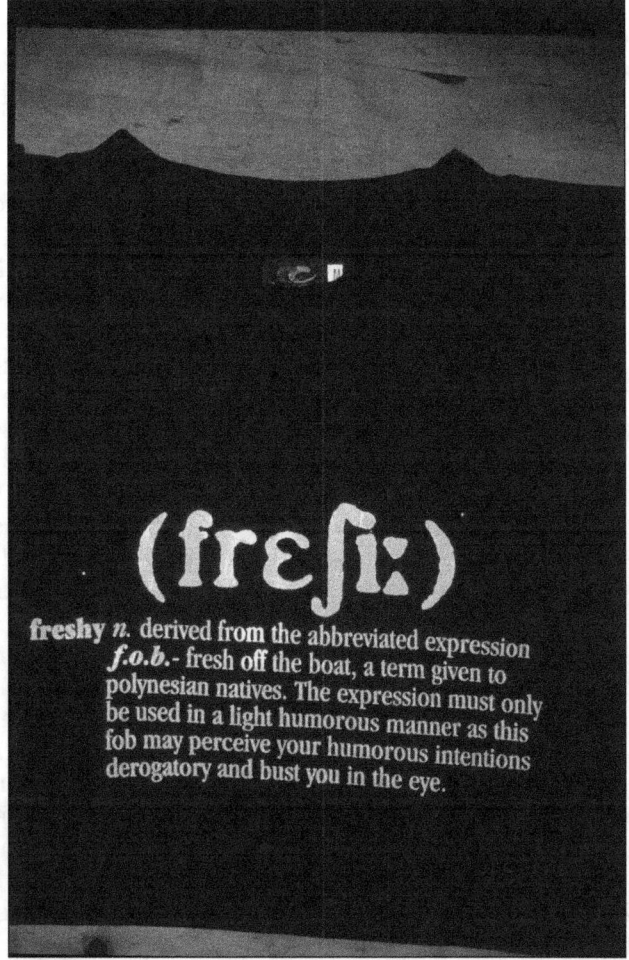

Plate 8.4   *T-shirt design by Popo Hardwear, 2001*

alike. The same designer has also experimented with T-shirts for Maori and Tongan wearers.

Humour and conflict resolution

In parts of the Pacific where authority figures are afforded great respect and deference, humour may provide a rare conduit to convey criticism. What has been described as 'clowning' now plays an integral role in Polynesian public celebrations and gatherings, providing another dimension to the normative structuring of experience. Burlesque renderings of the sexually provocative gestures that were so frowned upon by the missionaries are now a ceremonial comic form that provide some relief from the repressive codes of conduct that characterise much ceremonial activity in the Pacific. At wedding celebrations in Samoa, Fiji and Rotuma older female guests may abruptly depart from their dignity and decorum to improvise a comical dance involving suggestive hip-wagging, rolling on the floor with their legs in the air, flipping up the back of their skirts and so on.

Caroline Sinavaiana, who is the director of the Institute of Inter-cultural Communication in Pago Pago has shown how scripted songs and comedy sketches (*fale atiu*, literally 'the house of spirits') 'provide the only public arena in Samoan society that traditionally allows for popular criticism and institutions of authority' (Sinavaiana 1995:193). Such sketches may be used to address internal conflicts but they are also used to ridicule Western figures and institutions of authority, expressing sentiments that would be denied formal expression in any other fashion. Given this, it is perhaps not surprising to discover that Independence Day celebrations in Samoa should be marked by a national comedy competition. They may include parodies of Western politics, potentates, religion, education, medicine and popular culture. Characteristic comic devices include verbal play such as punning and mimicry as well as *double entendres*. The tradition of *fale atiu*, which also has developed in New Zealand (see for example Lisa Taouma 2005) has I am sure contributed to the development of sexually provocative humour in T-shirt art. But here it is expressed in a typically more complex and self-reflexive way that uses logo subversion or perceptual tricks to reference conventions of social perception.

One of the interesting things about the use of humour as a device for venting criticism in Pacific ceremonies is that it is a form of indirect expression in which the comedian is perceived as *mediating* external ancestral expression. T-shirt art may be seen as an external form in this sense, for within Samoan culture, and aside from the *fale atiu*, there was no equivalent institution to the *fono* for resolving conflicts involving commoners or the young (Duranti 1990). But I think that it also may be thought as being an indirect form of expression in as far as most of the graphic jokes are a play upon form, that is upon people's reaction to the graphic presence of words and objects.

Existing studies of conflict resolution in the Pacific have shown that people living in the intimately interdependent communities that are characteristic of this region typically favour indirect modes of expression to voice criticism, instead of open debate or confrontation. There are many such forms of indirect expression in the Pacific. They include varieties of formal speech, divinely inspired speech and 'veiled speech' – that is rich in the use of metaphor and allegory – as well as diverse introduced forms such as extempore prayer. Objects and imagery can also be involved. The arrangement of a feast may be perceived as an image that allows people to gauge a given event (Strathern 1991:97). For example, a sprouting coconut may be presented in a marital exchange so as to invite interpretation and speculation on the current state of relations between inter-marrying kin (McKellin 1990).

All these kinds of expression use forms that act as mediators between the protagonist and their audience, thereby encouraging the development of a co-operative perception of events. For example, the inherent ambiguity and enigmatic nature of metaphorical forms of expression allows people to test the relevance of what is presented without making any clear commitment of intended meaning or interpretation.

In many ways these observations are relevant to T-shirt art. T-shirt art is a form of graphic humour without a punch line. It is intrinsically interactive: it provokes interpretation depending for its effects on the temperament of its viewers, or the specific relation between wearer and perceiver. Many of the most sophisticated designs deploy meta-level humour: one laughs and then realises that one is laughing at one's own interpretation, perhaps laughing at oneself. As has so often been observed in the Pacific, designers are reluctant to advance their own interpretations of the meanings of their designs, preferring to conceal their sympathies as best they can, and encouraging the audience to make their own interpretation.

Conclusion

I would like to return to the problem that I sketched out at the beginning of this paper, regarding the nature of the connections manifest in T-shirt design. Chris Tilley has recently suggested that metaphorical expression, which involves understanding and experiencing one thing in terms of another, shows the extent to which mental imagery derived from our active engagement with the material world pervades our speech and thinking (Tilley 1999). Yet metaphor is pre-eminently a feature of language in which the analogies drawn between one conceptual domain and another often tend to be fairly conventional, as well as being generalised or abstract. The kinds of auditory and visual analogies that feature in many T-shirt designs are significantly different from this, since they involve the discovery of similarities of surface detail in ostensibly unrelated objects. It is this use of analogy to mediate conventionalised cultural oppositions between modernity and remote Pacific cultures that I have attempted to describe here. What interests me is that the visual and verbal puns in graphic humour are the result of the arbitrary correspondences that can be perceived in the outside world when the surfaces and detailed features of different material and cultural worlds overlap. In these cases marking connections between the details provides the key to specific associations and to a deeper reality, which may be inaccessible by other methods. I would suggest that the empirical attention to specific detail distinguishes them from the kinds of analogy that are more typically used in poetic expression and it is this which makes T-shirt art relevant to the particular experience of occupying a cultural position in between island communities and modern, settler societies.

I would like to conclude by returning to a question that I touched upon earlier. Is T-shirt art and with it this way of drawing visual analogies a foreign introduction, or did it resonate with something that had a longer heritage within Pacific thought? An historical perspective of Pacific Islanders' responses to European impositions suggests that both indigenous clothing and cloth achieved a newly prominent position in the Pacific in the wake of European intrusion. Both at the level of ceremonial performance as well as at the level of the patterns on individual pieces of cloth the nature of the connections evinced through cloth images has grown increasingly elaborate in the wake of religious and social change (Küchler 2003; Colchester 2003).

Greg Dening's discussion of Bligh's drawing of the Tahitian feather girdle *maro ura*, which incorporated a piece of the scarlet standard that was used to claim Tahiti for George III shows how the importance attached to discovering such connections between European and Pacific cloth marked the encounter between Europeans from the outset (Dening 1996:130). Moreover it would seem unlikely that visual analogy was introduced to the Pacific from Europe, given the prevalent European preoccupation with describing particularity and difference through the use of naturalism and empirical description (Stafford 1999). Conversely, one could perhaps see systems of pattern in the Pacific as an instance of very strong visual analogy, where the pervasive tension between figure, or object and ground conveys the point at which all differences are dissolved. I would suggest that the kinds of analogies in T-shirt art would appear to draw upon both of these genres, though how this highly political and self-reflexive form of humour contrasts with other synthetic forms that have emerged in the islands would seem to merit some analysis.

Bibliography

Appadurai, A. (1986) *The social life of things,* Cambridge: Cambridge University Press.

Babadzan, A. (1993) *Les depouilles des dieux: essai sur la religion Tahitienne a l'epoque de la decouverte*, Paris: Editions de la Maison des Sciences de l'Homme.

Bartlett, W. (1932) *On Remembering*, Cambridge University Press.

Borofsky, R. (2000) *Remembrance of Pacific Pasts*, Honolulu: University of Hawaii Press.

Brunel, C. (2002) *The T-shirt and Book,* Paris: Assouline.

Colchester, Chloe (ed.) (2003) *Clothing the Pacific*, Oxford: Berg Publishers.

Dening, G. (1996) *Performances,* Chicago: University of Chicago Press.

Duranti, A. (1990) 'Politics, Grammar and Agency in Samoan Political Discourse', in K.A. Watson-Gegeo and G.M. White (eds) *Disentangling: Conflict Discourse in Pacific Societies*, Stanford: Stanford University Press.

Empson, W. (1953) *Seven Types of Ambiguity* 3rd edition, London: Chatto and Windus.

Gell, A. (1998) *Art and Agency: An Anthropological Theory*, Oxford: Clarendon Press.

Kaeppler, A. L. 2002. 'The Structure of Tongan Barkcloth Design: Imagery, Metaphor and Allusion', in A. Herle, N. Stanley, K. Stevenson and R.L. Welsch (eds), *Pacific Art: Persistence, Change and Meaning*, Honolulu: University of Hawai'i Press.

Kneubuhl, V. (1986) 'Traditional Performance in Samoan Culture', *Asian Theatre Journal* 4:166–76.

Kneubuhl, J. (1993) 'Interview with John Kneubuhl', *Manoa* 5(1): 99–105.

Keane, W. (1997) *Signs of Recognition: Hazards and Risks of Representation in an Indonesian Society*, Berkeley; London: University of California Press.

Koestler, A. (1989 [1964]) *The Act of Creation*, London: Penguin Arkana.

Küchler, S. (2003) 'The Poncho and the Quilt: Material Christianity in the Cook Islands' in Chloe Colchester (ed.) *Clothing the Pacific,* Oxford: Berg Publishers.

Mageo, J. M. (1992) 'Male Transvestisism and Cultural Change in Samoa', *American Ethnologist* 19(3): 443–59.

McKellin, W. (1990) 'Allegory and Inference: Intentional Ambiguity in Managalese Negotiations', in K. A. Watson-Gegeo and G. M. White (eds) *Disentangling: Conflict Discourse in Pacific Societies,* Stanford: Stanford University Press.

Mitchell, W. (ed.) (1992) *Clowning as Critical Practice: Performance Humor in the South Pacific,* Pittsburgh: University of Pittsburgh Press.

Sinavaiana, C. (1992) 'Comic Theater in Samoa as Indigenous Media', in K. Nero (ed.) *Pacific Studies* 15(4).

―――― (1995) 'Where the Spirits Laugh Last: Comic Theatre in Samoa' in *Clowning as Critical Practice: Performance Humor in the South Pacific,* Pittsburgh: University of Pittsburgh Press.

Stafford, B. (1999) *Visual Analogy,* Cambridge, Mass.: MIT Press.

Shore, B. (1978) 'Ghosts and Government: A structural Analysis of Alternative institutions of Conflict Management in Samoa', *Man* 13:175–99.

Strathern, M. (1991) *Partial Connections,* Savage, MD: Rowman and Littlefield Publishers.

Taouma, L. (2005) 'Doubleness of Meaning : Pasifika Clothing Camp and Couture' in S. Küchler and G. Were (eds) *The Art of Clothing: A Pacific Experience,* London: UCL Press.

Tilley, C. (1999) *Metaphor and Material Culture,* Oxford: Blackwell.

Thomas, N. (2003) 'The Case of the Misplaced Ponchos; Some Speculations about the History of Conversion in Samoa' in C. Colchester (ed.) *Clothing the Pacific,* Oxford: Berg.

Watson-Gegeo, K. and White, G. M. (eds) (1990) *Disentangling: Conflict Discourse in Pacific Societies* Stanford: Stanford University Press.

Williams, J. (1984) *The Samoan Journals of John Williams* edited by R. Moyle, Canberra.

9

Decorated being in Huli

Parleying with paint

Laurence R. Goldman

*Inaga dumbi yalu bi te wandarirunaga halepangealedago mbira agi
lolebere?*

Your forehead is shining like the pearl-shell necklaces of the 'folk-
story girls', so what have you got to say?

[Addressed to someone who approaches with a beaming smile as if
they are about to convey good news]

Introduction

This saying from the rich ethnographic vein of Huli colloquialism reminds
us that much of our everyday behaviour takes place against a backdrop of
narratively defined representations. The self presents here as a 'decorated
being', the meanings of which are in part parasitic on mythically inscribed
experiences. Simply expressed, the speaker here imparts cultural knowledge
that the contours of one's adorned existence are often 'storied'.

But there is more than mere analogy and allusion to the way in which
such oral genres can scaffold the meaning of individualised decorative
performances. Developments in genre theory (Bakhtin 1986; Miller *et al*
2000; Goldman 1998) have sensitised us to the ways in which social actors
embed genres in each other – intertextuality – use genres to envision
specific realities, and reconstruct personal accounts through interanimation

(activation and interweaving of genre based behaviour). These findings have a particular resonance for understanding the tension between the oral narrative of *bi te* (story) in Huli and folk readings of decorated being in this culture. Decoration is here very much a whole-body renarrativisation of one's social activity; that is, in the flow of genre upon genre each performer's enactment invariably refracts the fund of semiotic resources found in *bi te*. Storied fragments and values about decorated people become both animated and appropriated within the context of often non-oral dance performances.

Anthropologists have of course long argued that the decorated beings that inhabit any fantasy economy crystallize that culture's imaginative dreams and aspirations. When actors create similar self-images they do so in a manner that manufactures a unique slippage between real and irreal worlds; that is, between an actor's perceptions of what-they-now-are and what-they-might/would-like-to-become as incarnations of high aesthetic and/or moral achievement. The decorated being attempts a 'dissimilar similarity' (Rapp 1984:143) in which the representation is partly fictional, and partly anchored to the context of some social performance. What a Huli encounters in the engagement with decoration or decorated beings is a modality of experience that, whatever else it may signify, always attests to the permanence of illusion in life. The decorated person is thus always a storied incarnation necessarily invoked in the sense-making activities of both actor and audience.

This is not to suggest that the backcloth of folklore exhausts the realities envisioned by decorated performers. Like many of the Highland cultures of Papua New Guinea, the Huli are in transition to modernity and many of the traditional contexts and rationales for decoration have undergone radical transformation. Often today the contemporary decorated/dancing being has drifted free of its traditional social and ritual moorings to now embody a mélange of images defined by the postcolonial predicament. In this paper I want to explore the above themes by way of posing the following question: in Huli, what role does this performing of a decorated being play in the general being of 'decoration/adornment' itself? Answers to this question can be found somewhere in the vineyard of the semiotic pre-eminence of paint.[1]

This project of understanding commences then with the premise that the adorned being is encumbered by, inflected with, and often shaped afresh from folklore resources. In Huli these genred representations define the 'decorated' in contrast to, and often as a mutation of, the 'undecorated'. Both of these images embed attributes concerning physical and spiritual well-being. What is thereby elucidated by way of scanning the narrative ethnography is a shared knowledge structure about adornment – a script theory of the decorated which implies the following: 'I am decorated and everything you know about the narrative construction of decorated being applies to your judgement of me'. What is hereby defined is a cultural baseline of intersubjectivity about decoration, about paint. My initial task is thus to unpack this baseline of intersubjectivity.

My second task is to progress the argument by examining how the forces of modernity have accentuated essentialist images of ethnicity now portrayed in decorated performances known as *Máli*. It appears that a process of natural selection has occurred in Huli to leave only this surviving dance genre from the gamut of pre-colonial dance types (see Table 9.2). The question is thereby begged as to why this has occurred, and whether Huli have thereby clad their traditionalist centre with a tourism-inspired veneer. Are the masons of *Máli* no longer adhering to authentic architectural blueprints? Rather, as I shall suggest below, the *Máli* dance repositions the customary dialogue about indigeneity[2] to more directly incorporate present agendas about land rights, tribal status and regional power. The individualised performer in *Máli* has renarrativised the performance to promote an ethnic iconicity. The whole endeavour becomes a new form of myth-making wherein decorated beings are actors in, as well as authors of, their own real-world documentaries. The *Máli* is thus a good example of interanimation, the embedding of traditional concepts in contemporary ethnic agendas.

For some readers, this discussion will no doubt appear squarely located at the intersection of the literature on tradition, history and identity (Thomas 1992, Jolly 1992, Linnekin and Poyer 1990, White and Lindstrom 1993), and the now voluminous discourse on embodiment and skin (Gell 1993, O'Hanlon 1989). The approach developed here is, I would argue, more oblique. I prefer to view the metaphysics of adornment as part of a larger ethnographic project about illusion, the real and the irreal. For this reason, I draw on genre theory to suggest the decorated being is a mimetician of as-if vignettes – 'fictional spaces are created into which audiences are invited by means of implicit solicitations –"let's say x is the case...let's pretend...let's treat as if..."contained in the artistic product ' (Goldman 1988:27). The decorated being reproduces a sense of passing into another body, of corporealisation, of 'taking the role of the other'. They have a story-like reality infused with the seepage of meaning from an imaginal economy itself often read as history. Analysis is thus very much about uncovering the genetic linkages forged between genre inflected representations of decorated being. The actor's interanimations segue the roles of redactor, historian, as well as advocate of regional agendas. Irrespective of the political messages about alterity and identity encoded in *Máli* dance, it is in essence an invitation to engage in and project hypothesised worlds – mythically defined states of person-hood and culturally etched aspirations.

Let me close this introduction with a few orienting words on the Huli people. Inhabitants of the Southern Highlands Province, the Huli are among the most populous of the ethnic groups in Papua New Guinea, numbering more than 100,000 speakers. As the foregoing implies, they exhibit to a high degree the interest in self-adornment characteristic of many groups in Papua New Guinea. In the pre-colonial period young Huli males would enter a bachelor cult known as Haroli in which they would nourish their bodies, skin and hair. Equally, young unmarried girls would draw from a number of make-up repertoires to signal various stages of betrothal. As will become evident, and as I have explored in earlier works (Goldman 1983), the Huli are also noted for their preoccupation with highly elaborate, standardised verbal forms. Finally, it is important to note the extent to which the general area inhabited by the Huli has in the last twenty years become the focus for gold-mining (at Mt. Kare) and for gas and oil extraction (from the Hides gasfield and Moran, Mananda and Kutubu oil fields respectively). This broom of social change has contributed to the re-positioning of self-decoration in Huli life as will become apparent later.

Decorated being: a narrativised identity

What then do I mean by the statement that Huli imaginal economies are often read as history? The Huli certainly mark terminologically a distinction between 'historical talk', *bi tene/tene te* (talk (*bi*)/account (*te*) + source/origin (*tene*)) and 'fictional talk', *bi te* (talk + account) that superficially appears to parallel similar distinctions drawn among the Kewa (*ramani: lidi*: LeRoy 1985), Duna (*pikono: hapiapo tse*: Stürzenhofecker 1998; Haley 1993), Daribi (*namu: po*: Wagner 1978) and many other Highlands societies. However, such emic categories have the capacity to confound ready classification as 'fact' and 'fiction' both for indigenes, where unanimity on genre rubric may be unimportant, and indeed for analysts alike. In the context of Huli oral tradition, this appears related to the profound understanding that 'from historical speech fictional speech will later emerge' (*tene te mani mo bi te holebira*) – that perceived history is subject to processes of poetic fictionalisation. Importantly then, a historically true tale can in Huli have its 'facts' embellished by inclusion of non-factual referents and events from a stock fantasy landscape. Huli narratives are constantly transforming artefacts moving between truth as what endures (*henene*) and pretence (*tingi*) as what is transient.

What this implies is that the domains of the 'real' and 'irreal' are not relatively autonomous but are mutually referential, mutually implicative and mutually incorporative in any single narrative. The same events and even personae can occur across the two categories with an oscillation between what we ordinarily gloss as fiction and non-fiction. This lack of genre discreteness implies then that the bifurcated categories are better thought of as indications of how information in any narrative should be understood. The terms denote not a property of some text but rather an attitudinal or propositional stance of pretence or non-pretence to be taken towards a set of discourses.

Bi te can be told by men or women, usually at night, and to an audience that invariably includes children. Aesthetically valued performances are those where the story is chanted and which rely on several poetic synonym systems (see Table 9.1). This genre is always a co-production because the audience is enjoined during specific phases of the narration to indicate their acknowledgment of information through interjection of segment-terminal 'yes' refrains. I have shown elsewhere (Goldman 1998) how children are able to participate in this folk genre from an extremely early age (3–4 years) through interanimation in their fantasy play. In this culture, story telling plays a developmentally critical role in how children come to understand or envision reality as genre inflected.

Ubiquitous inhabitants of the Huli Weltmärchen world include cyclopic ogres, shape-shifting tricksters, omen birds and, importantly for the present paper, the human-like hero and heroine *Iba Mulu Lunguya* [IML] and *Bebogo*

Wane Pandime [BWP] respectively. These two figures represent the acme of 'decorated being' in Huli culture. All of these narratively recurrent figures can occur in both aetiological and fictional passages. Significantly, for both narrator and audience, there are conventional textual cues – i.e. bracketing devices – which signal how information about their appearance is to be processed. These devices include:

[1] Explicit solicitations to suspend disbelief – e.g. *ogo(bi)alebe toba hea* (like you can't imagine)

Text 1

(Goldman 1998:vii–viii)[3]
Narrator: Giame – Yaluba 1993
Description of Bebogo Wane Pandime

> *Huli agali mbira layago laro*
> There was one man there, I am saying
> *agali igini ibu one mende laya laro*
> This man's son had a wife, I am saying
> *ibu waneore mabura mabuage tebone laya laro*
> His young daughter was a third person there, I am saying
> *mabuage ogodege agali wane la tago tago o nabi laya laro*
> This young girl was not like any man's daughter, I am saying
> → *kewa tangi urume ogoalebe toba hea laya laro*
> With string hats like you can't imagine, I am saying
> → *hale kuni payada urume ogoalebe toba hea laya laro*
> With arm-bone bracelets like you can't imagine, I am saying
> *limale mabu urume pugu lalu togo lea laro*
> With feathered cassowary claws as nose plugs, I am saying
> *kewa tangi pugu pugu lea laya laro*
> Wearing these string hats, I am saying
> *baya wane purugu laya laro*
> This wonderful girl who was so good as to dazzle and confuse, I am saying

Text 1 reveals the quintessential attributes of female beauty in Huli represented by *Bebogo Wane Pandime*. It is an image clearly drawn around the material culture of adornment (→). The diacritics of decorated female being in Huli are thus contained in a stock repertoire of accoutrements whose efficacy lies in their capacity to confuse and blind onlookers – this articulates the aspirations of the undecorated. The items of adornment are not in type or range removed from the everyday realm, but are at a level of excellence normal humans can only aspire to. Paradoxically they are both 'beyond imagination', but easily appreciated as also historically veridical representations.

[2] Working in tandem with such explicit disbelief markers are statements, invariably couched in the negative, which further portray the abnormality

of decorated figures by rendering impossible certain behaviours which in the normal course of things are unproblematic – negated normality.

Ordinary people cannot talk to, sleep with, or be included (*tago*) or mentioned (*la tago*) in the same company as decorated beings like *Iba Mulu Lunguya*:

> → *agali iginiale tago tago nabi ibiniya laya*
> Like this man's son one can't mix and he came it is said
> this wasn't like any ordinary man's son and he came it is said
> ...
> *honogagaru mani gudi layagola*
> cassowary feathers flow down the back of his (Iba Mulu Lunguya's) neck
> → *agali igini la tago howa nabi*
> he cannot be referred to as like any ordinary man's son
> → *igiri labona agali iginila paliaba loa nabi*
> this impossible boy, an ordinary person couldn't say to him 'Let's sleep together'

These storied 'others' are set apart as interactionally unequal with non-storied Huli; they cannot be conversed with, and are not genealogically derived from mortal origins:

> *Gongodale lame Togome lame walime gime bini ndo*
> his (Iba Mulu Lunguya's) mothers Gongodale and Togome were not from a woman's hands
> [they appeared born of another kind of woman]
> *ilu hali yule bini nu dambale Gabialu ilu hali yule bini mbira biarume*
> they used to make bags and aprons from the flying fox bones from Gabialu
> *walirume bi labenaheya*
> → it was impossible for women to talk to him
> .
> .
> *Iba Mulu Lunguya iba gurubuni dibarago biya*
> Iba Mulu Lunguya was shining like the reflection on the water
> *Wali igini bi di biabe naheago*
> → Women's sons couldn't talk with him

These bracketing devices project the decorated being not simply as unimaginable, but as also someone with whom conventional behaviour is simply inappropriate or impossible. Whilst the cumulative effect is to quarantine the decorated from the ordinary and mundane, the diacritics of this adorned status also reflect real-world decoration by real-world counterparts.

[3] In apposition to what I have called 'negated normality' – in which conventionality is explicitly denied – the narrator may, conversely, positively indicate the 'extraordinary' either by means of the content contained in the characterisations, or by incorporation of hyperbolic terms like *hiriribi* ('frighteningly/amazing'), *kulu mege* ('intimidating'), *gibi* ('enormous/incredible'), or *labona* ('extraordinary') – as a form of positive abnormality

TEXT 2

(Goldman 1998:204–5)
Narrator: Giame – Yaluba 1993
Description of Iba Mulu Lunguya

> *Uyuguria handa tagi halu heria*
> While they were looking outside
> *gulu babu gulu barabu gulu pilipe pili logobe o lama igiri mbira ibiya*
> One boy came blowing these pan pipes
> *igiri ibiyaria ai ibiyabe toba hayagola*
> As the boy came she didn't know who was coming
> *wali biago ibu gi howa handalu heria igiri ale la tago tago howa nabi layago*
> When she saw him she was frightened because this boy was not like other boys
> ✖ *! unduni hundu mandaru ogobialebe toba hea layago*
> With a wig coiffure like you can't imagine
> *ulu babu gulu barabu gulu ogoalebe toba hea layago*
> With cordyline leaves like you can't imagine
> ☞ *honagaga lagoli uru ogoalebe toba hea laya*
> With brown cassowary feathers fixed on his wig like a kneecap on a knee, such as you can't imagine
> ✖ *pulu yabe kindiru ogoalebe toba hea laya*
> With a flapping bag decoration like you can't imagine
> *geni ge haleru ogoalebe toba hea laya*
> With leg bands on the legs like you can't imagine
> ☞ *pagabua mano gu gau learu ogoalebe toba hea laya*
> With the apron ends making sounds like that made by pigs when moving, like you can't imagine
> ☞ *gelabo mandibu gugu ndibu learu ogoalebe toba hea laya*
> With the apron sitting tightly on each thigh like you can't imagine
> .
> .
> ¤ *amu daramabi biagoria dugu yalu tagira ibiyagola igiri labona agali iginila*
> *paliaba loa nabi nahea*
> When he came out of the red lake he was an utterly amazing man such that you couldn't
> tell another person to go and sleep with him

Precisely as was the case for Text 1, the above provides a finely graded curriculum in the art of becoming a male decorated being that is both timeless and standardised within the culture. Moreover, these indexical features appear to impart a quite separate level of meaning from associated textual cues about how such information is to be processed in respect to modalities of the real or irreal in any story. The text also betrays the intermeshing of form and substance. For example, there are layers of meaning associated with the poetics of expression – use of praise (kai ✂) analogues (see Table 9.1) for everyday lexicon, and invoked natural imagery (☞).

Item	Everyday Term	Praise Analogue
Tail Flap	Puluyabe	Kindu
Pearl Necklace	Halepange	Gulu mama/pa yaba
Oil	Mbagua	Tola amuname
Wrist Bands	Gi ndole	Ibabi
Arm Bands	Gi payida	Gi poro
Leg Bands	Ge hale	Dabu/lagu
Daisies	Aulai	Kalakambu

Table 9.1   *Huli Praise Terms for Decorative Items*

Decorative items can thus be verbally rendered in alternative poetic vocabularies that again offer up a level of aesthetic appreciation quite distinct from concepts of inherent beauty signalled by the decorative items. These in turn are compounded with reproduction of Huli aesthetic ideals about how decoration should 'sit'. There is here an aesthetics without any superarching theory of art *per se*. The attributes of decorated being[4] are worn on the text.

Succinctly stated, male decorative apparel includes pearl-shell necklaces (*halepange*), arm bands (*gi payida*), leg bands (*ge hale*), woven string aprons to which are attached pigs' tails (*nogo ere dambale*), a bark tail flap suspended from string bags (*pulu yabe*), and not least of all the coiffured wigs (*mànda*) for which the Huli are rightly famous. All of these items should be worn close to the body, feathers should be iridescent standing proud of the coiffure, and body paint should glisten – *migi mege* (reflective), *kiau* (bright), *limi limi deda* (radiant), *domdo domone* (gleams), *loai leda* (glowing), *da/wa* (shining).

TEXT 3

(Goldman 1998:204–5)
Narrator: Kadia – Yaluba 1977
Description of Iba Mulu Lunguya

☞ ! *Kiliaba ketene uru pelo biange lo heria*
These feathers were standing upright and planted on the wig like split pieces of wood
☞   *Uru tugubili liru lemo lemo*
The leg bands were tightly laced around his limbs like the *tugubili*

vines around trees
Bara pagabua mabi diwabi diwanre ma dambale urume tambi tugule hearia
The pigs' tails on the aprons in these places were folded in four over the thighs
☞ ! *Ega yagama uru anda andobe lo heria*
Feathers were glistening like the hanging soot from inside house roofs which often reflect light from the fireplace
☞   *Pau yabarume daga hana ngo ho heria*
The kina shell necklace was shining like a half-moon
.

.

Iba Mulu Lunguya larogo nde
I am talking about Iba Mulu Lunguya
Mbuli ambua Mbaguale ambua Hogale ambuarume de minu heria
The yellow clay from Mbuli, Mbaguale and Hogale was used as eye-shadow
!   *Ega Yagama uru biange lo heria*
The feathers on his wigs were fanned out
☞   *Giliaba gedeneru anga dabu bu heria*
The Giliaba feathers on his wigs were in rows like the stepped platforms on trees used to stop possums
Iba Mulu Lunguya pagabua nai Mobi Dibawi Tibini Tiwabe mara mbalue urume tambi tugulo ka
IML was wearing white pigs' tails that were flat across his thighs like the old adzes from Mobi, Dibawi, Tibini and Tiwabe
☞   *Gulu beberayaru andigi bu hearia lama hendene*
Wearing *beberaya* leaves in his arms as if they sprouted naturally from that place on his body

Significantly, these decorated beings are explicitly drawn in terms of outward appearance rather than inner mental states or dispositions. Furthermore, they are not articulated with stereotypical behaviour patterns or enumerative lists of deeds, causes or ideologies. So in what precise sense then can we consider these images of decoration as expressing, or constituting a conduit for, culturally etched aspirations? This inflection is embedded in the texts in two ways:

[1] by allusion to the motility of decoration which can literally 'knock-out' onlookers – they are rendered dumbstruck, confused (*purugu*) and unconscious (*oda buwa*)

TEXT 4
(Goldman 1998)
Narrator: Giame – Yaluba 1993
Description of *Bebogo Wane Pandime*

    danda irane bada keba mbira unu andaga winiyago
    she (BWP) got the digging stick that was inside the house
    giri layagola ede unu pango pango yu pea hene lama agini
    she held it and went about the valley
    pari dabale biya yagi
    ☞ she was going very fast in a blur of colour like snakes (*pari*) when
    they extend their necks causing the skin colours to blur into each
    other
    igiri emene biago oda bowa ede
    and the small boy was made unconscious (from the colour)

[2] by the nuanced manner in which speakers juxtapose decorated and undecorated representations. The colloquialism which opens this paper illustrates quite transparently how states-of-the-body are used to read off states-of-the-mind – that deportment betrays disposition. In part, these interpretations repose on the knowledge that Huli decorate for specific reasons (listed in the text below) and more often than not have to 'borrow' items from others –

    Hiri màlibe laya[5]
    Are they having a Màli?
    Tawa tege barabe laya
    Are they holding *Tege*? (traditional and major fertility rite)
    Mbirali homo horo harabe
    Are they burying someone?
    Ai hambiya Hela obenali Hiri màli larago poliya
    Brother they are having Màli in Obena so I'll go
    Gibi ega, hagibi ega, hayabe ega mbira wagalo pu lene
    Go and ask to borrow these feathers for the occasion

Equally, it is implicitly understood that the decorated being is impregnated with 'attitude' – self-belief, confidence, strength and machismo. In the following previously published passage from a dispute transcript an older litigant uses sarcasm when referring to his younger 'painted protagonist'. The individual is portrayed as cocksure and as someone holding the view that his elder antagonist is weak, of no consequence and poorly adorned. The speaker reiterates that despite appearances compensation will be paid.

TEXT 5
(Goldman 1983:272)

Gulu pobe ge laga yi dege degeru
With pan-pipes and leg bands
Dumbi yalu da dege degeru
With shining foreheads
! Manda parebi dege dege ru
With decorated wigs
Bolangua harugula denge payabu handale hayeni howa
You passed me and saw I wore a bad leaf-dress
'I won't kill pig' (i.e. give a pig in compensation), did you say that?
The day after tomorrow you'll kill pig
.

.
o hula pungua hiru ebere kegonigo
With decorated charcoal you are coming and there
o agali I nogo bo ngulebere
O man you'll kill a pig for me
o ko dambale uru galawangabi burayu bi o bedagome
(you said to yourself) 'that man there has an uneven apron dress and
bronchitis'
dawaliya
nevertheless we'll cook

The decorated bespeaks a 'what goes without saying' message about power,
physical well-being and individual identity and status. The undecorated is
not simply unadorned, or representing a body in some neutral state, but
presents as negatively valued. What the above passages reveal then is the
baseline of intersubjectivity about decorated and undecorated being. At
this juncture suffice to indicate that the second skin is but a translucent
veil on the mind, and in this array of indexical items the coiffure assumes a
somewhat privileged place.

Huli and hair

While the ethnography of Huli hair is semiologically complex, and has
been treated elsewhere (Goldman 1983), I want here to briefly review some
previous findings which bear on the present discussion.

Pre-colonial Huli males from about fifteen years of age entered an
initiation cult in the bush known as Haroli. The object was to promote inner
and outer beauty through various cleansing rituals and by growth of hair
shaped first into a **black** (*mànda tene*), down-turned coiffure, and then later
shaped into an up-turned style and coloured **red** (*mànda hare*). Following
graduation to this second stage of the cult, initiates would leave the cult,
cut their hair and make two replica wigs worn respectively on everyday and
special celebratory occasions. The coiffures were bedecked with a variety of
bird of paradise feathers each with their own special symbolism for wearers.

The anthropological/sociological understanding of 'hair' is of course anything but a *terra incognita* (Leach 1958, O'Hanlon 1992, Sillitoe 1988, Barthes 1973). The capillary meanings of Haroli are – like those of most other Melanesian initiation cults – inextricably gender inflected: women's blood gave the power and name[6] to this male cult signalled by colouring the wig 'red'.

Almost all the important semantic fields associated with decorated being can be subsumed under three critical lexically contrasted pairs:

YÁRI [cassowary] : [decoration] *YÀRI*
{The sense in which 'I am decorated' is related to 'I am a cassowary'}

MÀNDA [coiffure/wig] : [knowledge] *MÁNDA*
{The sense in which wearing one's hair/wig is related to wearing one's knowledge}

MÀLI [celebratory dance] : [death platform] *MÀLI*
{The sense in which this dance relates to the death platform for skeletal remains}

Tone contrasts in Huli language here mark the sense in which the etymologically related lexemes are also semantically connected:

- *Yari* – The cassowary is a symbol of strength and aggression in Huli culture and thus the decorated being implicitly assumes attributes of this other. There is nothing artificial about the relation of sign to the signified in Huli language.

- *Manda* – The maturation of a male through the attainment of capillary status is also an achievement and display of 'knowledge', truth and customary lore. The state of one's hair is a gauge of the state of one's health. Narrative conversations between genders are revealing of the manner in which females look to hair-states for moral or emotion dispositions

Igiri mbalu mbalupa giliwango biridaru agi biribe laya lama hendene
Boy your hair is knotted and crooked so what have you done?
[I can tell from your hair that you are sad and depressed]

often also ensuring males do not exert themselves in work which will affect their hair

Igiri mbalu nolebirago[7]
Boy your hair will go bad
Mbalupa nolebirago, Gogoro nolebirago, ngaluma nolebirago
Ebere habe
You stay there (and I'll do the work)

As a sacred site on the cartography of body symbolism, male 'hair' is also the first resource used by women when they want to insult men. Hair is an index of the pathology of the body. In this vein the oral traditions of the Huli are replete with narrative motifs that chart Cinderella-like transformation from corporeal images of the undecorated to decorated. Females are metaphorically likened to rotten log mushrooms (*nano ombe; nano homai*) with loose fitting apparel

> *Wali ainyeli biago mende godamberu hira dalidali biyagola*
> The mother's loose grass skirts continued to slide down her body

Men are described as having festering sores and scales (*duru, dere, wayu, togayu, kindu, kembera*), and as using in decoration birds whose plumage is not conventionally used as they are considered unappealing.

Text 6

(Goldman 1998:198–201)
Narrator: Giame – Yaluba 1993

> *Emene biagome*
> This little one (with the sores)
> *Gibi ege hagibi ega tugume ega yabe ega helabe ega*
> Wore feathers from Gibi, Hagibi, Tugume, Yabe and Helabe birds
> (i.e. feathers from birds considered unaesthetic)
> *Ni biaruni mani yini yalu ibu dai biyagola*
> He carried them back and tied them together on the back of his neck
> *Daba pu gimbu o*
> Tied them together on a string
> *Tege gaiyaru li mayagi mende yagi lene o*
> Pigs teeth were tied around the front of his neck
> *Gabale biaru mayagi o weno yagi lene o*
> Feathers were put everywhere in random scattered fashion
> *Gurai tangi biaru li mayagi o weno yagi lene o*
> The head-dress feathers were just placed everywhere in random
> scattered fashion

The transition from these states-of-being to 'decorated' is effected in narrative texts by a symbolic passing through from 'black' to 'red' lakes (see Text 2: ¤) – just as in the Haroli cult initiates graduated from black to red wigs.

Text 7

(Goldman 1998:198–201)
Narrator: Giame – Yaluba 1993

> *Iba amiguria daramabi mbira mindibi mende lowa bereneyagoria*
> There were two lakes over there, one black and one red
> *O biagoria yu pea howa amugureni udu mindibi biagoria minu ba pea hene*
> Over there where the black lake was she grabbed him (the little one
> with the sores) and pushed him in

Mini miyagola unu biagoria gudau la ha hene amu daramabi biagoria
dugu yalu tagira ibiyagola
She got him and pushed him so he splashed and came up the other
side out of the red lake

.

.

Gi payele kuniru
His armbands were fantastic
Manda biago gini dege bialu amuguria aube toba howa
His wig was fixed beautifully like you can't imagine
O gulu mamu baru liguria puni dawene lama agini
He wore pearlshell necklace close to his chest and it was sunburnt
[suntanned?]
O pagabua ere dambele biaru liguria haiya lo pea hene
The pigs' tails on his apron were laying flat
O mini aibe lama laya agini
What is your name, boy?
Ibu Mulu Lunguya lene o
He said, "Iba Mulu Lunguya"

In all the *bi te* texts collected where such transitions occur, women invariably
appear as the prime agents of change (*mo beregeda* – to turn around) by
preparing male decorations or cajoling them to enter into the 'red' lakes
while uttering the refrain '*abai hangabo yule angida* ('it is time to hold the hair
comb') – an oblique reference to the need for the male to enter the Haroli
cult.

Irrespective of the presentational context in which the decorated being
operates, it clearly instantiates a series of rhizomatic connections to these
storied counterparts. The above is a window onto this intersubjective
knowledge about decoratedness, and onto how narrative organises the
structure of such experiences. The decorated being is inflected by these
storied representations, can be understood only in terms of such script
theories of decoration, but only ever partially embodies meanings from this
cultural realm.

The 'Hela' and 'Huli' in Màli

The Huli – prophetically referred to by Sinclair (1973) as the 'Wigmen of
Papua' – are very much *the* face of Papua New Guinea for the outside world.
As Timmer (1993) has remarked, in the last decade Huli have eclipsed the
Asaro 'Mudmen'[8] as an evocative image of the tribal and exotic in Papua New
Guinea. A number of circumstances explain this propulsion to a national
marketing image:

- The Huli have continued to prove an enduring Mecca for anthropologists,
  ornithologists, film-makers and tourists. Their territory is promoted as
  one of the last areas in PNG to have been 'opened' up despite first
  contact occurring as long ago as the 1930's. This gives the Huli a quite

unprecedented level of exposure[9] in which they have become subject to commercial processes.

- As noted at the outset, since 1990, there has been increased attention on the Southern Highlands Province as a centre of resource development for gold (at the Mt Kare goldfield), gas (Hides) and oil (Moran, Mananda and Kutubu petroleum fields). In this cauldron the Huli numerically dominate their neighbours such as the Foi, Fasu, Onabasulu, Wola and Ipili. They are regularly flown to America and Australia on corporate promotion tours, and their 'decorated' images are used by the multinational developers on computer mouse mats, screen savers and clothing.

- As well as being regarded as a resource-rich province, the Southern Highlands is also one of the most violence ridden areas in Papua New Guinea. Its reputation reflects endemic tribal factionalism and the growing divide between the resource development 'haves' and 'have-nots'. Public and media attention continues to be fed images from this region, and separatist political agendas in the province have now been co-opted by Huli.

- Lastly, there is an embedded and perhaps ineffable aesthetic encapsulated in the Huli decorated being which appeals to the Western imagination in ways not matched by other regional analogues.

Significantly, pre-colonial Huli, like their Duna counterparts (Haley 1993:73), objectified salient cultural differences in stereotypical speech forms often used on the occasion of making compensation payments, at disputes or in war. These speeches foreground the repertoire of decoration items used as diacritics of alterity:

The Huli with hair bound with rope/decorated with yellow everlasting flowers/purple everlasting daisies/arrows with decorated shafts/with aprons of pigs' tails

The Duna with their form of axe/aprons made of this species of bark/ feather worn in the hair/string-cap

The Dugube (Papuan Plateau peoples) with their tree oil/axe/bow/ species of cane/dogs-teeth-necklaces/bamboo through their nose/ hair style/killing stick (cf. Goldman 1983:67–8, 297).

Ballard (1995), Clarke (n.d.) and Timmer (1993) have all cited my previous ethnography to indicate that Huli displayed a self-reflexivity about their cultural identity and distinctiveness long before colonialism. This consciousness of similarity and difference as embodied in varying 'decorated' styles was undoubtedly enhanced by vigorous inter-cultural trade, the migrational processes that spawned huge population enclaves, and the rich interaction between these neighbours predicated on shared sacred geographies and origins. This objectification process extended not only to knowledge of apparel, but also house styles, language and dance: Duna noted for the dance style *tele te*; Dugube for their version called *gereye*; and the Obena for their dance performance referred to as *Poro màli*. When the 'light coloured' (*honebi*) men [i.e. Europeans] came these speech forms about the material culture of decoration were adapted to include trousers, etc.[10] Clarke (n.d.) was thus right to interpret these data as a challenge to the notion that Pacific ethnic identities only emerge with colonialism and selective reifications of culture (cf. Linnekin and Poyer 1990). The ethnography points to how Huli rendered decoration as critical in the reproduction of identity, of Huli-ness – it thus speaks to the relationship between decorated being and decoratedness in this culture as an ethnotheory of ethnicity.

Huli perceive themselves as a culturally homogeneous unit because they share *mana* (custom) – *ina mama mamalinaga mana ogome mo mbiyaore kemagoni*: the *mana* of our ancestors makes us one (Goldman 1983:67). *Mana* embodies a symbol of identity, integrity, a criteria for self-definition from the individual to the tribal. The material culture of decoration is but one realisation of *mana* itself. Etymologically the meaning of the term reflects the morpheme *ma* ('past, before, neck, behind') – so that there is embedded here the idea of present convention and praxis linked to an ancestral past. *Mana* derives its epistemic validity and status from association with history, and was always part of the self-conscious rhetoric of Huli ethnicity. Clearly, those neighbouring 'others' were differently decorated in accordance with their own *mana;* but equally they were reproducing this with a dissimilar similarity. This is the dialectical interplay between the construction of otherness and sameness much commented upon by Highlands ethnographers. In other words, there was an implicit apprehension on the part of the Huli about the being of decoration as an expression of history. A culturally reflexive metaphysics fashioned in light of 'difference or externality' (Thomas 1992:213).

For both Huli and Duna, this awareness about decorated being was further encoded in two features of mythic structure. (1) It was common for stories to have a coda whereby there was a population diaspora leaving Huli in the 'middle' ground. These accounts often relate an ancestral distribution of *mana* to the ethnic groups[11] as an explanation of difference. (2) Pre-colonial Huli loosely encoded their belief about a world populated by four major groups through use of the honorific prefix *Hela* – Hela Huli, Hela Duna, Hela Obena (Ipili) and Hela Dugube (Papuan Plateau) (cf. Glasse 1965:33; Goldman 1983:113; Ballard 1995:55). Huli ideas about their cosmic centeredness and balance with outsiders was marked by this appellation. In some eschatological narratives, Hela is an original Huli progenitor, though other informants understood the prefix simply to reflect an assumption of commonality or descent.

Longitudinal ethnographic data are now clearly indicating a revitalisation of this belief harnessed to new agendas about regional and local land rights. A movement to split the present Southern Highlands Province into two with the creation of a new Hela Province has gathered momentum in the last five years. It is a now a strong political force articulated, driven and owned by Huli politicians and a sizeable constituency of the grass-root Huli population.[12] The public press statements include the following explanations:

> We are one ethical[13] unit. We are born of our common ancestor
> Hela...from time immemorial we have maintained the Hela identity...
> the name Hela also means, let it be, preserve, conserve, let it live;
> do not touch, keep off...The Hela province issue – is an issue in the
> heart throb, bone marrow and blood vein of all and every Hela (Press
> Statement – *The National 19/9/2000*).

In this new myth-making enterprise, Huli use the traditional rhetoric and
idioms of descent ('blood, bone, heart') to promote a political agenda by
melding these with the indigenous predilection to draw meaning from the
homonymy between a proper name – Hela – and an imperative form of the
verb 'to leave alone' (*hela*). What is thereby suggested is that the agenda of
this movement was decreed by the ancestors – that Hela should be preserved
as a unified regional group.

Is it cynical of me to suggest that there is a strong economic rationale
to this new political movement? Importantly, the new Hela myth talks not
of four but *five* core members – Huli, Duna, Dugube, Obena and the Lake
Kutubu people traditionally and collectively referred to as *Hewa Wane*. The
new Hela flag is thus to have five stars to include the Kutubuans who are
now referred to as *Hela Hewa*. That is, the changed terminology now aligns
them with the other Hela constituents. What is thereby created is an entirely
new artifice of the sacred cosmology of Huli. What we are witnessing is
the transformation of an old myth into a new one endorsing conventional
wisdom about the malleability of myths to reflect the present in the past. It
appears no coincidence that the new Hela province would thus embrace the
electorates of Komo-Margarima, Tari-Pori, Koroba-Lake Kopiago in Southern
Highlands), and Laigap-Porgera and Kandep in Enga Province. The resource
grids of Porgera and Kare gold, gas in Hides, and oil and gas at Moran,
Mananda, Kutubu and Gobe, overlays perfectly onto these proposed Hela
electoral lines. Huli have been able to monopolise this movement by virtue
not simply of their relatively massive population base – more than 100,000
speakers – but also because the same myth is in part shared by Duna.[14] Other
commentators (Clark n.d.) have talked of aggressive Huli chauvinism and
territoriality, and there is little doubt that the Huli language is set to become
the *lingua franca* of the southern highlands.[15]

Whilst it is no longer easy to tease out what is purely Hela and what is
Huli, the symbolic power of contemporary dance performances such as *Máli*
inscribe such concepts of identity. This is a context when Huli ethnicity is
presented, contested and delineated with respect to, or against the backdrop
of, Hela regional agendas. The sentience of the decorated being in *màli* is
thus bound up with a conjoint affirmation of individual status and Huli
nationhood in all their primordial and historical distinctiveness. An overture
is thereby made to onlookers and over-hearers to enjoin in a shared fantasy
about cultural aspirations. The dance creates a fictional space as a poetics
of the possible. It is not slavishly dependent on its traditional narrative
embedding, but nor is it comprehendible outside such mimetic rationales.

The Màli

The *màli* dance usually consists of two opposing lines of decorated dancers –sometimes terminated by a young boy or female holding a stick – who chant a two-tone shout (*màli iwa*) while beating hand drums in a syncopated beat-and-a half stroke. The dancers take short hopping steps in unison and in one direction – the routine is recommenced periodically after short breaks. The performance has no words, is highly repetitive, but is perceived now as the quintessential manifestation of decorated being. Traditionally *màli* was one of a number of Huli dance styles summarily listed in Table 9.2 below.

Decorative/ Dance Style	Description
Máli	Celebratory dance traditionally in anticipation of an enemy death and in fertility cycle rites of *Tege. Ira Mali* in pre-colonial times required small central stake around which dancers moved. A two-tone shout with syncopated drum beats was made by two opposing groups of dancers who hop in one direction.
Bilagu	Also known as *Dawe Haga* performed as climatic conclusion after divination and *Nogo Hagua/Kolo* to restore good health. One or two practitioners would dance through the night to deter spirits (*dama*). Primary feathers were cloaks of black cassowary from which were suspended hornbill beaks, beads (*dade*) and rattles. The head-dress consisted of white sulphur cockatoo feathers (*abuage*). Song verses plot the geography of surrounding areas and the associated natural fauna and flora.
Komia1	Performed as part of the drought fertility rites (*gaiya tege*) in which two dancers would jump over the cult fence known as *ali damba*. Apart from drumming, no verses accompany the performance. Decoration is dominated by plumes from the Lesser Bird of Paradise after which the dance takes its name.
Kabugua	The "wrapped"(*kabu*) ones were figures of fun who acted with licensed aggression against children in *Tege* rites – a kind of ritualised ogre (Goldman 1998:182) of pantominic proportions. Black is predominant in colour and cassowary feathers.
Hewabi bi	Not recognised as Huli in origin, appears to derive from the Lake Kutubu region. Large fronds of sago palm are worn at the back very reminiscent of Papuan Plateau dancers.

Decorative/ Dance Style	Description
Haroli	First stage initiates wore the base black coiffure (*manda tene*), whilst second stage neophytes wore the 'red' coiffure (*manda hare*)(see Goldman 1983).
Iba Tiri	The Huli trickster imitated in the *Tiri Yagia* rite performed as part of oblation to the supernatural to cure 'water'-based illnesses in Koroba region. Dancers dress up in ferns and suspend two Ribbontail feathers from their heads while encircling a male transvestite (*ega wandari*) (Goldman 1998:246).
Baya Horo	The Huli ogre which is often imitated by older boys and caretakers to frighten and entertain children (Goldman 1998:183) in a game called *baya horo ibira* ('Baya Horo is coming').

Table 9.2   *Traditional Huli dance/decoration styles*

For several decades after sustained contact in the 1950's, most of these dance/decorated styles were still performed albeit separated from their traditional anchorages. On occasions such as political rallies, school or hospital openings, or other celebratory occasions such as regional shows, Huli continued to display these styles. However, since the late 1980's only Màli appears to be regularly performed. The reasons for this survival are no doubt complex, but certainly include the fact that it alone allows for an undetermined number of participants to form groups. Moreover, it does not require any control of esoteric song forms (unlike Bilagu) or intricate decorative styles.

The Màli was traditionally performed prior to an impending war, when a warrior would drive a small sharpened stake into the cleared dancing ground (*hama*), and mark it with rings of coloured clay to signal the number of men that he would kill in the battle. When we draw on the same linguistic resources used to explicate Yari and Manda

MÀLI [celebratory dance] : [death platform] MÀLI
{The sense in which this dance relates to the death platform for skeletal remains}

it becomes clear why this dance is now an arena for the assertion of ethnic status, power and land rights. Skeletal remains were usually laid on a platform to dry (*mo màli*) in preparation for placement in limestone caves or raised coffins (*homa màli*). These same internment boxes now carry the names of those attributed responsibility for the death (see Plate 9.1).

The Màli, in either of its manifestations, was a preparatory, anticipatory and prospective rite; it was a kind of mnemonic about proclaimed intentions

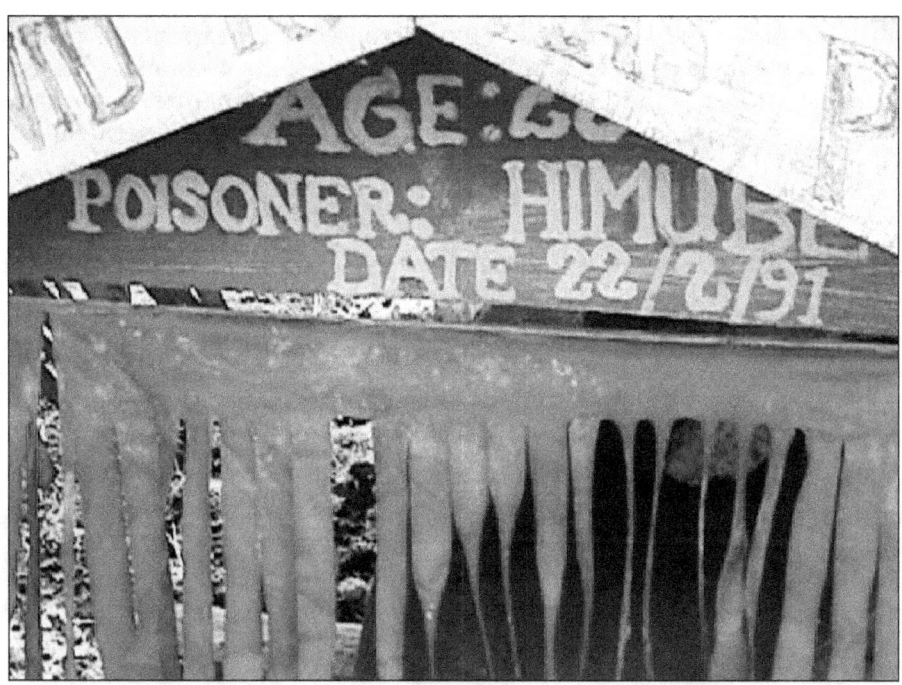

Plate 9.1   *Huli internment boxes now carry the names of those attributed responsibility for the death*

connected with the dead. In the same way that a *màli* platform prepares the dead spirit for its journey to the land of dead souls, so the Màli dance prepares for a coming death of an enemy. Màli was thus always a collective statement, and always performed on the open public clearings (*hama*). Just as the modern *màli* may signal an intention to claim compensation rights for a death, so too the modern Máli dance reasserts the claims of ethnic identity and politico-economic agendas. The ethos of display on public grounds requires that only the finest presentational mediums be used – pigs, paint or parlance are here interchangeable currencies of symbolic capital. In this regard, it is significant that of all the stylistic forms listed in Table 9.2, 'red wigs' are worn only for the Máli.[16] What is thereby suggested, is that in Máli the performers have passed through the mundane of the black lake, and emerged from the 'red' lake – a decorated being whose meaning is inscribed with and by blood.

Màli performances now mark political rallies, festival openings and large inter-clan and inter-tribal compensation exchanges. The decorated remain imbued with narrative authenticity as storied beings, but invested with the political potency of Hela. That the emergence of this pre-eminent symbol is perhaps tourism inspired – a representation of the frozen landscape of exotic culture – merely replicates processes engaged in by Huli themselves. The decorated beings are thus very much authors of their own newly adapted fictions. We witness here again the seemingly silent interanimation between 'màli' genres. The performers have renarrativised their experience to reflect political agendas. The communicative practices of decoration or being decorated can be seen to be inalienably intertextual in nature. But whatever the situated context of an individual's performance, at some juncture it draws meaning from having been 'storied'.

NOTES

In the writing of this paper I felt very much like a stranger in the woods of my own ethnography as both Clark (n.d.) and, later, Timmer (1993) had used my earlier data to traverse many of the themes broached within. While the views expressed here are my own, I acknowledge a debt of gratitude to both these Huli anthropologists for providing a set of boundaries and key concepts around which to weave this particular fiction.

1 In earlier work I talked of the significant continuities in the way Huli operate with pigs, paint and parlance as 'modal forms of presentation of self' (Goldman 1983:272).

2 See Magowan (2000) for a discussion of the poetic politics of dance and Aboriginality.

3 All the textual passages used in this paper are drawn from the twenty transcripts briefly described in Goldman 1998:187–88, 198–201.

4 This speaks in part to the perennial problems encountered by analysts concerning the verbal exegesis of decorative iconicity (cf. O'Hanlon 1989, Gell 1993). What this kind of narrative scanning offers is a unique window on decorative behaviour that analysts have found notoriously difficult to access because indigenes rarely self-reflect on such behaviour.

5 This list of occasions forms a standard narrative refrain of the omen bird Ega Mbe Hiwi. It provides an exhaustive traditional enumeration of exactly when Huli would decorate.

6 In some aetiological versions of the Haroli myth the founding female instructs the male to take her blood, 'stay in the bush' and call the cult Haroli – which means 'I customarily stay' (Goldman 1983:326). This tendency of Huli to provide narrative etymologies for proper names based on their synonymy with everyday verbs is also illustrated below in relation to the political movement of Hela.

7 Young boys who were sick would have their hair shaved leaving just a tuft known as *mbalupa* covering the fontanel to prevent spirit loss.

8 Asaro dancers used to construct elaborate masks for their faces made from mud, hence the coinage 'Mudmen'.

9 Timmer (1993) has charted the use of Huli faces on German telephone cards, Lipton tea adverts, CD covers, T-shirts and even the cover of Cultural Anthropology (Keesing and Strathern 1998).

10 The Dugube with their *wagia hale* (tree sap lights), the Huli with their *Bai hale* (split wood from bai tree) and the Honebi (colonial) with their lamp.

11 cf. Goldman 1983:129 for a passing down of *mana* between related genealogical lines.

12 During the writing of this paper I was made aware by Placer Dome Pacific – the company who own Porgera gold mine – that the group calling itself Hela 2000 had just cut down two of the pylon lines carrying electricity from Hides. There are branches of Hela organisations at the Technology College of Lae and the University of Papua New Guinea known as the Hela Gimbu Association (gimbu means 'to join').

13 This appears to me as a typographic error, and clearly should have read as 'ethnic'.

14 Known in this language as Hala

15 Estimates suggest an average 30% of all Duna, Fasu, Onabasulu and Foi are now bi-lingual in Huli.

16 The use of 'black' coloured up-turned wigs (*manda mindi*) is a recent innovation inspired by Engans.

Bibliography

Ballard, C. (1995) The death of a great land: ritual history and subsistence revolution in the Southern Highlands of Papua New Guinea, PhD dissertation, ANU.

Bakhtin, M. (1986) *Speech Genres and Other Later Essays*, Austin, Texas: University of Texas Press.

Barthes, R. (1973) *Mythologies* London: Paladin.

Clark, J. (n.d.) *Mana* from Heaven: Ethnicity and Knowledge in Tari.

Haley, N. (1993) Altered Texts and Contexts: Narrative, History and Identity among the Duna, Unpublished Honours Thesis, Macquarie University.

Gell, A. (1993) *Wrapping in Images: tattooing in Polynesia*, Oxford: Clarendon Press.

—— (1998) *Art and Agency: an anthropological theory*, Oxford: Clarendon Press.

Glasse, R. (1965) 'The Huli of the Southern Highlands', in P.Lawrence and M.Meggitt (eds) *Gods, Ghosts and Men in Melanesia*, Melbourne: Oxford University Press.

Goldman, L.R. (1983) *Talk Never Dies: the language of Huli disputes*, London: Tavistock.

—— (1988) *Premarital Sex Cases among the Huli: a comparison between traditional and village court styles*, Sydney: University of Sydney

—— (1998) *Child's Play: myth, mimesis and make-believe*, Oxford: Berg.

Haley, N. (1993) Altered texts and contexts: narrative, history and identity among the Duna. Unpublished honours thesis, Macquarie University.

Jolly, M. (1992) 'Spectres of Inauthenticity', *The Contemporary Pacific* 4 (1):49–72.

Keesing, R and Strathern, A. (1998) *Cultural Anthropology: a contemporary perspective*. Fort Worth: Harcourt Brace.

Leach, E. (1958) 'Magical hair', *Journal of the Royal Anthropological Institute* 88 (2): 147–64.

LeRoy, J. (1985) *Fabricated World: an interpretation of Kewa tales*, Vancouver: University of British Columbia Press.

Linnekin, J. and Poyer, L. (1990) *Cultural Identity and Ethnicity in the Pacific*, Honolulu: University of Hawaii Press.

Miller, P., Hengst, J., Alexander, K. and Sperry, L. (2000) 'Version of Personal Storytelling/Versions of Experience', in K. Rosengren, C. Johnson and P. Harris (eds) *Imagining the Impossible: magical, scientific and religious thinking in children,* Cambridge: Cambridge University Press.

Magowan, F. (2000) 'Dancing with a difference: reconfiguring the poetic politics of Aboriginal ritual as national spectacle', *The Australian Journal of Anthropology* 11(3):308–21.

O'Hanlon, M, (1989) *Reading the Skin:adornment, display and betrayal in the Wahgi,* London: British Museum Publications.

―――― (1992) 'Unstable Images and second skins: artefacts, exegesis and assessments in the New Guinea Highlands', *Man* (N.S.) 27:587–608.

Rapp,U. (1984) 'Simulation and Imagination: Mimesis as Play', in M. Spariosu (ed.), *Mimesis in Contemporary Theory,* Philadelphia: John Benjamin.

Sillitoe, P. (1988) 'From head-dresses to head-messages: the art of self-decoration in the Highlands of Papua New Guinea', *Man* (N.S.) 23:298–318.

Sinclair, J. P. (1973) *Faces of New Guinea,* Milton, Q.: Jacaranda Press with Robert Brown Associates.

Stürzenhofecker, G. (1998) *Times enmeshed: gender, space and history among the Duna,* Stanford: Stanford University Press.

Thomas, N. (1992) 'The inversion of tradition' *American Ethnologist* 19(2):213–32.

Timmer, J. (1993) Inclined to be Authentic: Altered contexts and body decoration in a Huli society, SHP, Papua New Guinea. MA Thesis: University of Amsterdam.

Wagner, R. (1978) *Lethal speech : Daribi myth as symbolic obviation,* Ithaca, N.Y.: Cornell University Press.

White, G. and Lindstrom, L. (1993) 'Custom today', *Anthropological Forum* 6 (4):467–606.

10

'Island dress that belongs to us all'

Mission dresses and the innovation of tradition in Vanuatu

Lissant Bolton

In Vanuatu, many women wear a style of dress known in the national lingua franca, Bislama, as *aelan dres* (island dress), or much less commonly as *matahabet* (Mother Hubbard). These are loose wide dresses with a plain V-neck and puff sleeves, often decorated on both the front and back of the bodice and on the sleeves, with lace and ribbon. Ni-Vanuatu women wear island dresses in both island and town: they wear them at church, to go to the garden, to work in offices or to sell food at the market, to weddings and funerals. They almost invariably wear them when pregnant (a bodily state to which the dresses are particularly suited). Not all women wear them, but the majority of adult women would own at least one, while some women only ever wear island dresses.

Tourists and other expatriates generally interpret island dresses as an archaism, as the long reach of Victorian missionary influence on ni-Vanuatu life, as a past introduction which must surely be overtaken by further introductions – the clothes with which the Western world has long since replaced Victorian fashions. What many such observers probably do not know is that upon independence, island dresses were identified as national dress for women. If they do know it, then it would be easy to see this as the final embodiment of such archaism: very often there is nothing so out of date as national dress. For expatriate observers (myself, until recently, included) island dresses are pre-modern, belonging to an era before changes in fabrics, lifestyle and fashion created modern, and post-modern, clothing; but this is a pre-modernity which is nevertheless not tradition. The dresses can be seen as neither indigenous nor part of contemporary global influence. They seem to sit somewhere between the two, neither one thing nor another. But this kind of assessment, based on Western ideas about clothing, misses the point. For ni-Vanuatu women, the dresses have a meaning and significance which is entirely local.

In places like Vanuatu, it is easy to define modernity by means of a binary opposition between indigenous practice and expatriate introductions. Indigenous practice is tradition, and all that has arrived from elsewhere, and especially all that has arrived from the West, is modern. Ni-Vanuatu effect a similar binary opposition through the Bislama term *kastom*, used to indicate indigenous knowledge and practice. There is now no strict opposite to this term, although practices defined as exogenous, as coming from outside Vanuatu, are most usually described in Bislama as *fasin blong ol waetman*. Island dresses are not, however, defined as expatriate practice. Among expatriate women only missionaries, anthropologists and rural aid workers tend to wear them. Some ni-Vanuatu women, especially women from Presbyterian central Vanuatu, go so far as to describe island dresses as *kastom dresing blong yumi* – as our traditional dress. There is no other way to describe the extent of their incorporation in local practice.

Not just incorporated locally, island dresses have become important to popular imagination, and seem to be the subject of widespread sentiment. In 2001 a ni-Vanuatu string band, Dausake, recorded a song that became the first genuine hit in the country. The song '*Aelan dres*' was written by a man from Emau island, Joel Kaltang. It has a cheerful tune and very simple lyrics, which translate: 'You can be found in every place/ island dress that belongs to us all. /Your patterns are very colourful/ making people happy/ smiling a little./ Sing around in every place/ island dress that belongs to us all'.[1] The song could be heard everywhere for nearly twelve months, and did itself seem to make people smile a little.

Island dresses thus demonstrate the fault lines in binary classifications of practice. If they appear to have been introduced from the outside, they are now seen by many people as emblematic of inside – 'island dress that belongs to us all'. The dresses raise issues about the flexibility of indigenous practice and the extent to which it can and does accommodate introductions, and about the relationship of *kastom* to *fasin blong ol waetman*. Their history also provides insights into the process of incorporation – about how something from the outside is gradually transformed into something inside. This paper then, is both about island dresses, and the formulation of ideas of *kastom* and not-*kastom*. It also sets out to trace something of the process of incorporation. I begin with some background, and a discussion of *kastom*, turning eventually to consider the dresses themselves.[2]

Some background

Vanuatu, for those not familiar with the region, is a small Melanesian nation in the south-west Pacific: at the beginning of the twenty-first century over 200,000 people live scattered across an archipelago of some eighty islands. The archipelago lies roughly north-south over 850 kilometres of ocean, to

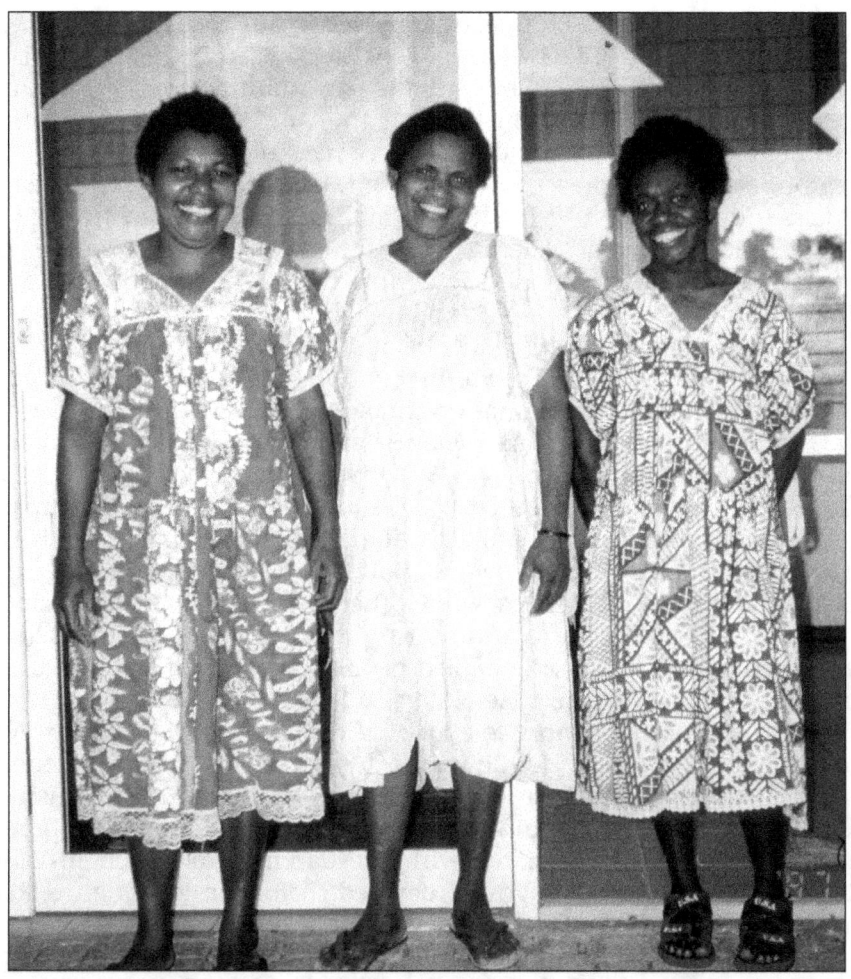

Plate 10.1   *Sera Peter, Irene Lini and Kathleen Vetamana, in everyday island dresses, decorated with some ribbon and lace. (Photograph by L. Bolton, November 2001.)*

the east of northern Australia. Those 200,000 people speak 113 languages between them: almost all of them also speak Bislama, a neo-Melanesian pidgin, as well as either or both of the languages of their colonial experience: English and French. There are two towns, the capital, Port Vila, in the centre of the archipelago, and Luganville, often also known as Santo, in the north, and both towns are growing rapidly. The bulk of the population continues to live in the islands, where people support themselves primarily through food-gardening, and through largely casual cash-cropping of copra, kava, cocoa and coffee.

Europeans, in the person of the Spaniard Ferdinand de Quiros, first appeared in the region in 1606, but he stayed only three weeks, and subsequent settlement was long delayed. In 1774 Captain Cook sailed through the archipelago and named it the New Hebrides. It was however only after about 1820 that Europeans appeared in any quantity in the region, and not until around 1840 that they began to settle there. The islands were never colonised as such, but were jointly administered by Britain and France between 1906 and 1980 through the Anglo-French Condominium Government of the New Hebrides. Neither nation was much interested in the region, each being present mostly to protect the interests of their own nationals. Indeed a Swiss visitor to the archipelago observed in 1913 'The Government has so far had practically no influence on the lives of the people … for nine-tenths of the people Government does not exist' (Felix Speiser cited in Jacomb 1914:30–1).

Missionary activity began in the region in 1839 with the work of the London Missionary Society. The Presbyterians appeared in 1848, and rapidly became the dominant denomination, making converts through south and central Vanuatu. The Anglican Melanesian Mission worked primarily in the north of the country from 1849. Other denominations arrived later, and squeezed in where they could. If missionaries made a major impact on islanders, the other significant impact was made by the labour trade. Between the 1860s and the early 1900s over 40,000 labourers were taken to work in the Queensland sugar cane fields, while other men worked in New Caledonia and Fiji and, after 1882 on plantations within the archipelago itself. This pattern of going away to work enabled people to maintain some measure of autonomy in their own places (see Jolly 1981:288).

I provide this potted history to explain the salience, and the construction, of the concept of *kastom*. As I argue at more length elsewhere, the introduction of the word *kastom* to designate local practice seems to have been a missionary strategy (Bolton 2003). Certainly, until the 1980s, *kastom* was primarily a term of opprobrium, associated with the darkness in which ni-Vanuatu lived before the light of the gospel dawned. Before Independence, *kastom* was paired with the Bislama *skul,* a word which economically encompassed education, church and denomination. *Kastom* and *skul* were widely perceived as being two different roads which people could choose to follow. The transformation effected during the 1970s by the leaders of the independence movement, was their redefinition of *kastom* as a good thing, and as a basis for a new national identity, uniting islanders and distinguishing them from both colonial powers. Crucially, this redefinition of *kastom* was achieved with the support of the churches. Most of the Protestant churches were self-governing and locally led from the 1960s, and the independence movement received strong support from them. Thus the context which first negatively defined *kastom* became a key influence on its positive revaluation.

Western commonplace understandings of tradition and modernity have a chronological character to them, the one being generally understood to precede the other. *Kastom* and *skul* were distinguished differently, divided in terms of place of origin – the practices of the place – *kastom* – opposed to those introduced from outside – *skul*. This locatedness has continued to be a strong element of *kastom* in the first several decades after independence. *Kastom* is best defined as referring to the practices of the place.

Introduced clothing

As has been observed, missionaries saw the adoption of European clothing as a sign of conversion (Jolly 1996:271; Douglas 2002:4). The Presbyterian newsletter, *Quarterly Jottings from the New Hebrides South Seas Islands*, expressed this idea thus 'A heathen requires moral courage to don a shirt. It is a declaration of new desires, a breaking with the hideous past, an "outward and visible sign of an inward and spiritual grace" ' (1901:23). Clothing not only exhibited conversion, for women especially it also exhibited denominational affiliation. The Anglicans introduced blouses and skirts for women, a style that remained characteristic of women's dress in the Anglican north until independence (although sleeves and hems shortened over the decades). At the start of the twenty-first century Anglican women still wear T-shirts and skirts more commonly than dresses. The Presbyterians introduced dresses to central and southern Vanuatu. The Presbyterian author I just quoted continues by making a plea for donations of clothes and fabric. He comments 'For women's dresses, the most suitable and becoming are loose robes, the material gathered around a yoke at the neck like a nightgown, but wider and not so long.' (1901:23).

European clothing was by no means adopted completely: people continued to wear local clothing for a number of not always ideological reasons. Limited supplies of cloth prevented people from dressing in European style, people often had to make do with small amounts of fabric, and to cobble together what clothing they could. Missionary accounts of labour in the New Hebrides are often illustrated with photos of neatly clad converts, but the reality was often considerably more ragged. Local clothing also suited better people's ideas of modesty in dress. The Presbyterian missionary James Lawrie observed of Aneityum in 1880, that 'although every woman and girl wears a large print garment, she would have the feeling of being unclothed without the native-made fringes, of which three or four are worn together' (James Lawrie 1892:305, cited in Douglas 2002:5). Even today, Anglican women, recalling the first time they put on an island dress, often report that they felt uncomfortably naked in it, with no fabric fast about their waists (Jean Tarisesei pers. comm. 2001).

Women remember a number of different dress styles which were introduced by missionaries and other expatriates. These include dresses known in Bislama as *foapis, fulpis, malmalkot, franis frill, mak franis, taetfit,* and *bataflae* or *stingre dres*. Of these, *foapis* and *fulpis* seem to be the oldest styles, while both *taetfit* and *bataflae dres* seem to be styles from the 1960s. *Malmalkot* is a central Vanuatu name for what is often known in English as a sundress (a sleeveless dress with a round neck and dropped waist), while *taetfit* (sometimes *taetdres*) is Bislama for mini-dress, and *bataflae dres* Bislama for caftan. Island dresses may appear to follow on from the nightgown style advocated by *Quarterly Jottings* but their pre-eminence among these other dress styles can not be explained only in these terms. Ni-Vanuatu women have chosen to wear them in preference to the other dress styles available to them. Indeed in most places women can recount the history of the introduction of island dresses to their own area. Their histories of how island dresses came to their region points to Nguna (a small island off north Efate) as the place where island dresses were developed.

Missionaries initially introduced not dress styles but ready-made clothes, which they produced from mission boxes, and acquired by donation from supporters in Europe, Canada and Australia. As the quotation from *Quarterly Jottings* suggests, clothes were often made specifically to be sent to the mission field: they arrived ready-made. However, the training in the domestic arts provided by missionary wives included lessons in sewing, which were often eagerly taken up by potential converts. Initially women were taught to make dresses using paper patterns to cut the fabric: these were particularly necessary for cutting the bodice or neck of the dress. The innovation which makes island dresses so valuable was that the fabric can be cut entirely freehand, without patterns, and that the cut pieces are easy to sew together.

Island dresses

There was a significant Presbyterian training centre at Tikilasoa village on Nguna for most of the twentieth century. Ni-Vanuatu Presbyterians were trained there as 'teachers', and were subsequently sent to work with local congregations around the country. Teacher's wives were trained in skills including sewing techniques, and when their husbands were sent as teachers to other islands, these women passed these skills on to their new congregations. It seems that the island dress was introduced to or developed on Nguna at the end of the 1930s, and was taught to women there from that period onwards.

The distinctive character of the island dress depends both upon the bodice of the dress and on the way in which the skirt is constructed: the merit of the style lies in the fact that it can be so easily cut and sewed. This applies particularly to the bodice, the only part of the dress which is lined. Two pieces of fabric are placed together (right side in) and a simple neck comprising a square plus a triangle is cut in them together. They are then sewed together around the neck hole and turned right side out, through the hole, to create a hemmed edge around the neck. As far as I can piece together the evidence, it seems that that this technique for creating the bodice is, in construction terms, the most important characteristic of the island dress, and that this technique was first developed or introduced on Nguna.

Island dresses consist of four parts, the bodice, the sleeves, and the two segments which make up the body of the dress: a tube of fabric sewed to the bottom of the bodice, dropping to about hip height, and a second tube of fabric sewed to the first, extending to just below the knees and finished with a hem. The circumference of the first tube is greater than that of the bodice, and the circumference of the second considerably greater than that of the first. In each case the top of the tube is gathered in as it is sewed to the one above, so that the dress fits quite neatly to the wearer's shoulders and billows wide around her knees. The degree to which it billows depends on how much fabric is used. Early dresses seem to have been cut quite narrowly. A woman from Anglican north Vanuatu recalled for me the time in her childhood, in the late 1950s, that some central Vanuatu women wore larger dresses to her island for the first time. Ambae men, watching the women jump down from the back of a truck, commented that the dresses were like parachutes (Tarisesei pers. comm. 2001).

The four elements from which the dress is constructed are named in Bislama with terms that are known primarily to those women who actually make them. The terms translate as the arms, neck, body and frill (*ol han, nek, bodi, fril*). Significantly, there are also terms for these four elements in central Vanuatu languages: in the Nakanamanga language spoken on Nguna the terms are *naruna, nakau da leona, namalona* and *natuana*, which translate as hands, neck, body and legs. The idea of a dress having legs is amusing to an English speaker, and has some ironic overtones in contemporary Vanuatu (where women wearing trousers are deplored) but this reference to legs points to a further idea about the dresses which seems to derive from Nguna itself. This is a terminological identification between the dresses and flying foxes. Women constantly modify the basic format of these dresses, but one of the ways of cutting the neck, a style that may be going out of fashion, involves folding back the corners of the fabric cut to make the V-neck, and sewing them down on the front of the bodice. These small folds are known as *sora blong flaeng foxis* – the ears of the flying fox. Thus the terms for the elements of the dress take on a new significance – hands, neck, body, legs and ears.

There is a fifth and optional element which is a feature of many island dresses – flaps of fabric which are sewed onto either side of the dresses at hip height. These are known as the wings. Some women specify this more precisely: they are flying fox wings. The bottom of the wings are often cut in large scallops, making a visual reference to flying fox wings, which, when spread out, have the same scalloped appearance. One Nguna woman, Leisaruru Tanearu, explained to me that the wings are called flying fox wings precisely because of this visual resemblance. The hems of dresses are often also scalloped. It is hard to interpret cause and effect in this resemblance. The hem style may have engendered the analogy: it is probably fanciful to imagine that the association may have generated or encouraged the style of hems.

Nevertheless, the analogy with flying foxes is immediately comprehensible as visual metaphor: even just the breadth of the dresses suggests a flying fox with outstretched wings. The metaphor has a kind of touching domestic character to it – reminding one of flying foxes wheeling at dusk above the fruit trees in a hamlet. A young white woman who went to Nguna a couple of years ago told me she was given an island dress there and that people then made lots of jokes about flying foxes which she did not understand (Rousseau pers. comm. 2002). The analogy is thus still active, although when I asked Nguna women about it they had no particular commentary to offer. Ellen Facey's 1988 compilation of Nguna histories and stories does not include any which refer to flying foxes. However, not only does she make no claim to providing a comprehensive archive of Nguna stories, but all the stories she records were told to her by men. It may be that there are or were women's stories about flying foxes, which I on a short visit, and working only with certain women, was unable to elicit. Interestingly, the women's meeting house in Malaliu, a Nguna village, is called Flying Fox.

This issue is the usual problem of anthropological analysis. People's explanations are always framed within their own experience and frame of reference, and so are always at some level illuminating, but one needs long experience of particular individuals to know what the probable source of their explanations might be. In the case of comparatively new practice, like island dresses, it is possible to see knowledge in the process of being constructed. Leisaruru Tanearu, is a Vanuatu Cultural Centre fieldworker for Nguna: in her report at the first island dress workshop in 2001, she observed that island dresses used to be called Mother Hubbards, and that the origin of this name was that the dresses were a habit of women – 'hem i wan habit blong ol mama'.[3] In Bislama ol mama is the more respectful way to speak about, and especially to address, adult women, so that the 'mother' in Mother Hubbard references all adult women for Bislama speakers. 'Habit' is not a Bislama word. Leisaruru is here drawing on her knowledge of English. The explanation appears to be her own conclusion. When I asked Leisaruru about the association between island dresses and flying foxes on Nguna, she commented that it is based only on visual resemblance. This may be so, but it may be her confident conclusion on the basis of her own experience. It is in her village that the women's meeting house is called 'Flying Fox'.

I have often asked women from throughout Vanuatu about the origin and significance of the wings on island dresses, and have received a considerable variety of replies. The Nguna analogy with flying foxes is not necessarily shared by other ni-Vanuatu women, some of whom did not mention flying foxes in their explanation at all. Most people refer to these flaps as wings, although just a few describe them as ears. Most women said that the wings are there only to decorate the dress, although many commented, as on a self-evident truth, that they are sewn-on handkerchiefs, attached to the dress in order to wipe one's hands, or the sweat from one's brow. Women also tie them together to fasten the dress to their bodies, and shorten it a little. They usually do this to facilitate some specific physical work, like gardening or gathering shellfish on a reef. On Paama island, in the past, some women had pockets hidden under the wings, and this role seems to be coming into fashion again in Port Vila at present.

At the same time, the wings can be seen to reflect an indigenous central Vanuatu concern with wrapping bodies. At key moments, such as at marriage, women were wrapped in many lengths of bark cloth, and are now wrapped in lengths of fabric from trade stores. Susanna Kelly reports for example that in Tongoa, brides are wrapped in a 42 yard length of cloth which has two or four yard pieces of cloth tied all along its length. This cloth binding makes the bride 'heavy' in preparation for being carried to the groom's home (Kelly 1999:296). 'Heavy' in this context means weighty, significant or perhaps even powerful. The wings, which create layers on the body, seem to allude to this wrapping aesthetic, although no one has ever articulated this to me.[4]

Alternatively, or additionally, the wings could parallel the contemporary practice I have observed in north Vanuatu, of pinning new handkerchiefs to the new clothing of a bride. In this case the explicit intention is decorative, and the handkerchiefs substitute for the sweet-smelling leaves and flowers which would formerly have been stuck in her armbands and other body

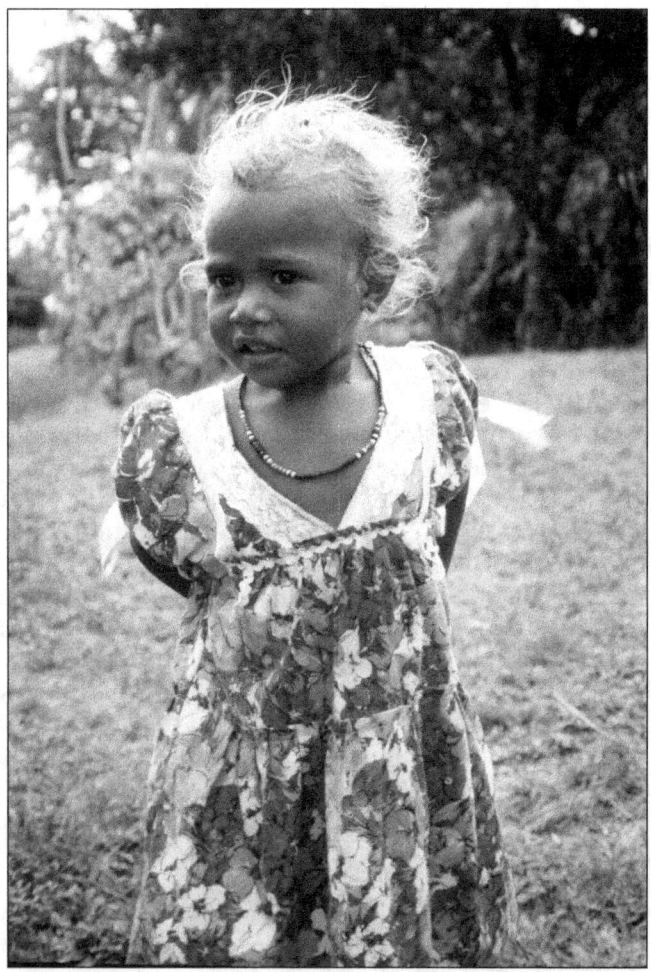

Plate 10.2   *Lissant Hango wearing an island dress*
– the ribbons ready to fly out behind
her. (Photograph by L. Bolton, November
1994.)

ornaments. In her report on the history of island dresses, Leisara Kalotiti, a
fieldworker from Mangaliliu/Lelepa, north Efate (central Vanuatu), observed
that in the past, when island dresses had long sleeves, Lelepa women would
buy nylon handkerchiefs and attach them to the sleeves. Leisara said that this
practice had no meaning, but was only decorative in purpose – it was, she
said, just a style of our grandparents in past generations, as were wings.[5] Such
uses of handkerchiefs may also reflect on earlier times when cloth was not
readily available, except via mission boxes, and when small pieces of cloth
were put to many uses.

The ribbons and lace sewn onto bodice and sleeves, like pinned-on
handkerchiefs, are explicitly identified as decorative. Mody Vatoko, an
elderly woman from Mele, a large village on the edge of Port Vila responded

to questions about the decoration of island dresses by saying that they intentionally imitated white women's nightdresses.[6] Mele has always provided domestic servants for expatriate women in Port Vila, Mele women were presumably laundering white women's nightdresses for many decades of the twentieth century. Mody commented that seeing how good the ribbons hanging on nightdresses looked, Mele women were prompted to sew ribbons on their island dresses. The assessment that this looked good may reflect on the way in which local body decorations throughout Vanuatu exaggerate bodily movement. Leaves and flowers, notably those worn for dancing, move with and against the body, as do the ribbons on island dresses. This is most evident when one watches small girls, running and swerving. The ribbons on their dresses fly out almost horizontally behind them.

Part of the significance of such associations between the use of cloth and local forms of body treatment and decoration, as with the flying fox analogy, is that they represent an indigenisation of island dresses – an accommodation of them to the practices of the place. If cloth was introduced to the archipelago, the way in which it was adopted and understood reflects on existing ideas and aesthetics. Throughout Vanuatu local practice constrains the wearing of body decorations. In most cases, the right to wear an item – a feather in the hair, a particular design on a textile, a certain kind of flower or leaf in one's hair or belt – is a privilege which has to be earned or bought in a ritual context. In north Ambrym, the wearing of red and yellow was a privilege which women had to earn. At least into the 1960s, women applied this rule not only to local clothing, but also to introduced clothing: at the 2001 workshop Lucy Moses from north Ambrym described how women there tried to wear red or yellow on dresses according to their locally defined rights to those colours, a short term attempt to apply a local restriction to an introduced medium.

Significantly, it appears that investment of meanings into introduced clothing is a primarily female practice. Missionaries directed their teaching about cloth to women: they did not often teach washing and sewing to men. To some extent, this echoed indigenous practice: throughout the archipelago, the manufacture of textiles, both barkcloth and plaited pandanus textiles, was the prerogative of women. Although some women can make men's shirts, in general, most men's clothes (trousers, shirts and T-shirts) appear to be purchased. Making men's clothes is more technically complex than making island dresses. And although suits are required wear for men with high status in introduced contexts such as government and church, in general, men's clothing does not seem to be invested with the locally specific meanings such as are attached to what women wear. However, the post-independence generation of young men (those coming to maturity from the mid 1990s) seem increasingly to invest meaning in the arrangement of their hair, drawing to some extent on traditional practice, and to some extent on international reggae culture.

Trade and transmission

In most of the islands for which I have so far done research, women recall very well who it was who first introduced island dresses, and when they did so. On Paama, for example, this style was introduced by a woman called Lezbet, from Piliura village on Nguna, who moved to Tahanesa village on south Paama with her husband, Talang, in 1939. She taught Paama women this new way of making a dress, which was known on Paama for many years as 'Nguna style'. Lezbet seems to have cut the fabric for the body and frill differently to other Nguna women, so that the join between the two lay not on the hips, but below them. Paama women continued to make dresses like this until after Independence, so that while Paama women talked of these dresses as Nguna style, women in the rest of the country recognised and referred to this as Paama style. In recent years this low-slung style has completely disappeared and I have yet to see a dress cut this way, but many women from other areas have anecdotes about the Paama style. One woman I talked to recalled that she had a dress made for herself in the Paama style, because she was interested in it, but never felt comfortable in it, and hadn't worn it. Other women remarked that the style looked awkward on pregnant women: because the Paama style is narrower over the length of the torso, a pregnant belly pulled the back of the dress tight against the behind.

Histories of the introduction of island dresses to other islands, to Ambrym, to the Maskelynes and to Futuna, nearly always name the person who first brought and made the dresses, and the route by which they acquired their knowledge. Sinlemas Kalo, from Emae island, in the Shepherd group, described the introduction of island dresses to her island at the first island dress workshop in 2001. She observed that it was missionary wives who brought European fabric, needles and thread to the archipelago and taught women how to sew several kinds of dresses. They brought only plain fabric, without designs or flowers on it. Before World War II, she said, they taught women how to make *fulpis, malmako, taetpis, franis fril* and *bataflae dres*.[7] They also taught women how to make skirts and tops, which in her language are called *nasimi ne na raverau*.

Island dresses came to Emae by an indirect route. Mrs Milne, wife of the Nguna missionary Peter Milne, showed a woman on the adjacent island of Makira how to make an island dress precursor which had a square neck, like the contemporary *robe mission* of New Caledonia. The Milnes were on Nguna between 1870 and 1924. The Makira woman Mrs Milne taught was called Leisandi Marie Bobongi, and she transmitted her knowledge to Leimala Lesi. Leimala Lesi was from Magarisu, Tongoa island, but had married a Makira chief, Naviti Maraki. Leisandi and Leimala made dresses with a square neck like Caledonia dresses. Leimala subsequently introduced the V-neck, a style she learned from Nguna. She was able to learn the style because in the past people from Emae and Makira used to make sailing canoe voyages to Nguna. Then Leimala went to south Emae, where people speak Namakura language, and taught two woman there, Isabel Matagova and Leisongi Elsie. After they changed the neck, Sinlemas said, they also started to add the wings and the ribbons to the dresses, this was after about 1950.[8] On Emae, wings are called *natalien nasugor*, meaning literally the ears of the dress.

Such histories echo the myths and histories which record the movement of objects and rituals formerly traded from place to place in the archipelago: the details of who brought a ritual to a place, and where and who it came from, are long remembered. Sinlemas' account is interesting for a number of reasons, not least that Makira, along with the small islands of Buninga and Mataso, were the three places in the Shepherd group where special plaited pandanus textiles for wear were made, and from which they were traded (David Luders, pers. comm.). So the transmission of island dresses from Makira to Emae follows, as far as I can establish, the traditional route for the acquisition of clothing textiles in that region. Local names for island dresses also reflect transmission histories: if the Paamese referred to island dresses as 'Nguna style' women on Futuna in the far south of the country described them as *moenga Vila* – clothes from Vila, because it was through Vila that the dresses moved to Futuna.

Joel Kaltang, who identified himself to me as the author of the hit song *'Aelan dres'*, suggested to me that it was his song which first introduced to many people in the country the name *'aelan dres'*. He argued that before the song burst upon their imaginations, most people knew the dress by a local language term. This may be an exaggeration, or it may be that the song introduced the term particularly to men. Kaltang suggested that the term *aelan dres* is itself an approximation of many of these indigenous terms – dress of/from an island. It is certainly the case that the very name suggests that the dress is of the place, from an island, rather than as coming from outside the country. Significantly, Dausake, the band which recorded the song, is itself from Nguna island, reinforcing the link between the dresses and Nguna itself. In this sense, the island in 'island dress', could at some level refer to Nguna specifically.

Island dresses have also been made structurally equivalent to local material forms through trade and exchange. In many areas of central Vanuatu, dresses are presented during major rituals such as marriage and funerals, often at points where textiles (bark cloth or plaited pandanus) would have been presented in the past. In Central Vanuatu dresses have become very significant items of exchange at marriages, and many dozens of dresses exchange hands on these occasions.[9] Dresses exchanged as valuables must be new, they cannot have been worn. Significantly dresses for exchange must be island dresses. Dresses in other styles are not an acceptable substitute.

Dresses are also traded between women in central Vanuatu, but only ever against plaited pandanus textiles. Women in the Vila peri-urban villages trade dresses to women living further away from town, in exchange for pandanus textiles. The same groups exchange men's shirts against kava. Only pandanus textiles can be exchanged for dresses, and only kava can be exchanged for shirts. Women also often exchange dresses with each other in friendship. The admiration of a dress, as with the admiration of other personal possessions, is generally understood as a guarded request to acquire it. The receiver will make a return gift from her own resources, giving an item such as a mat or a fowl. Women remember very well the source from which they acquired each of their dresses, and can recount the nature of the return gift they made.

Regional variations

It is in central Vanuatu, where women formerly wore pandanus textiles or bark cloth, that European clothing, and ultimately, the island dress, has been most deeply incorporated into local practice. It is in this area that women most readily speak of island dresses as *kastom dresing blong yumi*, and it is there that there is most pressure on women to wear them in preference to other European clothing styles. If island dresses are national dress, women from central Vanuatu see them as their special property.

I was given an account in 2001 of a long dispute about this very issue. A girl from the north Vanuatu island of Pentecost married a young man from Tongoa, in the heartland of central Vanuatu. They lived together not on Tongoa but in Port Vila. Pentecost is an island where women hardly ever wear island dresses, even today, and this young woman was reluctant to adopt the practice. Her reluctance was the focus of a significant marital and community dispute. Her husband tried to force her, somewhat violently, to wear the dresses, on the basis that by marrying him she had become a Tongoan (a standard assumption in contemporary Vanuatu). Eventually he took the issue to a *kastom* court – a community hearing before locally appointed leaders. Fined for not wearing island dresses, the girl nevertheless persisted in her rebellion, occasioning further meetings and further fines. Without doubt the issue was a focus for wider problems in the relationship, but it is nevertheless a mark of the importance of the dresses to Tongoa that it was considered to be a legitimate focus. I have not spoken to the girl herself, but my understanding is that, a young urban resident, she was more comfortable in jeans.

The situation in southern Vanuatu was and is somewhat different. There, as James Lawrie observed, women chose to wear mission clothing over the top of their fibre skirts. A visitor to Erromango in about 1940, Kathleen Woodburn, describes women wearing a number of ankle length skirts one on top of the other, surmounted by a Mother Hubbard (1944:139). The last Futunese woman who wore fibre skirts her whole life died in 1984, but some Futunese still don the skirts to work in their food gardens, finding them more practical to the purpose. Women from south Vanuatu were less interested in my island dress research than were women from the rest of the country.

Only women from central Vanuatu would suggest that island dresses are *kastom dresing blong yumi*. Women from the north would not relate at all to this suggestion. What they would accept is that the dresses are national dress. When island dresses were adopted as national dress for women soon after independence, this had a significant impact on women in Anglican areas. Not themselves having the skills to make island dresses, Anglican women often tried hard to acquire them. Women from the Banks islands in the far north of the country, for example, sought to obtain island dresses because they had been designated national dress, buying them mainly from trade stores in Luganville. At the first island dress workshop in 2001, one fieldworker from Pentecost attended the workshop with the explicit intention of learning about the dresses because she felt her own ignorance on the topic. When my colleague Jean Tarisesei, who comes from Ambae in north Vanuatu, visited

Europe in 2002, she readily responded to a request that she bring her national dress by providing herself with her best island dress.

In 2001–2 a Vanuatu Cultural Centre research group, the Young People's Project, undertook research on young women's attitudes to beauty, under the direction of the Canadian researcher Maggie Cummings. A report on the project findings observes that while young women appreciated the dresses for their beauty and as national heritage, they were not themselves comfortable with wearing them (Cummings 2002:25–6). The report findings suggest that island dresses are associated with motherhood, and thus represent something these young women were not yet ready to embrace.

Stealing with the eye

If the fact of island dresses has remained constant since before World War II, the detail of them has involved constant alteration. Subtle differences in hem, sleeve, bodice and wing have been constantly appearing, spreading and disappearing again. These are partly a function of fashion, and partly of available materials. The availability and cost of fabric and other materials has had a very significant effect. In the 1960s and 70s trade stores stocked the very thin fabrics such as nylons and muslins which were popular internationally in that period. Dresses made from these fabrics tended to be transparent; they had to be worn with heavy underdresses. Recalling these fabrics women are rather disparaging – they shrank. Before the 1970s, most decoration was created using bias binding: the fashion for decorating dresses with ribbons and lace developed from this during the 1970s and 80s as a consequence of the availability of cheap supplies of these commodities during that period. In the last few years, however, a 'new' style has become more and more fashionable, especially in Port Vila. Making use of a new range of strongly coloured fabrics, these new island dresses are un-embellished, decorated with neither ribbons nor lace, but only with pleats in the same fabric.

This fashion is a response to a variety of factors. Since the introduction of Value Added Tax in Vanuatu in the mid 1990s, ribbons and lace have become more and more expensive. Moreover, as several women pointed out, lace is very vulnerable to the vigorous scrubbing brush approach to hand washing used in Vanuatu, and lace on the bodice is equally easily torn when the wearer carries something abrasive, like a branch of ripe bananas. However, the decision to wear this plain post-millennium style is also a matter of fashion: the dresses are very popular, and have been quickly passed between women in Port Vila as the admiration of a dress has led (as it very generally does) to a gift of what has been admired. Like most fashion, this is in fact a reworking of something from the past; the first island dresses were similarly undecorated.

In the era before independence, an era in which women moved about the country far less than they do today, certain features of island dresses were recognisably characteristic of certain areas – as the Paama style was of Paama, for example. Women in Port Vila's peri-urban villages also differentiated themselves through features of their dresses. The women of Ifira used distinctive patterns in the ways they decorated the backs of their bodices, for example, and were instantly recognisable to those in the know. Even today,

Mele village women are easily identified in the Port Vila market by the bright, purposefully clashing colours of the ribbons with which they decorate their dresses.

The idea of distinctive styles belongs primarily to the indigenous way of thinking in which body decorations are privileges to be earned. Distinctiveness is in this context symbolic of personal status and achievement. There seems to have been some attempt in the second half of the twentieth century to control dresses and to accommodate them to indigenous systems of right and privilege. But such controls were not successfully established. Instead, dresses are vulnerable to what is known in Bislama as *'stilim wetem ae'*, stealing with one's eyes. A woman seeing a dress with a particular feature will copy it herself. Thus a style created in a trade store in Luganville, in which the back of the neck is fastened with a button, was seen by a Paamese woman visiting Luganville, and taken back to Paama. Now a seamstress on Paama is adding this feature into dresses on request.

Herein lies the distinctively modern aspect to island dresses, or, at least, the distinctively not-of-the-place character of them. Island dresses are vulnerable to stealing with the eye, and there is no one with either the inclination, or the authority, to control such thefts. That features of the dresses should be transmitted without reference to the person who devised them is entirely uncharacteristic of indigenous Vanuatu, even as remembering the source and route of transmission is a practice of the place.

Kastom, kalja mo tredisin

In the heady days of the independence movement, the single national shortwave radio station was the most significant source of information for rural ni-Vanuatu, and was consequently very significant in influencing public opinion. The chief of the Bislama Section, French Residency Information Service, Paul Gardissat, a fluent Bislama speaker, was passionately committed to the importance of *kastom* for the fledgling nation. From about 1976 he made a program which he called *Kastom, Kalja mo Tredisin* ('custom, culture and tradition'), consciously introducing the terms *kalja* and *tredisin* into the Bislama vocabulary. For Gardissat, these three terms each had distinct meanings and he often explained the distinction he made between *kastom, kalja* and *tredisin* in the program. He used *kastom* to denote indigenous knowledge and practice, *tredisin* to denote introduced practices which had been incorporated into people's lives – his example being the singing of New Year (*Bonne Année*) songs – and *kalja* to refer to all contemporary practice, whatever its source. He made programs devoted to each of these three terms and attempted to reinforce the distinction between them in a number of different ways.

Gardissat's phrase, *kastom, kalja mo tredisin*, was adopted mostly by educated ni-Vanuatu such as government officials, or people involved in one way or another in the Vanuatu Cultural Centre. They use it as a reinforcement of the idea of *kastom*, rather than as a set of distinct terms. The phrase has not developed wider currency.[10] Gardissat's formulation seems to me to be quite an interesting attempt to give to Bislama terms in which it is possible to accept things which have become incorporated into ni-Vanuatu practice, without defining them as *kastom*.

The fact that these terms were not widely accepted reflects on the political importance of the idea of *kastom* at that period, but it could also be fairly readily concluded that his formulation struck no chord with ni-Vanuatu. The binary opposition between *kastom* and *fasin blong ol waetman* seems to have been not just a political tool, but to have satisfied most people's classificatory requirements. Indeed although I have often asked people about their use of the phrase *kastom, kalja mo tredisin*, I have come across only one ni-Vanuatu who distinguished these terms. This was the feminist and intellectual, Grace Molisa. She set out her distinction between these terms in a 1991 publication, defining all three as relating to indigenous practice: she does not include in the definitions any explicit reference to what has been adopted from outside.[11]

For national occasions, especially those held in places such as Port Vila, women often feel it important to appear in an island dress, no matter their island of origin. The importance of the dresses as a national symbol seems to be widely respected in rural Vanuatu. This suggests an interesting third to the binary opposition between inside and outside, between *kastom* and *fasin blong ol waetman*. This is *nasonal* – national. National is something distinctively of Vanuatu, but which may have been adopted in, rather than being autochthonous. But if there is, in practice, such a third, it is not in any way acknowledged as a third in discussion in Vanuatu. Rather, as the song suggests, island dresses are regarded as something of the place ('you can be found in every place'), and as a source of pleasure or comfort ('making people happy/ smiling a little'). If island dresses are strongly associated with adult women as mothers – so strongly that unmarried girls are less willing to wear them – then Leisaruru's gloss on *matahabet* is relevant to this association. The dresses worn by adult women (who are by definition mothers), are a habit of mothers. They can thus be seen as deeply associated with people's sense of home, of place and of belonging.

Tradition and modernity seem to me to be like a pair of armies skirmishing over the same ground. What is held by one, may easily and soon be held by the other. Modernity is not a term used in Vanuatu, but if an equivalent must be found, then it would be found in the idea of things which are from outside. As island dresses demonstrate, the relationship between things from inside and things from outside is by no means a simple one. Even stealing with the eye, which in contemporary Vanuatu appears to be a practice from outside, may yet be captured by *kastom* and made local. Island dresses underline some of the complexities which that binary opposition makes simple, and illustrate some of the ways in which ni-Vanuatu are thinking about their own practice. The process of incorporation is complex and continuous, as meanings are invested, accepted and often ultimately forgotten, overtaken by something else. Island dresses are, at the beginning of the twenty-first century, seen by many ni-Vanuatu as reassuringly indicative of home.

NOTES

1 The lyrics in Bislama are, with multiple repetitions; '*I go raon long evri ples, aelan dres blong yumi/ Kala blong yu i kalaful/ mekim man i hapi /laf lellebet./ I go raon long evri ples/ ilan dres bilong yumi*'. The song was recorded and released on Dausake's album *Volume 3 "Dawn of February"* Recorded by Vanuatu Productions Limited (P.O. Box 142 Port Vila, Vanuatu). The album notes thank Alphonse Jack for allowing them to record 'Island Dress', suggesting that Joel Kaltang's claim to have written the song may be disputed.

2 The research for this paper was conducted with and through many of the Vanuatu Cultural Centre's female volunteer extension workers, known in Vanuatu as fieldworkers. I work with these women every year as a volunteer advisor to the Women's Culture Project at the Vanuatu Cultural Centre (VCC). I mentioned my interest in island dresses to them in July 2001, and was overwhelmed by their interest in the topic. In relation to this paper I am indebted particularly to Leisaruru Tanearu, Leisara Kalotiti, Numaline Mahana, Sinlemas Kalo, Leinare Kalmet, Lucy Moses and Lonette Tasale. I also thank Jean Tarisesei and Martha Kaltal (VCC staff) for their assistance with research. This research was funded through the ESRC funded London University/British Museum project *Clothing the Pacific*. I thank my colleagues on that project, Nicholas Thomas, Susanne Küchler, Chloe Colchester and Graeme Were. I also thank Ralph Regenvanu, VCC Director, for research permission and support.

3 Island Dress Workshop recordings Tape 1 Side A 19 November 2001. National Film and Sound Archive, Vanuatu Cultural Centre.

4 As I have discussed briefly elsewhere (Bolton 2005), central Vanuatu seems to have been influenced by settlement from western Polynesia prior to European settlement. Wrapping the body at key moments of transition is a widespread Polynesian practice (see for example Gell 1993:88–91).

5 Island Dress Workshop recordings Tape 1 Side B 19 November 2001. National Film and Sound Archive, Vanuatu Cultural Centre. It seems unlikely that handkerchiefs would be nylon. Although the Bislama dictionary defines *angkejif* as handkerchief, I suggest that the word may mean 'small square of cloth' to a Bislama speaker.

6 Mody Vatoko was interviewed by Numaline Mahana and Jean Tarisesei as part of Numaline's research for the second island dress workshop. (Island Dress Workshop 2–4 October 2002, Tape 3 Side B. National Film and Sound Archive, Vanuatu Cultural Centre).

7 Sinlemas's terms differ slightly from those I have given above, reflecting regional variation in Bislama.

8 Sinlemas dated the introduction of island dresses to Emae as being about 1900. This must refer to the Caledonian neck version of the dress, and perhaps refers to the period when Makira women could make them, but not, according to Sinlemas, any women on Emae itself. However, dates such as '1900' can be used to mean an indefinite but long ago period, as well as a specific year. It may be that Sinlemas used '1900' in that sense.

9 I discuss aspects of this in a little more detail elsewhere (Bolton 2005).

10 Crowley's (1990) Bislama dictionary listed neither *tredisin* nor *kalja*, and translated both tradition and culture as *kastom*, listing as an alternative rendering of culture *fasin blong laef* (way of life). The 1995 edition of the dictionary listed *kalja* and translated it as culture, suggesting that this word has gained in currency during the early 1990s. However, the 1995 edition did not list *tredisin*, translating tradition as *kastom*. Throughout the decade most people only used *kastom*.

11 Molisa (1990) defines *kastom* as 'something which we all accept as good practice' while her rather lengthy definitions of both *tredisin* and *kalja* reiterate the idea of knowledge and practice

Bibliography

Bolton, L. (2003) *Unfolding the Moon: Enacting Women's Kastom in Vanuatu*, Honolulu: University of Hawai'i Press.

—— (2005) 'Dressing for Transition: Weddings, Clothing and Change in Vanuatu', in S. Küchler and G. Were (eds) *The Art of Clothing*, London: University College London Press.

Crowley, T. (1990) *An Illustrated Bislama–English and English–Bislama Dictionary*, Vanuatu: Pacific Languages Unit and Vanuatu Extension Centre, University of the South Pacific.

Cummings, M. (2002) *Young Women Speak: A Report on Young Women, Beauty and Self-Image*, Vanuatu Young People's Project, Vanuatu Cultural Centre, P.O. Box 184, Port Vila, Vanuatu.

Douglas, B. (2002) 'Christian Citizens: Women and Negotiations of Modernity in Vanuatu', *The Contemporary Pacific* 14(1):1–38.

Gell, A. (1993) *Wrapping in Images: Tattooing in Polynesia*, Oxford: Clarendon Press.

Jacomb, E. (1914) *France and England in the New Hebrides: the Anglo–French condominium*, Melbourne: George Robertson and Co.

Jolly, M. (1981) 'People and their Products in South Pentecost', in M. R. Allen (ed.) *Vanuatu: Politics, Economics and Ritual in Island Melanesia*, Sydney: Academic Press.

—— (1996) 'European Perceptions of the Arts of Vanuatu: Engendering Colonial Interests', in J. Bonnemaison *et al.* (eds) *Arts of Vanuatu*, Bathurst: Crawford House Publishing.

Kelly, S.K. (1999) Unwrapping Mats: People, Land and Material Culture in Tongoa, Central Vanuatu, Ph.D. Thesis, University College London.

Molisa, G. (1990) *Kalja Buklet: Nasonal Festivol blong ol woman 1980 – 1990*, Port Vila, Vanuatu: Vanuatu Nasonal Council blong ol Woman Festivol Infomesen mo Pablikeson Komiti.

Quarterly Jottings from the New Hebrides, South Sea Islands, [Woodford, England] : John G. Paton Mission Fund, 1895–1961.

Woodburn, M.K. (1944) *Backwash of Empire*, Melbourne: Georgian House.

Index